PRINCESS ALICE

By the same author

THE GREAT LOCK-OUT
ENA: SPAIN'S ENGLISH QUEEN

Princess Alice at Osborne

GERARD NOEL

PRINCESS ALICE

QUEEN VICTORIA'S FORGOTTEN DAUGHTER

CONSTABLE LONDON

First published in Great Britain 1974
by Constable and Company Limited
10 Orange Street London WC2H 7EG
Copyright © 1974 by Gerard Noel
Paperback edition published 1985
ISBN 0 09 465980 X
Printed in Great Britain by
St Edmundsbury Press
Bury St Edmunds, Suffolk

TO ADELE

CONTENTS

Contents

ILLUSTRATIONS

FOREWORD

I was brought up on tales about my grandmother, Alice, not only by my mother but by her sisters and brother and from time to time by distant reminders from my great uncles and great aunts, the brothers and sisters of Alice. With one accord they accepted her as the most remarkable of Queen Victoria's remarkable children. Had she not died so very young her impact on liberal history would obviously have been far greater.

To me she was a fascinating personality and I was often told my mother took after her in progressive thought and ceaselessly taking the lead in discussions and conversations. She replaced her at the age of fifteen as 'mother' to her sisters and brother and they were brought up in the aura of their mother's wonderful personality.

As recently as 1967 I attended the centenary celebrations of the Alice Frauenverein (Alice Women's Union) in Darmstadt and had the privilege of speaking to a large gathering of citizens, none of whom could have known her personally, but all of whom were interested in carrying on the work she had started with the various organizations which bore her name. From the other speeches it was clear how strongly the impact of this high-minded practical Princess was still felt in Hesse.

So I am glad Gerard Noel has written this first full biography to record her short but most significant life.

MOUNTBATTEN OF BURMA

ACKNOWLEDGEMENTS

Alice, Grand Duchess of Hesse, Princess of Great Britain and
Ireland, was the third of Queen Victoria's children to be born
and the first of them to die. The expression 'forgotten daughter'
is obviously a relative one; and it is probably natural that
more should be known and that more should have been written
about her longer-lived brothers and sisters. But it remains
true that meagre attention has so far been paid to Princess
Alice, about whom no full biography has ever been written.
No research, moreover, has previously been undertaken into
the mass of original and hitherto unpublished material as to
the long-hidden details of her life. The two principal sources
of such material are the Archives at Windsor and those at
Darmstadt.

By the gracious permission of Her Majesty the Queen, I have
been given unhindered access to all documents relating to
Princess Alice in the Royal Archives at Windsor. For this I
am deeply appreciative and must express my sincere gratitude
for the advice and help in this regard of Mr Robert Mackworth-
Young cvo, the Librarian at Windsor Castle and Assistant
Keeper of the Queen's Archives. I am particularly grateful to
Miss Jane Langton mvo, who as Registrar in day-to-day
charge of the Royal Archives was of immeasurable help thanks
to the kindness and efficiency of herself and her assistant, Miss
Frances Dimond, and to the fruits of her own very considerable
knowledge and scholarship.

For information regarding the second half of Princess Alice's
life I owe an enormous debt to Her Royal Highness, the
Princess Margaret of Hesse and the Rhine. Of her friend hip
and kindness over the obtaining of material for this book it is
difficult to do justice in the expression of my appreciation.
Princess Margaret was not only a most generous hostess at
Wolfsgarten, where she lives, allowing me to see, and in some
cases borrow, certain relatively unknown but vital information

regarding the Princess; but she also arranged for me to visit the State Archives in Darmstadt to seek the kind help of the Archives' Director, Dr Franz, to whom I am greatly indebted.

By the generous permission of Earl Mountbatten of Burma, and that of Lord Brabourne and the Broadlands Archives Settlement, I was able to consult the Broadlands Archives, and there found some valuable supplementary material relative to Princess Alice. And I am very grateful indeed to Lord Mountbatten for the personal interest he was kind enough to express in this life of his grandmother and for the advice and encouragement he gave me on the occasion of my visit to Broadlands. I am no less grateful for the suggestions he made after reading through the typescript and for the Foreword he has so kindly written to the book.

From the strictly practical point of view, there is no single person to whom I am more particularly beholden than Mrs Geoffrey de Bellaigue. Having formerly, as Miss Sheila Russell, assisted Miss Langton at the Royal Archives while I was working there, she subsequently agreed, with great magnanimity, to take on for me a task of vital importance. I had found on my visit to the Darmstadt Archives that the volume of material therein relating to Princess Alice was enormous. My own working but distinctly non-expert knowledge of German would not have enabled me to undertake, unaided, anything like an adequate examination of all this material. In relieving me of this aspect of the background work Mrs de Bellaigue has helped me to an extent for which I can never be sufficiently grateful. She not only visited Darmstadt but also worked for a considerable period thereafter on the translation of xeroxed copies of innumerable letters, diary entries, notes, memoranda and many other miscellaneous documents. For her scholarly and systematic assembling of such material my gratitude is profound.

For invaluable research and detective work on previously published and other miscellaneous material I am considerably indebted to Mrs Olive D'Arcy Hart, with corresponding appreciation of the ever-efficient help of the staffs of the British Museum and the Public Record Office. And for additional translation work my thanks are due to Mrs Rita Moore, as also to her typing agency for work on the final typescript.

I must also record my thanks to Mrs Raymond Burnaby and Miss Jennifer Hassell; the former's encouragement and the latter's advice were positively inspirational before pen was even put to paper.

For the loan of two booklets I am very grateful to Mr David Duff, whose extended attention to Princess Alice in *Hessian Tapestry* (1967) has been the only important effort to date to remedy the absence of collected biographical data about her. (A sketch published in 1884, and the substantially similar memoir edited by Princess Helena the following year, consisted mainly of letters to Queen Victoria. But a complete picture of the Princess does not emerge from this or any other of the hitherto published sources that deal with her life or mention it in passing.) It is hoped that the gap may to some extent be filled by this portrait whose four parts correspond to four facets which were separated from one another in a more than merely chronological sense.

In dedicating this book to my wife I must pay tribute to the helpfulness of her comments on the draft and her patience over my periodically going into *purdah*, getting up in the small hours of the morning and causing the other annoyances to family life attendant on writing a book in one's 'spare time'.

London, January 1974

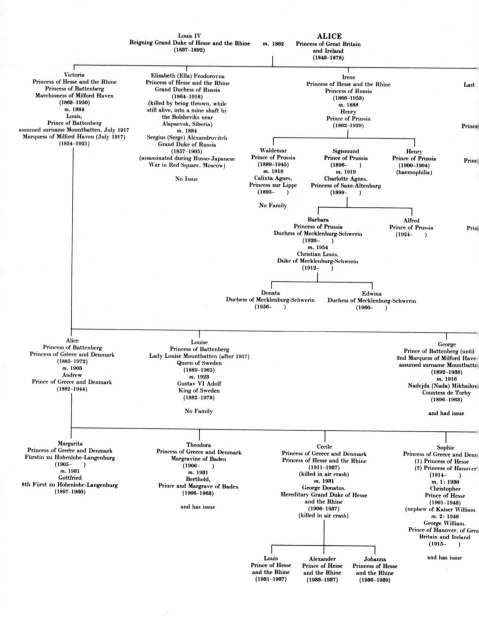

Louis IV
Reigning Grand Duke of Hesse and the Rhine
(1837–1892)   *m.* 1862

ALICE
Princess of Great Britain
and Ireland
(1843–1878)

Victoria
Princess of Hesse and the Rhine
Princess of Battenberg
Marchioness of Milford Haven
(1863–1950)
m. 1884
Louis,
Prince of Battenberg
assumed surname Mountbatten, July 1917
Marquess of Milford Haven (July 1917)
(1854–1921)

Elizabeth (Ella) Feodorovna
Princess of Hesse and the Rhine
Grand Duchess of Russia
(1864–1918)
(killed by being thrown, while
still alive, into a mine shaft by
the Bolsheviks near
Alapaevsk, Siberia)
m. 1884
Sergius (Serge) Alexandrovitch
Grand Duke of Russia
(1857–1905)
(assassinated during Russo-Japanese
War in Red Square, Moscow)

No Issue

Irene
Princess of Hesse and the Rhine
Princess of Russia
(1866–1953)
m. 1888
Henry
Prince of Prussia
(1862–1929)

Last

Prince

Waldemar
Prince of Prussia
(1889–1945)
m. 1919
Calixta Agnes,
Princess zur Lippe
(1895–   )

No Family

Sigismund
Prince of Prussia
(1896–   )
m. 1919
Charlotte Agnes,
Princess of Saxe-Altenburg
(1899–   )

Henry
Prince of Prussia
(1900–1904)
(haemophilia)

Prince

Barbara
Princess of Prussia
Duchess of Mecklenburg-Schwerin
(1920–   )
m. 1954
Christian Louis,
Duke of Mecklenburg-Schwerin
(1912–   )

Alfred
Prince of Prussia
(1924–   )

Prin

Donata
Duchess of Mecklenburg-Schwerin
(1956–   )

Edwina
Duchess of Mecklenburg-Schwerin
(1960–   )

Alice
Princess of Battenberg
Princess of Greece and Denmark
(1885–1972)
m. 1903
Andrew
Prince of Greece and Denmark
(1882–1944)

Louise
Princess of Battenberg
Lady Louise Mountbatten (after 1917)
Queen of Sweden
(1889–1965)
m. 1923
Gustav VI Adolf
King of Sweden
(1882–1973)

No Family

George
Prince of Battenberg (until
2nd Marquess of Milford Have
assumed surname Mountbatte
(1892–1938)
m. 1916
Nadejda (Nada) Mikhailov
Countess de Torby
(1896–1963)

and had issue

Margarita
Princess of Greece and Denmark
Fürstin zu Hohenlohe-Langenburg
(1905–   )
m. 1931
Gottfried
8th Fürst zu Hohenlohe-Langenburg
(1897–1960)

Theodora
Princess of Greece and Denmark
Margravine of Baden
(1906–   )
m. 1931
Berthold,
Prince and Margrave of Baden
(1906–1963)

and has issue

Cecile
Princess of Greece and Denmark
Princess of Hesse and the Rhine
(1911–1937)
(killed in air crash)
m. 1931
George Donatus,
Hereditary Grand Duke of Hesse
and the Rhine
(1906–1937)
(killed in air crash)

Sophie
Princess of Greece and Den
(1) Princess of Hesse
(2) Princess of Hanover
(1914–   )
m. 1: 1930
Christopher
Prince of Hesse
(1901–1943)
(nephew of Kaiser William
m. 2: 1946
George William,
Prince of Hanover, of Gre
Britain and Ireland
(1915–   )

and has issue

Louis
Prince of Hesse
and the Rhine
(1931–1937)

Alexander
Prince of Hesse
and the Rhine
(1933–1937)

Johanna
Princess of Hesse
and the Rhine
(1936–1939)

Descendants of Grand Duke Louis IV of Hesse and the Rhine, and Princess Alice of Great Britain

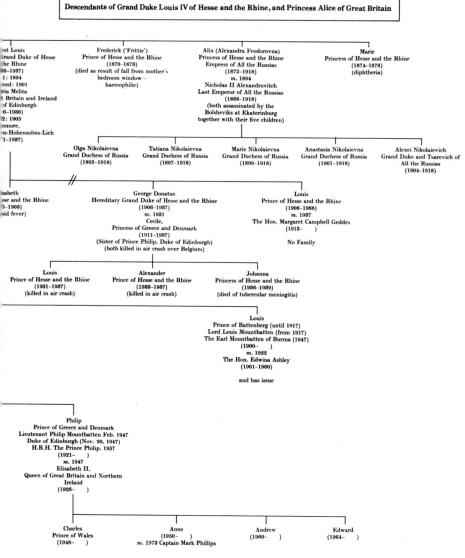

est Louis
rand Duke of Hesse
the Rhine
38–1937)
1: 1894
ced: 1901
ria Melita
Britain and Ireland
of Edinburgh
6–1936)
2: 1905
eonore,
ns-Hohensolms-Lich
1–1937)

Frederick ('Frittie')
Prince of Hesse and the Rhine
(1870–1873)
(died as result of fall from mother's
bedroom window –
haemophilie)

Alix (Alexandra Feodorovna)
Princess of Hesse and the Rhine
Empress of All the Russias
(1872–1918)
m. 1894
Nicholas II Alexandrovitch
Last Emperor of All the Russias
(1868–1918)
(both assassinated by the
Bolsheviks at Ekaterinburg
together with their five children)

Marie
Princess of Hesse and the Rhine
(1874–1878)
(diphtheria)

Olga Nikolaievna
Grand Duchess of Russia
(1895–1918)

Tatiana Nikolaievna
Grand Duchess of Russia
(1897–1918)

Marie Nikolaievna
Grand Duchess of Russia
(1899–1918)

Anastasia Nikolaievna
Grand Duchess of Russia
(1901–1918)

Alexei Nikolaievich
Grand Duke and Tsarevich of
All the Russias
(1904–1918)

tabeth
sse and the Rhine
5–1903)
oid fever)

George Donatus
Hereditary Grand Duke of Hesse and the Rhine
(1906–1937)
m. 1931
Cecile,
Princess of Greece and Denmark
(1911–1987)
(Sister of Prince Philip, Duke of Edinburgh)
(both killed in air crash over Belgium)

Louis
Prince of Hesse and the Rhine
(1908–1968)
m. 1937
The Hon. Margaret Campbell Geddes
(1913–)

No Family

Louis
Prince of Hesse and the Rhine
(1931–1937)
(killed in air crash)

Alexander
Prince of Hesse and the Rhine
(1933–1937)
(killed in air crash)

Johanna
Princess of Hesse and the Rhine
(1936–1939)
(died of tubercular meningitis)

Louis
Prince of Battenberg (until 1917)
Lord Louis Mountbatten (from 1917)
The Earl Mountbatten of Burma (1947)
(1900–)
m. 1922
The Hon. Edwina Ashley
(1901–1960)

and has issue

Philip
Prince of Greece and Denmark
Lieutenant Philip Mountbatten Feb. 1947
Duke of Edinburgh (Nov. 20, 1947)
H.R.H. The Prince Philip, 1957
(1921–)
m. 1947
Elizabeth II,
Queen of Great Britain and Northern
Ireland
(1926–)

Charles
Prince of Wales
(1948–)

Anne
(1950–)
m. 1973 Captain Mark Phillips

Andrew
(1960–)

Edward
(1964–)

Part One

SISTER

Chapter One

TO THE PRINCESS ROYAL

On 3 September 1878 the majestic paddle steamer, *Princess Alice*, was churning up the waters of the Thames on an excursion trip from Sheerness to Woolwich. She was one of that popular fleet of 'Butterfly Boats' – as the deep-water mariners called them – which had been so prominent a feature of London's river life since the end of the Napoleonic age. The *Princess Alice* was one of the most popular of all. She had carried the Shah of Persia on a visit to Greenwich and had become nicknamed 'the Shah's boat'. More importantly she was named after the Grand Duchess of Hesse-Darmstadt, Queen Victoria's second daughter, just then, as it happened, on a visit to England.

The Princess was thirty-five at the time. Had she been a spectator by the river bank she could not, for very special reasons, have failed to be proud of the craft bearing her name as it plied the Thames that particular autumn afternoon. The boat was majestic yet democratic, even as she was herself; and the scene was very much a part of the romantic – as opposed to the grimly realistic – side of Victorian life. What could be seen on the surface was comfortable, happy and blameless; what was hidden beneath, in muddy waters, was uninviting and potentially lethal. Princess Alice had experienced both types of surroundings and knew that if anyone was suddenly toppled from one into the other, daydreams became nightmares.

She was, in fact, unusually conversant with these diverse elements in the life of her day. She had tasted its uplifting but sometimes stifling respectability at royal as well as less exalted levels; she had plumbed, by personal and peculiar choice, many hidden depths of its squalor in terms of human suffering. Her own life was itself an exquisitely painful amalgam of innocent pleasure, cruel shock, idyllic romance, brutal reality, life-giving compassion, psychological limbo and overshadowing tragedy. Though no one knew it at the time, it was this last element that dominated that September afternoon both for Princess Alice herself and for the boat that bore her name.

Alice was spending this autumn in Eastbourne. She was exhausted but could not relax, a pattern that had been building up for some time during her life at home in Darmstadt. Instead of resting (as intended by her mother, who had made her a present of this holiday) she spent a large part of her time visiting hospitals. She was full of plans for her future as a result of such visits. As she passed from sick bed to sick bed the gilded years must, young though she still was, have already seemed like a very distant dream from a totally different world. The intensity of life's demands in between had been the substitute for that long, hazy summer-into-autumn 'plateau' of middle age that dims earlier memories for most people in their later years. For in Princess Alice's case there had been no such halcyon interlude. Instead there had been a virtual transition from spring to winter and her whole life-span was only half the 'three score and ten' years proverbially allotted to mortals.

Remote, however, as may, in 1878, have seemed the carefree days of youth they were real enough and very recent. They coincided moreover with the heyday of Victorianism, with the happiest years in the life of the monarch and her consort, and with the pristine glory of a rather different, more triumphalist type of pleasure craft, the *Victoria and Albert*. This famous royal yacht was launched on 25 April 1843. Earlier that same day, at five past four in the morning, Princess Alice had been born.

'It was customary that when a Royal baby was born either the Home Secretary or a Cabinet Minister should be in residence at the Castle, Palace, or house, where the child was to make its appearance. This custom has recently been discontinued.'[1] So, as late as the 1950s, wrote Princess Marie Louise, daughter of 'Lenchen'* (Princess Helena), the sister closest to Alice, whose volume of letters to the Queen she edited in 1885.

* The German diminutive for 'Helen' was 'Helenchen', which was abbreviated by Queen Victoria for her third daughter to 'Lenchen'.

Alice's birth, however, came quickly. And though the Queen suffered considerably it was all over much sooner than had been the case with her sister the Princess Royal ('Vicky') or her brother, 'Bertie', the Prince of Wales. Official personages, in fact, were conspicuous by their absence. Only the Lord Steward of the Household was present at Buckingham Palace that early morning in the spring. This point was of great import to Queen Victoria, surprising as it may seem. She recalled in her Journal for 25 April 1843 (written up, with the help of notes, on 14 May): 'The only person who was there to whom the child could be shown was Lord Liverpool.'[2]

The expression 'male chauvinism' was of course unheard of; in fact the very word 'chauvinism' was not coined until 1870. But the expressions used by George Edward Anson are revealing, and perhaps quaint-sounding to us:

This morning at 4 o'clock the Queen was safely delivered of *another* Princess. Her Majesty was so speedy in her proceedings that only one of the great officers or Ministers had arrived at the Palace before the event was over. . . . It is a disappointment to both the Queen and the Prince that the child is not a boy; and I think there was a general wish in the country that the succession should have been strengthened by another male descendant; but there is time enough for that yet.[3]

How Anson could have known (writing within a few hours of the event) that the baby's sex was a matter of 'disappointment to both the Queen and the Prince' it is difficult to know. But he certainly expressed, if instinctively, a general feeling of a society even more male-dominated than our own. On the day of the birth a proud father, Prince Albert, received at a Council meeting 'addresses of congratulation *and condolence* from both houses'.

Queen Victoria's own account of the occasion was rather different: 'After getting hardly any sleep, soon after midnight Dr Laycock was sent for and at five minutes past four a fine healthy girl was born and all my sufferings came to an end! . . . I felt extremely quiet and comfortable afterwards and slept a good deal. My beloved Albert who had watched so tenderly over me the whole time, had many people to see and such numbers of letters to write.'[4]

Prince Albert was punctilious indeed in making the news known to various individuals. Of these Lord Melbourne was one of the most important in the eyes of the Queen, if not in terms of official protocol. For Melbourne, it will be remembered, was Prime Minister when the bewildered but determined eighteen-year-old Princess Victoria came to the throne in 1837. And the three-year partnership between them has been called 'one of the romances of history'.[5] Theirs was certainly an extraordinary relationship, fascinating to study and to try to analyse, but directly relevant to Alice's story only in two particulars. One of these relates to the quality which – according at least to one rather perspicacious observer – attracted Queen Victoria to Melbourne in the first place. And this was: 'A femininity which made her, for all her strength of will, the reverse of independent in coming to a judgment in general and impersonal matters. The fact that she was a woman also meant that she sought for her guide among the male sex.'[6] Almost the same words could be used to describe Princess Alice's state of mind nearly thirty years later when she came under the spell of another 'father figure', one David Friedrich Strauss. This strange and intimate – but innocent – relationship was vitally stimulating to Alice, even though it caused her to abandon temporarily some of the most cherished and fundamental beliefs of her earlier life.

The other relevance to Alice of Melbourne's influence concerns the choice of names for Queen Victoria's second daughter. These have invariably been accounted for by taking at face value what the Queen wrote to her Uncle Leopold, King of the Belgians: 'Our little baby, who I really am fond of for she is so very forward for her age, is to be called *Alice*, an old English name, and the other names are to be Maud, another old English name and the same as Matilda, and Mary as she was born on Aunt Gloucester's birthday.'[7] Alice may well be an old English name but almost certainly this was not Victoria's main motive in choosing it. Some years before, during one of their innumerable conversations on a wide variety of subjects, the Queen and Melbourne had talked about Christian names. Two of the names that had cropped up had been Alice and Louise. The first, according to Melbourne, was beautiful, though he thought the second fastidious. When Alice was born Queen Victoria had by no means outlived the influence of Melbourne, though he had ceased to be her Prime Minister two years previously.

Thus was chosen the 'beautiful name of Alice'. Poor Melbourne, never the same after his stroke in 1842, was deeply touched. To be one of the first to be told the news was the kind of gesture most likely to make up somewhat for the void during which he had missed the young Queen 'every hour of the day, missed her more even than he feared he was going to and more with every month that passed'.[8] 'I cannot sufficiently express my gratitude for the early communication of this auspicious intelligence,' he wrote in spidery writing from Brocket Hall.[9] When telling her uncle about the choice of names in the letter already quoted, the Queen went on to say: 'The sponsors are to be: The King of Hanover; – Ernestus Pious; – Poor Princess Sophia Matilda and Feodore.'[10]

The King of Hanover was the Queen's uncle, the much-hated former Duke of Cumberland; 'Ernestus Pious' was the ironic nickname (borrowed from a former Ernest of Coburg to whom it was more suitable) for Prince Albert's dissolute elder brother, Ernest, Duke of Saxe-Coburg-Gotha.

Very different were the individual ways in which these four godparents of Princess Alice represented a world that was totally alien from that of their godchild's subsequent ideals and experiences. Ernestus Augustus of Hanover was the heavyweight champion of the old order of things in Europe, the autocratic and implacable enemy of liberalism and social change. He died, as his most sympathetic modern biographer puts it, 'still trying to stem the flood which he had held back during his lifetime, and with his death one of the stoutest bulwarks against it was removed'.[11]

Prince Albert's brother Ernest, in his youthful days, represented if anything the brief 'spree' that some Europeans staged as a sort of conditioned reflex to the end of the Napoleonic era. Something of the pre-French Revolution hedonism tried to revive itself until the 1848 revolutions swept Europe on into a more down-to-earth and solemn phase. Queen Victoria compared Ernest to Gladstone in that 'he persuaded himself that things were right that were wrong'.[12] Many other people in the perverse moral climate of Alice's lifetime – and for that matter during the middle years of Ernest's own life – tended to persuade themselves that things were wrong that were right.

It was thought wrong, for example – in the sense of being 'not done' – for women to take up such jobs as nursing, to be interested in social problems and to espouse the cause of female emancipation. Alice did all these things with a spirit and determination that could only have appeared eccentric to her godmothers, Princess Sophia Matilda of Gloucester and Feodore, Princess of Leiningen, by then married to Ernest, Prince of Hohenlohe-Langenburg. Both of these ladies – the latter being Queen Victoria's half-sister – lived in the same rarefied world in which Alice herself was born. It was not until the death of her father in 1861 that her glasshouse-cum-gilded cage came crashing down. If bad nursing was a prime cause of that death, the fault for this did not lie at the inexperienced door of the eighteen-year-old Alice. She had no pretensions at this time to any nursing skills. It was a very different Alice, however, who, ten years later, ministered at the bedside of her brother, the Prince of Wales. For Alice had lived through (and been close to the consequences of) two wars by the time death's shadow had come to hang over her elder brother in 1871. This was the high-point of her especially tender and close relationship with this particular member of her own generation in the family. It was a relationship that budded during childhood years, never to lose its bloom. But during the very earliest years Alice was a sister primarily to the Princess Royal rather than to the Prince of Wales. They inhabited the same world – rather cut off from their parents – with strong feelings of solidarity and comradeship; this in itself made the 'sister' rather than the 'daughter' relationship the predominant one of Alice's infancy.

Ever faithful to her Journal, Queen Victoria kept notes during the periods when she could not write it up in full. Three weeks after Alice's birth she brought it up to date and continued it with her usual detail. On 26 April Alice was 'shown to her sister and brother and they were delighted with her';[13] but it was not until 17 May that the Queen was feeling that

she could 'begin to forget all I went through and think only
of all our blessings'.[14] And then, on 20 May, 'at half past two
we set off with our 3 children (!!) for Claremont'.[15]

Claremont in Surrey had been bought as a royal country
residence after the marriage of George IV's daughter, Princess
Charlotte, to Prince Leopold of Saxe-Coburg (who, in 1831,
became King of the Belgians); it was a place often used as a
retreat by Queen Victoria, even though it reminded her of
Princess Charlotte, whose death while giving birth to a still-
born baby sometimes preyed on her mind.[16] Such mental
distresses – including the occasional fear of going blind – were
in general the main causes of whatever 'illnesses' were suffered
by Queen Victoria, who was very robust physically. Similar
distresses – possibly inherited? – were to prove more deadly
to the psyche of Princess Alice. But at Claremont in May 1843
all was light and happiness and the twenty-fourth of the
month was the Queen's twenty-fourth birthday. Her most
unexpectedly pleasing gift was well stage-managed by Prince
Albert: the month-old Alice 'was looking so pretty and had a
little bunch of flowers to present to me'.[17]

Of longer lasting enjoyment was another surprise even more
carefully and secretly prearranged by Albert. This was 'a small
gem of a picture by Landseer* of the little baby in her lovely
Saxon cot with "Dandy" [their terrier] watching next to it.
It is a "chef d'œuvre".'[18]

Alice was something of a peacemaker even from the very
first weeks of her life. Her christening occurred on 2 June 1843
– 'a great and interesting day'. Such at least was the quaintly
reassuring description of the Queen's mother (and King
Leopold's sister), the Duchess of Kent, who added that Alice's
christening ceremony was followed by 'a great and beautiful
luncheon. It was very grand.'[19] She also records surprise at the
sudden and belated arrival of the King of Hanover, whom she
found 'more quiet' and 'very civil'. Even the Queen, despite

---

* Sir Edwin Landseer (1802–73) was a prolific and much-favoured
painter of mid-nineteenth-century royal babies. But as he was primarily
an animal painter, a dog was ingeniously introduced into most of such
compositions; some considered his 1844 study, 'The Princess Alice and
Eros', to be the best of his royal series. Alice, in her cradle, is here
guarded by a beautiful greyhound.

an unresolved feud over jewelry with King Ernest Augustus, showed signs of wishing, or rather welcoming, an incipient melting of the ice in this direction. Though unable to resist mentioning that he 'arrived just in time to be too late', she told King Leopold that the old King was 'very gracious for him'.[20]

By this time the Queen's Journal was once more in full flood. Her description of the christening goes on for page after page, even eliciting a rare excursion into religious dogmatizing: 'This ceremony is indeed a holy and most important one – "an outward and visible sign of inward and spiritual grace" and may God bless our dear little child.'[21]

Prince Albert was in his field marshal's uniform and the Queen in her wedding lace, while the baptismal register records the presence in the chapel at Buckingham Palace of the highest dignitaries of Church and State. Band and choir were 'stationed' in the gallery, and at the appropriate signal from Her Majesty the Lord Chamberlain withdrew to 'summon the child' to be baptized by the Archbishop of Canterbury. What followed was something of an anti-climax. The Archbishop forgot to make the sign of the cross on the baby's forehead and had to be reminded by one of the assisting bishops. When the moment came for the baby to be named there was dead silence from Princess Sophia – the only sponsor there in person. After some prompting by the Duke of Cambridge the baby was duly named Alice Maud Mary. There was another embarrassing hiatus when the leaves of the prayer book stuck together and the Archbishop and attendants struggled in vain to separate them. But all ended in final triumph to the strains of the Hallelujah Chorus.

Having quickly grown 'enormous and flourishing' Alice had acquired the nickname 'Fatima', which fortunately did not stick. It was the invention of Prince Albert, from whom high praise followed a couple of months later when, in a letter to Baron Stockmar, he referred to Alice as 'the favourite'.[22]

Life for Alice, as a sister with much to keep up with, quickened pace from now on. It was a three-faceted existence corresponding to the doings of her family life, her educational regime and her emotional development.

For the three eldest royal children* no event touching on family life was more important than that which occurred in 1845. This was the purchase of Osborne House on the Isle of Wight.

It seemed strange that yet another house was needed for the royal family. When the Queen married Prince Albert she already had three large houses to live in: Windsor Castle, Buckingham Palace and the Royal Pavilion at Brighton. The trouble was that all of these were more suitable for public than for private life. Windsor had no private gardens, and at Buckingham Palace the children and nannies had to be housed in the attics. Brighton Pavilion, apart from being in the middle of the town, had neither nurseries nor gardens. What was wanted, as the Queen put it, was 'a place of one's own, quiet and retired'. It is hard to imagine anything more ideal in all the circumstances than Osborne – secluded, though reasonably accessible from London, and near the sea, with its own private beach. (News of the latter feature, given by a delighted Papa, was greeted by ecstatic hand-clapping by Alice and the Princess Royal.) The house's setting, over-looking the Solent, put the Prince Consort in mind of the Bay of Naples; and having demolished the former building he decided, with the practical advice of the brilliant Thomas Cubitt, to design something entirely new: in fact his own elaborate version of an Italian villa. The main work of re-building took just over a year and the family first went there in September 1846. The month and the year were specially memorable for Alice, who was exactly three and a half at the time. Her later memories were hazy as to happenings before that date; but this was a major landmark and she was to dwell with heavy nostalgia in years to come on the 'happy days of our childhood at Osborne'. Indeed among the places, as opposed to the people, responsible for forming her emerging character, the retreat on the Isle of Wight was of special importance. The Osborne days helped Alice to pass fairly quickly through her shy state; but the description of one of the governesses, Miss Crawford, that she soon grew 'as wild as

* Victoria, the Princess Royal, known in the family as 'Vicky'; Edward Albert, the Prince of Wales, known in the family as 'Bertie'; and Alice herself. (Prince Albert was born in 1844.)

a fawn' is misleading by modern standards. It betokened little more than an increasingly carefree attitude to life mixed in with minor peccadilloes.

Alice's elder sister was already being groomed for stardom as future consort of the King of Prussia. As such she was subjected daily to the inhibiting kind of pressures never inflicted on Queen Victoria's less well-remembered second daughter. Though the Princess Royal adored Osborne, this was primarily because it was her father's creation. Alice adored it as a liberating playground for herself, her pets and her pony. The thousand acres gave wide scope for her lively imagination; and the wonderland element continued to predominate, even though her latent seriousness was becoming observable.

The famous chalet known as the Swiss Cottage was not actually built until 1853, when Alice was ten and the Princess Royal not far off her first official steps towards becoming a child bride. But it arrived (in sections from Switzerland) in time to be an endless source of delight to the children. Perhaps the only way of appreciating the full extent of such delight is to explore Osborne (as it is even today) and examine in parti-cular the Swiss Cottage and its contents. In this life-sized doll's house, complete with mini-kitchen and micro-grocer's shop, the princesses practised housekeeping and cookery – their parents being frequent guests for tea – while their brothers got their apprenticeship in carpentry and gardening. The adjoining thatched shed still contains the royal children's tools and wheelbarrows (each marked with the owner's ini-tials). Also nearby is the quaint contraption that is uniquely evocative of this period: Queen Victoria's bathing machine, a sort of mobile and regal-looking beach hut perched high on gun-carriage-style wheels. Five steps bring the bather down into the sea. The 'machine' was lowered down a sloping pier in Osborne Bay every time Her Majesty – attended by 'a very nice bathing woman' – felt like a dip. Some of the rooms of the Swiss Cottage are still set out exactly as when they were first used in 1854.

Osborne was, of course, for all its significance as a 'little paradise', in Queen Victoria's phrase, only a summer retreat. The major part of Alice's life, right up to the time of her marriage, was thus spent at Windsor Castle. Virtually her only playmates were the other royal children; the time spent with anyone else, even her own parents, was severely limited. And this applied as much to study as to recreation as Alice took her place beside her sister and brother for the gruelling schedule of class work that their parents had so carefully worked out.

Alice was not yet four when her educational life began in some earnest. The Queen, assisted by Prince Albert's trusted adviser and Uncle Leopold's hypochondriacal but sagacious *alter ego* Baron Stockmar, saw to this. He drew up an extensive memorandum[23] in English and German setting out the principles and practical aspects of the three elder children's education. It included a timetable decreeing that Alice (who occupied the third column) should spend each day as follows: 8, breakfast with Mlle Gruner, then downstairs to the Queen; 9 and 10, out; 11, lunch, sleep; 12, sleep; 1, English lesson, Lady Lyttleton; 2, dinner; 3, out; 4, French, Mlle Charrier; 5, German, Mlle Gruner; 6, tea with Mlle Charrier. Within a month an even more formidable document[24] had been issued and solemnly signed by both the Queen and Prince Albert. It presented a 'positive plan for the future management of the children's education . . . from the first month after their appearance in this world'. The Queen herself would take charge of Alice for religious instruction as soon as she was 'sufficiently advanced'. 'It is intended,' the memorandum concluded, 'that these classes and these persons are to do for all the children now extant and possibly to come.'

Foreshadowing of conflict and of certain unhappy corollaries of being the Queen's second daughter are traceable, however dimly, to these formative days. Queen Victoria's daily inspections of the nurseries were looked forward to by the Princess Royal but dreaded by Alice; the reason may well have been the lack of psychology on the part of her mentors, which is not unusual in such situations. To be considered 'slow' is often as bad as actually being so; and this is what depressed Alice most. In fact she learned most things with great facility, showing special talent for music and drawing. It was her sister's superiority in formal learning and memory that gave her the edge as far as her rather conventional elders and betters were concerned. But Alice combined sense with sensitivity in

ways beyond the ken of her elder sister. She was much more
tactful than her, and unlike her was seldom given to showing
off. Anecdotes of precocious exploits feature strongly in the
early life of the Princess Royal, ever conscious, especially with
servants, of her exalted position. One of the most characteristic stories of young Alice, on the other hand, is told by a
former dresser of the Queen. 'I remember well,' she relates,
'meeting the Royal children in the corridor, and, as I passed
on, the Prince of Wales making a joke about my great height,
the Princess [Alice] said to her brothers, but so that I should
hear it: "It is very nice to be tall. . . ."' Whenever she in the
least suspected that anyone's feelings had been hurt, she
always tried to make things smooth again.'[25]

One of the first 'outsiders' to strike up a close friendship
with the youthful Alice was Princess Louise of Prussia, the
sister of the Princess Royal's future husband, Crown Prince
Frederick William of Prussia. Her first impression was that
Alice was 'charming, merry and amiable' but 'always occupying
a subordinate place to her very gifted and distinguished
sister'.[26] This impression tended to overcloud subsequent
comment by others whenever a comparison was being made
between the sisters. But one particular 'science' then in vogue,
though discredited as such by future research, was responsible
for an uncannily accurate prognosis of Alice's intellectual
abilities. The science in question was phrenology* and its most
notable practitioner at that time was Mr George Combe,
author of the *Philosopher Frenologist*. He was commissioned
by Prince Albert to assist Dr Becker in studying the 'cerebral'
development of all his children. He reported that Alice (who
was then nine) 'will be less apt in learning the details of knowledge from observation and instruction, but she will, in time,
go deeper and further than the Princess Royal in discovering
or learning the causes and consequences of actions and events.
. . . She may at present appear more dull in intellect than the
Princess Royal; but, in time, she will become intelligent in her

---

* Originated in the early nineteenth century by Gall and Sparzheim, on
the theory that mental powers consisted of separate faculties each having
its organ and location in a different region of the surface of the brain;
on this basis, examination of the cranium became an index to the
development of the various faculties.

own way and may advance further, in a higher sphere of knowledge, than her sister.'[27]

Alice, in short, was a slower developer than her elder sister, but her intellectual gifts were no less sharp when they appeared. She meanwhile shared all joys and sorrows, as well as all studies and recreations, with her sister; any over-shadowing of one by the other was not apparent to them – at least not to Alice. If the Princess Royal got her way through a combination of charm and the exercise of strong feelings, Alice had a quieter and often more subtle way of making her-self appealing to others. She had the almost waif-like quality of one who was as merry as any at games and larking, but there was a certain sadness in the fine lines of her angular face, and her deep-set dark eyes (accentuated by the long nose) were more often cast down as if in solemn thought than was the case with the wide-eyed, round-faced Vicky.

The first important turning-point in Alice's emotional life came in her seventh year. 'Quite a little lady now . . . with funny little lady's manners,' is how she is described by the Queen's half-sister;[28] but Feodore also recalled the frequent blushing of days gone by: 'In what a state she used to be at dinner sometimes.' In fact she was suddenly growing up more quickly than her parents had expected she would. The revolu-tions of 1848 and 1849 and the Crimean War 'took place when the Princess was already old enough to feel their gravity'.[29] This was certainly true of the war, during which Alice accom-panied her elder sister and her mother when visiting the wounded in various hospitals. Such tours Alice then made as an innocent young lady; later in life she would make them as a war-weary woman. She was with her mother when on two occasions (in 1849 and 1850) the Queen was attacked while out in her carriage. In 1851 (the year of the Great Exhibition) and 1853 the Prussian court visited London; such visits brought a further flowering of Alice's friendship with Princess Louise, who wrote:

Alice was now drawn more into the circle of the grown-up members of the family; but, in spite of this, she retained all the fascination of her charming graceful ways. A great vein of humour showed itself in her, as well as a certain sharpness in criticising people who were not congenial to her. Many a little conflict took place in the schoolroom; but while the individualities of the sisters became more and more distinct, their happy relations remained unchanged. She was a great favourite with her brothers and sisters, though they knew she was fond of mischief. To a naturally engaging manner, quite exceptional joyousness and power of showing affectionate emotion imparted an especial charm, which revealed itself in the fine lines of her face, in her graceful movements and a certain inborn nobleness and dignity.[30]

Scarlet fever (in 1855) left her more delicate than should have been the case; but Queen Victoria was impatient of physical illness and seemed not to suspect at that time that Alice's health might well become a major problem. Nor did she fully appreciate in later years how much of her ill-health was due to mental stress of one kind or another. Despite the germs of a distinctly introspective make-up, she was still as outwardly exuberant as all the others, excelling particularly in the frequent family theatricals. But her desire to help those less fortunate than herself was unusually ardent. Though she had picked up one or two adolescent royal airs,[31] probably from the Princess Royal, her sensitivity to the suffering and feelings of others was distinctly more pronounced than that of either the Princess Royal or the Prince of Wales. Such proclivities found a ready outlet during their Highland holidays, when she spent a lot of time in the humblest of the surrounding cottages. At a Sunday service at Windsor she gave her governesses the slip and escaped to the public pews; she enjoyed the feeling of proximity to strangers.

Then at the vulnerable age of thirteen, Alice was hit by a minor bombshell. She was told, in April, of her elder sister's engagement to Prince Frederick William of Prussia which, according to her mother, 'she had never suspected'.[32] But she had 'cried violently'[33] at the Princess Royal's confirmation a month earlier; and now her realization that her sister was grown up and pretty, while she wasn't at that stage, was given a cruel sort of confirmation in her own mind. Though the Queen reported that Alice was 'very amiable about her dear sister's happiness', she noted that she could never speak about it without tears coming into her eyes.[34] Quite obviously, in fact, Alice was going through the first of many periods of her life during which she was thoroughly miserable, although no one realized it. To psychological setbacks were added physical ones. They were minor in themselves, such as hurting her arm in a bad fall in 1856; but the incident attracts attention because of her mother's attributing it to 'her usual bad luck', and praising her for bearing it with her habitual 'mildness and fortitude'. It was perhaps a pity that the Queen should have laid such stress on these particular qualities. It might have been better if, when viewing Alice's matrimonial prospects, she had assessed more shrewdly her second daughter's very individualistic temperament and talents. Instead she rather complacently assumed, from such things as the hurt arm episode, that the possession of an 'amiable character' was virtually her most pronounced accomplishment. This enabled the Queen to conclude that she would be 'a valuable gift to the man she may hereafter marry';[35] but it did not prompt her to delve too deeply into what kind of man was most likely to bring her complete satisfaction. King Leopold fell in with Queen Victoria's line of thought and, in an expression whose full aptitude he may not have appreciated at the time, referred to Alice as a 'wounded warrior'.[36] Not for the last time she was indeed fighting a private civil war between heart and head, her yearnings for fulfilment vying with a reluctance to cause trouble or hurt feelings.

She was, moreover, passing through that painful 'plain stage' at this time. 'I dare say she will improve in looks again,' the Queen wrote nonchalantly to her half-sister; then she added, unexpectedly but significantly, 'Of the young Prince of Orange I have heard only favourable reports.'[37] Here are detectable the opening – if abortive – moves in the campaign to find a suitable husband for Alice. Fortunately for her she could have no foreknowledge of the private hell into which – at certain times and despite outward appearances – this campaign would ultimately lead her.

Meanwhile the days of being her elder sister's chief companion were clearly numbered. As the Princess Royal, though hardly more than a child herself, became more and more engrossed in her coming marriage, Alice began slipping into a role that had previously been dormant. From 1857–8 onwards she became, more consciously, a daughter rather than a sister. But there was another very important relationship in her world, which played a special part throughout her whole life. Naturally enough, however, it was most observable during the early years. This was the relationship between Alice and her brother, the Prince of Wales.

Chapter Two

TO THE PRINCE OF WALES

Princess Alice's voluminous correspondence with her elder brother began at a time when the unfortunate Prince of Wales's youthful problems were beginning in earnest. He was quite happy up to the age of seven, when his upbringing was in the hands of the ladies. But after that, when the tutors took over, a veritable reign of terror began. Not that it was the tutors' fault; they were well-meaning and, in most cases, congenial. But his parents, particularly Prince Albert, were determined to force-feed him with knowledge at a speed far outstripping his rate of development, and to curb his temper and other shortcomings by exaggerated and often quite unsuitable methods. Prince Albert's ultra 'pure', heavily serious and intellectually acute approach to life, moreover, did not have much appeal for his eldest son, though the last-mentioned quality was distinctly inherited by Alice. The Princess Royal meanwhile shone so brightly in her father's eyes that the next two children might have suffered more in consequence had they not, unconsciously at first, formed a very close bond with one another.

Another factor was that the most impressionable period of Alice's childhood and adolescence corresponded to the golden years of their parents' marriage. They were years during which, despite more quarrels than was once suspected, the Queen and Prince Albert were almost exclusively wrapped up in each other. Or, to be more precise, Queen Victoria was almost exclusively wrapped up in her husband and he, in turn, was more and more wrapped up in affairs of State. Indeed it was this two-fold onslaught of ever-increasing emotional demands by his wife and widening political responsibility that so greatly contributed to the Prince Consort's premature death. All in all it was more than ever inevitable that Alice in her early life should be conscious of sisterhood rather than parental attention as the dominant element. And the resultant bond with her favourite brother persisted, as it turned out, for the whole of her life. It was thus the longest-lasting of her three most important relationships with members of the other sex, the others being – for the short time allowed – with her father, and then, much later on, with David Strauss. The relationship with her husband was of a different kind, being ultimately a rather sad and empty one.

Apart from being thrown together a good deal – and often in a kind of psychological isolation from their sister – the basic key to the bond between Alice and her brother was merely that they happened to like each other very much; and they also complemented each other extremely well. Alice as time went on was brighter and much more keenly intuitive than her brother. But the young Prince was manly, decisive and loyal, all qualities that Alice admired; and he brought out all his younger sister's budding maternal instincts, so that none could soothe and comfort him in his frets and rages as effectively as she. She was even able to defuse some of his caustic comments to or about others with an apt and generous rejoinder; and Queen Victoria had no difficulty in observing: 'Bertie and Alice are the greatest friends and always playing together.' Both were only tiny when on one occasion Alice, guilty of a rare breach of discipline, was confined to her room. Her faithful brother was caught trying to pay her a surreptitious visit, his rueful excuse being that he was going only 'to give Alee a morsel of news'.

Whenever they were apart Alice sent constant letters to the Prince of Wales; he was not quite so prolific as she in the childhood days but was a faithful correspondent during the long separation of adult life. Her earliest letters date from the time when she first learned to write; they contain many quaint expressions and formally phrased invitations such as 'to play your duet with me between 5 and 6';[1] and on one occasion, addressing her letter to 'HRH The Prince of Wales', she signs herself 'Your very dutiful sister, AMM'.[2] More than anyone else, regardless of age, she could even reprove and correct the heir to the throne without his resenting it.

Queen Victoria, little as she understood her eldest son during his boyhood, at least appreciated the efforts of Alice as an intermediary. 'Dearest Mama wishes me to mention,'

Alice wrote to the Prince, 'that *you as well as me* ought not to begin our letters with thank you very, etc., but *I* thank you very, etc.'[3] The ungrammatical phrase in (added) italics was inserted afterwards by Alice; and the word 'our' had originally been 'your', the 'y' being later crossed out. This youthful essay in tact may have been rather transparent, but was not without its effect. Between the ages of seven and ten the bewildered Prince of Wales had no doubt as to who was his principal ally. After this time Alice's letters were dated, and increased in frequency, length and degree of affection. Her writing lost its childish roundness and became forward-slanting and flowing, rather like her mother's. By the time she was ten herself surprising maturity had come to characterize not only the appearance of her writing but also the style and content of what she wrote. With shades of the future nurse she informed the Prince of Wales (in 1853, on an occasion when Prince Albert was ill): 'Papa had as good a night as could be expected; he was rather feverish but he is happily less so now.'[4]

Notwithstanding such maturity in one direction, Alice combined sophistication with simplicity in a way that was possibly peculiar to such highly insulated royal children. With virtually only her brothers and sisters as playmates, imagination had to work overtime. In writing from the fairy world of Osborne to the Prince of Wales in Dublin she still spoke of her dolls as if they were human beings.[5] By now, as she approached her teens, her handwriting underwent the interesting vicissitudes connected with trying to be more grown-up. The writing itself went through a rather uncertain, jerky phase (a bit like the hand of a very old lady); this happened when she was about twelve. Thereafter it settled down to a fluent free style, more than ever after the model of the Queen, as was the case also with the Princess Royal. In her letters, by now, Alice could switch fairly easily from English into German, and sometimes into French if required. As she opened up more with her elder brother than with others she allowed her natural affection full sway, pining in tears after the departure (before Christmas in 1855) of 'my *own own* darling Brother'.[6] She carried some of his hair in a locket she never took off, even when wearing a 'low dress in the evening', since it was the only thing she had of one 'whom I *so so dearly love* and *cherish*'. But not long after this, when just turned thirteen, she portends the future in letting philosophy temper sentiment: 'If there is anything in this world that I hate it is parting. But I suppose – as everything else – that it is some good to us.'[7]

That Alice had a great capacity for loving and a great need for strong, protective and inspiring love in return is nowhere more evident – in her younger days – than in these particular letters of hers. In fact, though patently pure and innocent, parts of many of the letters could well have come from the pen of an ardent lover. She misses him pitifully when they are separated and longs for the next meeting. Osborne and Windsor might be poles apart when she is in one and he in the other; to bridge the yawning gap she asks him to 'believe me ever, *Dearest dearest* Bertie, Your ever loving and affectionate Alice';[8] she treasures the trinkets he gives her, and carries round his latest letter all day in her pocket; she pleads with him more than once not to show her letters to anyone else, ostensibly because they are 'so badly written';[9] she frets moodily if a week goes by without hearing from him; she is desperately anxious for him to excel in all things and asks him always to 'be assured of the love I bear you'.[10]

By this time (1859) the Princess Royal* was married and Alice was willy-nilly assuming the part of dutiful daughter to the Queen. She had often successfully acted as an admitted intermediary between the exacting Queen Victoria and an eldest son whose charm did not always, in *her* eyes, redeem his waywardness. But there was a subtle change as both children advanced through their teens. Alice's advice to the Prince of Wales in matters affecting their mother was shrewd and revealing. If prevented by temperament – not to mention other circumstance – from impressing herself as formidably on others, she was basically cleverer than the Queen; she was thus as a rule fairly adept at 'containing' her mother's moods. It was ever, on the other hand, the Prince of Wales's misfortune that he found his mother difficult to please, and impossible to placate when annoyed. Alice was thus a key figure to whom, first of all, her brother could thankfully let off steam; there-

* Thereafter referred to as Princess Frederick William (of Prussia), until her uncle-in-law's death in January 1861, when she became the Crown Princess.

after her technique for pacification could come into play. She found his annoyance at the Queen excusable, but sometimes felt that 'the way you expressed yourself against Her was not quite respectful'; and in such a case she would burn his letter after reading it so as to have no 'false excuse for not showing it'.[11] She invariably agreed with her brother rather than with her mother, but understood them both particularly well; and her sympathy was increased by the fact that she had often herself been the victim of the Queen's lack of sensitivity or understanding.

One letter in particular from this period sums up her feelings on such matters (often trivial in themselves), when she writes to her brother:

> What you say is correct and unless Mama asks me whether I have heard from you, I shall not mention the subject; but when I do, I will tell her about what you say; but without showing her the letter. Yet for the future I think it would be better dear Bertie if, when she makes such remarks, and gives you such advice that you should not only thank her for it but tell her you *will follow it* – Those other things which she so often alludes to, I advise you to take no notice of, but to let them pass. You must remember she is your mother and is privileged to say such things; and though, as Vicky and I have often and long known, that [*sic*] they are not said in the pleasantest way, and often exaggerated, yet out of filial duty they must be borne and taken in the right way. . . .[12]

Alice was unquestionably the stuff of which martyrs are made. She was, to some extent, a martyr by temperament; but she was also a martyr by force of often the most emotionally crushing circumstances. It was a life sentence that had its beginnings in this period of trying to be a loyal sister as well as a dutiful daughter. And if what she wrote to her brother has been quoted somewhat extensively it is because in letters written to no one else – during the early part of her life – does she reveal so much of herself. (Her published letters to her mother have been relied on in previous books about Alice as the principal source for the details of her life in Darmstadt;

but in them she is extremely guarded and circumspect; she narrates without 'confessing', chiefly because the Queen often inspired her more with awe than with intimacy.) Even more revealing, in a very different way, are the innumerable letters written to her husband Louis in days to come. They came to be more and more like letters to a son or good friend than to a husband, let alone a true soul-mate, which Louis never was. She seldom disclosed to him her inner self; but on the rare occasions on which she did, the effect, as will be seen, was shattering. Such occasional revelations resulted from the building up of tension and were afterwards regretted. She was aware of her tendency to do this even in the relatively carefree days before marriage, when she wrote so often to her brother. She asked him on one occasion to burn a previous letter 'for I am so hasty that when I am frustrated I say more than I ought and am often sorry for it afterwards'.[13]

The frustrations of these days were distinctly minor compared with the years to come, but very much part of the same pattern. The Prince of Wales is once more her confidant when she blurts out: 'I am so eternally bothered with letters and commissions for other people that I have no time left to myself. . . .'[14] Alice's sweetness and generosity have always, rightly, been stressed by those writing about her; but it has often, quite wrongly, been assumed that she was placidly indifferent to being put upon and having her mildness taken for granted. More tactful and less demanding than her mother, she humoured the Queen more and more as the years went by.

The Queen meanwhile continued her reports to all and sundry about the children's progress, always with affection but often with strange lack of insight into the remoter depths of their character. The most frequent recipient of such reports was Queen Victoria's eldest, and now married, daughter, Princess Frederick William. 'Alice,' the Queen wrote to her towards the end of 1858,

> . . . is very like him [the Prince of Wales] in many things – but has a sweet temper and is industrious and conquers all her difficulties; she is such a good girl and has made much progress lately. She now takes lessons of an evening with

Papa and reminds me so of former times [Princess Frederick William having done the same thing] when she comes in at six – and often waits in despair for 'dear Papa'. Do you recollect? Papa says she is very attentive, whereas Bertie was stupid and inattentive and quite incapable of taking in or even willing to take in anything.[15]

But the eldest son took in more than his parents supposed, even if he did not always take in exactly the things they wanted him to. In the summer of 1856 he had been visiting Napoleon III's court in Paris and did not want to come home. The Empress Eugénie remarked that his parents could not do without their children. To this the Prince of Wales retorted: 'Not do without us! Don't fancy that! They don't want us, and there are six more of us at home!'[16]

The Prince was right, at least as far as Queen Victoria was concerned; for she did not at this period particularly relish the company of the elder children. There was thus increasing reason with the passing of these particular years – during Alice's early and middle teens – for her special bond with her brother to grow deeper. These in fact were the years when they were closest of all and during which their remarkable physical resemblance to one another was as noticeable to outsiders as were their widely differing personalities. 'I never saw a stronger likeness between brother and sister,' wrote Eleanor Stanley* to her mother. 'But they are not alike in character at all; he is retiring, shy, a little inclined to be overbearing, and rather obstinate; but with a sweet kind expression about his eyes; she, not apparently knowing what shyness means, very sweet tempered and not at all obstinate.'[17] The bond meant, of course, more to Alice than to the young Prince of Wales, who by now was beginning to move about – in and out of England – and to have an interesting and varied life. Alice, at home all the time, sensed that the days of youthful intimacy with a beloved brother were numbered. She was, in the late fifties, kept increasingly busy with the 'numerous and excellent lessons' that absorbed her more and more. She felt that she should have worked harder in the years before that, for now,

* Hon. Eleanor Stanley, maid of honour to Queen Victoria, 1842–62.

by 1859, she had been brought, as a brand new pawn, into the matrimonial chess game that never ceased to absorb the crowned heads of Europe; and to Queen Victoria the game was intoxicatingly exciting. Little did Alice know, at this date, what a cruel game it could be.

Part Two

DAUGHTER

Chapter Three

ELDEST AT HOME

Alice's relationship with her mother was a complex and extremely interesting one. It went through several clearly defined and distinctive phases, as well as many ups and downs later on. It was – in certain key respects – unlike the Queen's relationship with any of her other children. Queen Victoria, despite her faults, was immensely lovable to her daughters. Indeed, except as regards the rather capricious Louise, she exercised an almost mesmerizing effect on all of them, even the independent-minded Princess Frederick William and the long-suffering Princess Beatrice. Princess Helena ('Lenchen') shared Alice's good nature but, like Princess Beatrice, could not compete in terms of brainpower. It is arguable that Alice understood her mother better than any of the girls; and she had a deep love for her, despite the periods of quarrel, because of a compassionate comprehension of human nature in general, and in particular of her mother's fluctuating emotions and occasional unfairness. But it was a strange sort of love, based certainly on much affection but sometimes depending heavily on respect, if not awe, for its survival. One particular link, thought by some to be crucial, was missing from the start, in that Queen Victoria refused to breast-feed any of her children. In this respect, admittedly, the Queen was conforming to conventions of the day; and psychologists would be hard pressed to find clues of any significant turning away by Alice from her mother in favour of some other supply for her earliest emotional needs. It is true that the nursery (and eventually schoolroom) days were mostly spent with adults other than the Queen and Prince Albert. This was usual enough, and indeed still is in upper-class circles; but such separation unquestionably produces a certain barrier between child and parent, occasionally even ending in something approaching a love–hate relationship. That this never happened between Alice and the Queen was due largely to the genuine love that blossomed between mother and daughter after Princess Frederick William married, and ripened still more in the traumatic aftermath of the Prince Consort's death. Alice's fidelity thereafter survived even when her mother's actions caused her bitter unhappiness.

But of the Queen's loving care for all her daughters at every stage there is no doubt. It was based on strong natural affection supplemented by very clearly defined ideas of the upbringing proper for little princesses. In the earliest period the Queen's sentiments for Alice are tinged with no little detachment. Interest picks up when she feels able to hand over the Princess Royal's religious instruction to Miss Hildyard (in 1847) and take over personal direction for that of Princess Alice. The latter was slower at absorbing facts than her elder sister but more desirous of probing them deeply. She was thus a readier devotee than her younger sister to her mother's brand of religion, which was basic and Lutheran. Queen Victoria favoured the post-Reformation German custom of sitting rather than kneeling for prayer, and was upset that the royal governess Lady Lyttleton encouraged the children to kneel. But it was ultimately agreed that the latter posture was more in conformity with Anglican practice. (Alice naturally inherited a strong aversion to anything 'Roman' and was to express herself forcibly on this subject more than once later on.) The Queen moreover experienced none of the mystical yearnings – let alone agonizing religious doubts – experienced by her second daughter in subsequent years.

Though Alice from about this time on saw more of her parents, it was within the continued context of a detached and 'systematic' approach rather than anything more spontaneous or liberating. The Queen and Prince Albert inspected the schoolroom and visited the nurseries at set times, and 'kept themselves thoroughly informed of the minutest detail of what was being done for their children in the way of training and instruction'.[1] Princess Helena nevertheless speaks of Alice's 'happy daily intercourse with her parents; the many walks, drives, journeys with them and her brothers and sisters; the various occupations and amusements, all watched over and shared in by the Queen and the Prince Consort'. Thus was made up 'the sum of a most perfectly happy childhood and

youth',[2] during which, as already described, the Princess Royal
and the Prince of Wales, in their respective ways, provided the
main pivots for Alice's emerging cosmos. It was not until she
had entered her teens that there was any real change; fore-
shadowings of the future lay across the page on which Queen
Victoria wrote to her Uncle Leopold from Windsor Castle just
before Alice's thirteenth birthday. She asked him to make
discreet inquiries about the 'education, entourage and disposition' of the young Prince of Orange.[3] Alice herself was
blissfully unaware of any plans being made on her behalf in
regard to the Dutch King's eldest son, Prince William
Nicholas. She reported his visit to England that autumn in a
letter to the Prince of Wales[4] without attaching any particular
importance to it. But the following summer the Dutch
Prince's mother came on a visit to Osborne. Alice had dined
with her parents and the other grown-ups for the first time in
her life a few days before. (The occasion had been a treat in
honour of the marriage between Uncle Leopold's daughter
Charlotte and the Emperor Franz Josef's ill-fated brother, the
Archduke Ferdinand Maximilian.) Thus as the Queen of
Holland sat at dinner with the Queen of England she saw, in
singling out her hostess's second daughter, a princess who was
no longer a child. If her looks had not yet, unfortunately,
begun to blossom, her mother was optimistic by the time her
next birthday had come round. 'She is such a dear sweet child
and will I think be very pretty; she has such a slight graceful
figure.'[5]

The Queen was indeed now looking at a new and different
Alice, the first major turning-point of whose life had occurred
two months earlier. For on 25 January 1858 the Princess
Royal had married Prince Frederick William of Prussia. Up
to then Alice had shared virtually everything, including a
bedroom, with her sister; now all that had come to an end,
and 'her sister's departure for a new home wrought an entire
change in her life, throwing upon her, as it did, new responsibilities as now the eldest daughter at home, and placing her in
a new position in relation to her parents'.[6] Queen Victoria at
this time badly needed an intimate and soothing companion;
Alice turned out to be ideal in ways that her mother had
never suspected. They got to know and love each other, in

fact, as never before. The Queen was undergoing an emotional reaction to the vast amount of nervous energy she had expended during the two years between the Princess Royal's engagement and marriage. She was exhilarated but exhausted and now, while resting on her laurels, she applied the brake to such plans as were in the wind. Having pushed on her eldest daughter's matrimonial programme with almost indecent haste she became determined to hold things up in the case of Alice, for whom it was a difficult and bewildering period. She had much love to give, and was not unwilling to bestow it unstintingly on her mother. But the Princess Royal's marriage had seemed to imply that seventeen was not too young to start a new life, and romance was in the air. Admittedly it was the kind of romance that would nowadays be considered cruelly counterfeit, wholly depending as it did on parents' whims and/or political demands. Surprisingly often, however, the end results were happy, and certainly the Princess Royal and Prince Frederick William of Prussia were genuinely in love. Alice's position was potentially a rather dangerous one; as the Queen's *second* daughter her marriage candidature fell ominously in between two categories. Unlike her sister, she was part of no master plan that necessitated a 'brilliant' match: for the ultimate advent of an English Empress to a liberal-minded Germany was, in the mind of Prince Albert, to be an integral part of an emerging European pattern of peace and enlightenment. Alice, on the other hand, might have less freedom of choice as to a husband than was likely to be the case with the younger daughters. Was she then to be sacrificed, and fated to get the worst of all possible worlds?

At the age of fifteen Alice – naturally oblivious to such dangers – was all too susceptible to any hints of 'romance' that were allowed to penetrate the castle walls; and she knew by now that 'identikits' for various suitable candidates for her hand were circulating through the usual channels. At the same time the anchor of the schoolroom had suddenly been removed and, despite herself, she was buffeted in different directions according to the vagaries of unfamiliar currents. It soon became evident that a safe berth alongside her mother was to be her mooring-place for the time being. The Queen,

moreover, was now looking at her through new eyes, finding
her 'so tall', and 'so much more grown up than Vicky' at the
same age.[7] (The Queen, it may be noted, was not given to over-
praising or exaggerating her daughters' good looks.) On the
eve of her confirmation and sixteenth birthday, with her
'graceful fine figure' Alice was 'altogether much admired'.[8] So
'gentle, good, sensible and amiable' was she, in fact, and such
a 'real comfort' to her mother that the Queen readily abandoned the matrimonial intrigues to which she was normally so
addicted. 'I shall not,' she informed King Leopold, 'let her
marry for as long as I can.'[9] Alice was thus kept in a state of
somewhat suspended animation as far as her future was concerned. This brought out the rather interesting introvert–
extrovert side of her character. The Queen found her 'quiet
and posée . . . so unselfish and useful'; it seemed right to her
(writing to Princess Frederick William) that the second
daughter should 'wait at any rate till a reasonable age – but
she must not be so completely exiled as you, my poor child.
I could not bear that with all our girls'.[10] (And of course she
made quite sure that it did not happen.) Others, however,
looked on Alice as a potentially 'wild fawn', anxious to escape
from the gilded cage in which she had been brought up. Both
kinds of description were wide of the mark in the sense of
being too simple, for Alice was an intensely complex character,
not least in the extent to which she kept her deepest yearnings
a secret from most people; and from her mother she hid much
in order not to hurt her. Moreover, despite talk of marriage –
even if any actual plans were temporarily in abeyance – she
was still living in a somewhat unnatural world. To celebrate
her sixteenth birthday, for example, a 'very gay pretty little
dance' was held at Windsor; but, no men. Though Alice was
the 'little Queen' of the evening she was 'dressed much too old
for her, in a double skirt of straw-coloured silk, and a wreath
of daisies and violets'.[11]

Alice herself, theoretically at least, did not feel she was too
young for marriage;[12] but she was far from restless for the
frivolous reasons presupposed by Lord Clarendon in comparing
her to a bird in a cage beating its wings against the bars. ('If
she could get out wouldn't she go it!')[13] Most of the evidence
points to her being vivacious and talkative at this stage, but

if anything all too serious in what she had to say. The year 1859, for example, was the year of the war over Sardinia between Italy and Austria, which ended disastrously for the latter. Prince Clodwig of Hohenlohe,* visiting England, was placed at dinner next to the Foreign Secretary's wife, Lady Herbert, to whom he would have had much to say. 'But,' he wrote, 'I could only exchange a few words with her as Princess Alice, the Queen's second daughter, sat on my other hand and had much to tell me. She is very well informed for her age, is quick and lively, and her face, in spite of the long nose (which she herself regards as a calamity) is very pretty.'[14] (In regretting her long nose Alice may well have been subconsciously comparing herself with her elder sister, but this very attribute undoubtedly gave interest and character to a face that was more finely chiselled than that of Princess Frederick William.) The German Prince was not the only one to find Alice talkative; it was a trait that further exemplified the introvert–extrovert pattern, being largely a cover-up for the inward shyness that she and the Princess Royal, despite outward appearances, took a long time to shake off. Though welcoming the chance of meeting 'outsiders', she often preferred to keep the conversation on ground familiar to herself. Being musical she regaled the Foreign Secretary, Lord Malmesbury, at some length on this subject when he was dining at Buckingham Palace early in 1859. He found her charming but felt she must have thought him woefully ignorant as to the topic of conversation in question.[15]

However much Queen Victoria needed – and found in Alice – a restful and understanding companion, a decision on marriage could not be postponed indefinitely. Alice had been just the right age – and possessed the ideal temperament – to fill, temporarily, the gap left by the departure of her sister. But the arrangement was not meant to be permanent, for apart from anything else the Queen's third daughter, Princess Helena, was now in her teens and growing up quickly. There was even a moment when it seemed she might be pushed ahead of Alice in the plans for a matrimonial alliance with the House of Orange. But Alice made it clear that if anyone was

* Ultimately successor but one to Bismarck as Chancellor of the German Empire.

going to be Queen of Holland it would be herself. The issue was, however, far from clear-cut. King Leopold had sown doubts as far back as 1856, feeling that it was a pity that Alice could not marry Pedro of Portugal (a Catholic), since the Oranges 'have not turned out very good friends the last few generations'.[16] There was also talk of Prince Albert of Prussia, but Queen Victoria, on the strength of reports from Princess Frederick William's husband, felt he would not do: 'It would be a very secondary and bad position for one who deserves the very best.'[17] This appeared to leave the field to 'the Orange Boy', as Prince William came to be called. Feelers had now been going out for some time and Queen Victoria received favourable reports of him from her eldest daughter in Berlin;[18] but they were mixed with allusions to his 'bad loose habits', presumably learned from his somewhat dissolute father. Lord Clarendon, however, pushed the match for all it was worth and claimed to have 'improved Pss. Alice's prospects in a conversation with the Consort'.[19] The latter saw political advantages in the scheme and was evidently too innocent to see that the Orange Boy was, unfortunately, more than a mere drinker and gambler. Some months later Clarendon (writing to the Duchess of Manchester) had to report that he 'evidently had no sense of what was decent and proper'.[20] This was at the end of 1859, by which time similar information had seeped through to Alice's parents, who were now beginning to regret their earlier overtures. To bring matters to a head the Prince of Orange let it be known, in December, that he would be visiting England the following month. Panic stations were taken up in British royal circles and Queen Victoria contemplated her daughter's having to face for the first time one of the hard decisions of life. Princess Frederick William wrote to her mother that she was 'very much astonished and as little delighted as you seem at the approaching visit of the Prince of Orange. It will be a trying and exacting time for poor dear Alice whom I shall think of much. She has many more difficulties than I had. I only saw and liked one person and had no doubts and fears, no choice to make. Oh, I am so thankful to Providence and to you all for that!'[21]

The problem was solved by the Dutch Prince himself. Though at first ingratiating himself on visiting Windsor, his

gaucherie towards Princess Alice came as a rude shock to her.
When the time had come round for a farewell dinner at
Buckingham Palace she was cured of any desire to be Queen
of Holland. On the face of it she may be thought to have
escaped from an uncomfortable fate. But perhaps a chance
was missed of changing for the better – *and prolonging* – the
lives of both Alice and the young Dutch Prince. The stimulus
of life in liberal-minded Holland and the challenge of being
married to a spirited husband, whose waywardness might have
proved to be a passing aberration of youth, might conceivably
have spared Alice much of the illness emotionally induced by
a frustrating life in backward-looking Hesse-Darmstadt. And
with Alice at his side the Orange Boy would almost certainly
have found something to live for, crowned, in every sense, by
their becoming King and Queen of one of Europe's most
interesting and progressive countries. Nothing would more
ideally have suited Alice's particular tastes, talents and temperament. But it was not to be. And the rest of the Orange
Boy's life was one of the tragic dead-ends of the age. The
anonymous author of *Uncensored Recollections*, who appears to
have known him well, calls him a 'strange creature' but 'a
kind, good-hearted and very obliging chap'.[22] Despite many
efforts he never married, but turned instead to a life of dissipation in Paris that hastened his premature death. He had sadly
lacked any objective to change his ways and lead a meaningful
life. Had his upbringing not led him to early bewilderment,
compensated for by dissipation and resulting in social awk-
wardness, he might well have proved himself 'a man' in good
rather than useless causes and been a husband worthy of the
responsive and dynamic mettle – given a daunting but exciting task – of someone like Princess Alice. Instead he died,
debauched and forgotten, in Paris – only a few months after
Alice herself.

Relief, of course, was the emotion uppermost in Alice's
mind at the time. On her seventeenth birthday her mother
found her 'in very good looks' but with her future 'still un-
decided. She is quite free and all we wish is a good kind
husband, no brilliant position (which this is not to be got) [*sic*]
but a quiet comfortable position.'[23] This somewhat soporific
prospect matched King Leopold's well-meant observation that

Alice deserved to be happily settled and 'will make an amiable companion which is not so common as people would make one believe. The young Weimar* would be well if he was but a little older; he is born in '44.'[24] But the Orange débâcle had produced a respite, and as spring came round in 1860 Alice was 'full of lark' but not knowing what to do with herself, according at least to Lord Clarendon. He makes much, as have others, of one of Alice's practical jokes and of her bantering remarks that she might yet marry the King of Holland's heir, concluding that 'that damsel will give trouble before she has done'.[25] His attitude is a typical male one of the period, picturing her as he does as a rather empty-headed teenager in love with love. On the other hand, Alice could hardly fail to have been sensitive to the 'romantic' overtures now being aimed in a certain direction, based on favourable information from Princess Frederick William. As one account rather touchingly put it, 'Her Majesty was not unreasonable when the unerring Hand of Providence interposed, and the young Prince Louis of Hesse and Princess Alice met and formed a mutual attachment.'[26]

What had actually happened was that under the restless if not invariably unerring hand of Queen Victoria, Louis and Henry, nephews of Grand Duke Louis III of Hesse, had – after adequate 'screening' – been asked to stay at Windsor for the Ascot races. The visit was duly arranged by King Leopold. And by the end of June 1860 the garrulous Lord Clarendon had a good deal to tell the Duchess of Manchester: 'Princess Alice drove Constance† about for two hours yesterday morning, when she talked almost exclusively of her own anxieties and sufferings from excessive love for Prince Louis . . . he is now the "*one being*" the only man she ever did, shall, can or will love and Mama knows from his Mother that she (A) is the only girl he could ever bring himself to marry so we expect it to be all arranged when we go abroad in September.'[27] The reality was neither as fairy-landish in its background nor as cut-and-dried in its consummation. But the auguries were good. Princess Frederick William was pleased that her father had so obviously taken to these Hessian Princes, whom she

* Hereditary Grand Duke of Saxe-Weimar Eisenach.
† Lord Clarendon's daughter, Lady Constance Villiers.

thought 'the best "specimen" (as Sir William Hooker says) of young German Princes that I have seen. . . .'[28] By this she meant that Louis and Henry seemed to be clean-living, clean-looking, virile and patently pure young men – well calculated to prove sympathetic to Prince Albert. And the Princess added the hope that someone would soon marry Princess Marie of Baden to get her out of the way, as Louis's rumoured affection for her seemed the only obstacle to a successful courtship with Alice.

What was he really like, this young Prince Louis of Hesse? And what were his own true feelings for Alice after their initial meeting? His diaries are revealing and one can begin to build up, for the first time, an intimate picture of Alice's and Louis's contrasting personalities as they reacted to what they took to be love at first sight. Allowing for Lord Clarendon's embellishments, Alice was uninhibitedly ecstatic. She was five years younger than the twenty-three-year-old Louis, who was in no doubt as to the purpose of his visit and the intended object of his affections. In neat, rather cramped writing he described his arrival in London at the end of May and the sightseeing of the first few days. He is impressed by Madame Tussaud's in 'Backer St.', and by the fact that there were more French than English women roaming Regent Street around midnight: but 'only the numerous Frenchwomen accost one'.[29] Then comes the first meeting with Princess Alice, and Louis, contrary to his normal custom, enters the place and date in full in his diary, and underlines them: '*1 June 1860 London* . . . at ¼ to 10 we drove to Buckingham Palace wearing black suits with short trousers, shoes and stockings and tricorn hats.' Introductions followed and Alice's name, when first mentioned in the diary, is written in capital letters. Subsequent entries would not be so revealing, due to Louis's reticence and brevity, were it not for added thoughts. On 7 June there was a ball at Windsor after the day's racing at Ascot and he partnered Alice in a Sir Roger de Coverley. In very small writing in the margin are the bracketed words beside the name Alice: 'is very natural, agreeable, pretty and nice'.[30] It was evident that Louis was gradually coming out of his shell, and by the time of the farewell lunch the brothers were 'sorry to leave after being received in such a kind and friendly way'. And then Louis adds, in tiny spidery writing, as if to express a surreptitious afterthought: 'I sat next to Alice again, not for the last time I hope.'[31]

Louis emerges from this first encounter as an unsophisticated but thoroughly 'nice' and correct young man, uncertain not so much of his feelings as of what was expected of him by his powerful elders. No further hints emerge from his diaries about what the future might hold until October, his parents not yet having met Princess Alice. Almost pathetically dutiful in the matter, he awaited their verdict. But in other quarters it seemed to be presumed that the die was cast. Soon after Louis's departure from England Alice heard from her old friend, ally and favourite brother. He added an arch postscript to his letter saying, '*Private* I suppose you are sorry that certain *Princes* have left.'[32] Shortly after this the young Prince of Wales left for a tour of Canada and the United States, which was to be a spectacular turning-point of his formative years. The whirl of activities and tumultuous receptions did not prevent his sending fairly frequent letters to Alice. From the St Lawrence river in August he wrote:

> I have to thank you for two letters. . . . I also received a letter from Papa yesterday, in which he told me more fully than he had before of your future prospects; my only hope is, dear Alice, that you will be happy and that you will not choose rashly, as you may afterwards bitterly repent it. I think as far as I can judge that P. Louis seems a very nice person and I know [he] is very fond of you, and that what Papa told me in his letter about his conduct has raised him very much in my estimation, and I also agree that long engagements are not advisable, *though I am sure that you know that it will be a bitter pang for me to separate from you, as it will not be the same place without you, nobody will be able to supply your place, as Lenchen is so much younger and still so childish. . . .*[33]

The young Prince followed this with a letter the next month from Niagara Falls, which certainly appeared to presume a *fait accompli* on Alice's side:

I am sure that you have made a good choice, as I was delighted with the little I saw of Louis, and it also struck me at the time that I did not think it improbable that some day he would be my brother-in-law; I have not the least doubt that he will make you a good husband, and I am equally certain that you will make him an excellent wife, as I know *what a good sister and excellent friend you have always been to me.* . . . This letter will probably reach you in Germany; I shall be anxious to know what your impressions are of your future home, and I have no doubt that you will agree with me in thinking it a very inferior country to England, wh. I am John Bull enough to consider the best of all countries. . . .[34]

Meanwhile the verdict of Louis's parents on the match was favourable, and was communicated to Queen Victoria and the Prince Consort when, accompanied by Alice, they visited Coburg in September. Louis thereupon set off for Berlin and, with lighter heart, began talking seriously for the first time – with Princess Frederick William – about England and Alice. He was back in Berlin in November when the Princess, who was all in favour of him, gave him some photographs of Alice and a plaster-cast of her hand. Only then did he make up his mind irrevocably, though Alice had long since made up hers. Thus was the matrimonial fate of Victoria's second daughter settled, and no one was more delighted than the Queen. She naturally felt it was all her own work and had already, in the summer, reported optimistically to the ever-interested King Leopold. 'We have every reason to suppose that this affair will in due time be realised,' she wrote, adding with enthusiastic tautology, 'the feelings are very reciprocal on both sides.'[35]

By August Prince Albert had not felt it premature to inform his stepmother that Louis had asked for Alice's hand; and Princess Feodore, taking comfort from the 'good accounts' from Berlin, expressed eminent satisfaction at the prospect of 'Alice's future'. No one stopped to ask if the couple knew each other well enough for such plans and assumptions to be made; indeed it would have been amazing, at that date, if anyone

had. And of course the young 'lovers' knew each other hardly
at all. Alice could see in Louis a fair-haired young German
prince of military bent, regular-featured, with tidy and
modest-sized moustache and side-whiskers; obviously keen on
and good at sport, polite, likeable and unassuming. She could
never guess how oblivious he might be towards cravings for
things that were different, for philanthropy and reform, for
intellectual stimulation, and towards her need for sensitive
but rock-like support in times of emotional trauma. She
herself barely realized how deeply she would one day nurse
such cravings; and Louis could be forgiven for imagining
her to be, at this time, little more than a decorative, de-
mure, conventional, if obviously very warm-hearted, young
princess.

He was not, however, insensitive to his possible unacceptability, due partly to lack of personal fortune or position until
he succeeded to the throne, but above all because of doubts
as to whether Alice would want to cut herself off from England
and make her home in Darmstadt. Little did he know what
was in the mind of Queen Victoria, for whose special require-
ments the match was tailor-made. In favouring the cause of
Louis she had every intention of gaining a son but no intention
of losing a daughter. Hence the desirability of a 'quiet' position
for Alice, whose presence in England as often as possible after
marriage was very much envisaged by the Queen. And thus
was the stage set for a return visit to England by Louis at the
end of November, a visit that was meant to be decisive.
Though things could hardly have been going better for the
Queen – her vicarious thrill at the romantic elements not
being accompanied by fear of permanent loss – she began to
get apprehensive as Louis's visit approached. Memories of the
nervous tension over her eldest daughter's courtship alarmed
her and she wished the denouement could be deferred.[36] But
the 'honest and good'[37] Louis now knew exactly what was
expected of him from the moment he landed in Dover in the
small hours of the morning of 24 November 1860. He was in
Windsor by lunch-time, shortly after which he was walking
with Alice in the Home Park. Once more he writes her name
in big letters in his diary,[38] varying the procedure by surrounding it with dots in the entry of a few days later. But it was not

until the twenty-ninth that he spoke to Alice 'for the first time almost undisturbed'.[39] This he managed to do while sitting beside her after lunch, until they were interrupted by a lady singing songs. They were seldom alone and there was constant activity what with walks, games with the younger children, elaborate meals and entertaining, and shooting. The atmosphere of suspense was mounting, and Louis's nerves may well have been given an artificial boost by the slightly bizarre circumstances of breakfasting one day in full uniform. The date, which turned out to be the decisive one, was 30 November, the earlier part of which was spent inspecting troops. On the way to and from Aldershot in the train Louis spoke only to Alice. Soon after they got back to Windsor Prince Albert came and talked to him about 'the reason for my visit here' – as if he did not know! – 'and said he hoped that after a few days I would know Alice well enough'.[40]

Queen Victoria meanwhile had been far from idle. The Prince Consort's talk with Louis in fact had been at her prompting.[41] Her invaluable volume entitled 'Remarks—Conversations—Reflections' records how nervous they had all been, particularly Louis, after the first reunion of the two young people on 24 November;[42] but 'we took care that at meals they should sit together and when out walking they should be able to talk to each other'; and 'every day I saw that they seemed to come nearer to one another'. The Queen was in fact absolutely in her element. Indeed no approaching Christmas of the future would ever see her as fulfilled and content as she was at this moment. It climaxed the happiest decade of her life and the personal heyday of her reign. Her husband appeared (at least to her) to be happy and healthy; as Prince Consort (since 1857) he had consolidated that winning-over of the British public that had begun with the 1851 Great Exhibition. The Prince of Wales, after his triumphant tour of North America, had assumed an entirely new image in his mother's eyes; and there were now (after the three eldest) six more children to reflect matriarchal majesty and refuel maternal fires until far into the future. The Queen was brimful of zest for whatever tasks might lie at hand; and none could have been more congenial than that of stage-managing a princely request for her daughter's hand. The more elaborate production starring Prince and Princess Frederick William had been nothing if not, *inter alia*, an effective dress rehearsal; it had also ensured a minimum of first-night nerves for the Queen on subsequent occasions. Louis, on the other hand, had no such advantages, as, while dressing for dinner, he reflected on the conversation with the Prince Consort and felt all round him the palpable air of expectancy at Windsor Castle. The big moment, involving himself in a principal role, was only hours away. He was virtually speechless with agitation. But the 'secret' was already out in Darmstadt[43] and for Louis at Windsor it was a case of now or never.

The Queen liked to think she was quite *hors de l'affaire*[44] but her remote control of the situation was unerring; with the proprietorial confidence of an authoress describing two of her own characters she could write, on 29 November: 'Matters come daily nearer to a climax for one sees how both young hearts expand toward one another.'[45] On the next evening (after the day at Aldershot) she sat down after dinner in the Red Room as if taking her place in the royal box to watch a command performance that she herself had produced. Ten years – the golden years – had flown by since she had heard Alice in a 'voice sweet and penetrating like that of the Queen'[46] speak her parts in the numerous nursery theatricals. Now she was to witness that same daughter grappling with her first real-life drama. The supporting cast were strategically placed, nearest to Her Majesty being 'some of the Gentlemen'.[47] She engaged them in the kind of artificially animated conversation carried on by actors near the wings while a spotlight picks out the principal players. The latter, that is Louis and Alice, 'happened' – in the Queen's phrase – 'to be standing alone at the Chimney Piece'. They did not of course *happen* to be standing anywhere; they were left in splendid isolation by the excessive discretion of the others in the room, though the Queen's covert gaze did not for a moment leave the unfortunate couple. She could spot immediately when the psychological moment had come and gone; and at that precise point she ceased to be an apparent spectator. Recognition of her role as chief protagonist in the whole drama was implicit in the hush that fell as the Queen rose to leave. Her exit was deftly planned 'and when I passed to go to the other room Alice and

Louis whispered it to me. We had to sit quiet and crochet till
the evening was over and then Alice came to our room, where
we went in with Alice and here the confirmation of what
occurred took place, which was very moving, as poor dear
Louis was so completely *überwältigt** with his feelings as to be
unable to say a word; he seemed quite over-powered.'[48]
The Queen's impression of Louis's emotional state is certainly confirmed by his diaries. There is no doubt about his
almost childlike excitement and strongly sentimental feeling
about what was portended by the great day. The date, written
in larger letters than usual, has been underlined three times
in the diary, and next to it in the margin are six strokes of the
pen forming a pattern – a sort of homespun giant asterisk – to
mark the occasion and highlight the corresponding entry. But
he found it hard to articulate in any other direction (partly
because of lack of fluency in English) and seems to have played
his part throughout in a sort of stunned haze. His account of
the proposal, however – if there was any formal proposal in so
many words – is no less touching for its succinctness: 'After
dinner I talked to Alice by the fireplace in the Red Room.
Everyone else was talking too, and suddenly I had become
engaged to my dear Alice!!!'[49] As to the immediate circumstances of this decisive moment, he has no other observation
to add than: 'It was exactly ½ past 10.'

The scene that followed was the part dearest to the Queen's
heart, at this moment flowing over with warmth for a daughter, not yet quite eighteen and on the verge of married bliss –
that blessed state which, for the Queen herself, was a foretaste
of heaven. 'With heart full of joy, gratitude and emotion do
I write these few lines!' was how she started her 'Remarks'
volume the following morning.

This day or rather more last night was one of those of
intense emotion – not to be forgotten, like the 29th Sept. '55
and the 25th Jan. '58.† When we came to my room Alice
and I explained to Albert what had happened which was a
surprise to him. Alice said in much agitation – though quiet
all the time as she always is – and has since tried to repeat

* Overwrought.
† The respective dates of the Princess Royal's engagement and marriage.

it to me as exactly as her beating heart would allow – that Louis said he could no longer bear going on as they had done for this week, and then asked her if she did not think Germany too small and if she would exchange it with England; and that he was nowhere happy without her; did she like him enough to do that?

She answered without hesitation. She embraced her dear Papa and me and Louis was sent for to Albert's room. Albert went in first to him and returned to fetch Alice and me. When I came in I gave him my hand which he kissed and pressed for some time unable to speak, – while I embraced him. Then Alice went up to give him her first kiss and it was a very moving moment for the dear young man was so overcome with the depth of his feelings that he clasped her in his arms and bent his head on her shoulder. Such a moment is one most touching and moving to witness for Parents' hearts when 2 such fine and good young beings pour out the first confession of their mutual love . . . a foretaste of another and better world.[50]

Queen Victoria felt it was all somehow very different from the atmosphere surrounding the engagement of the Princess Royal: 'She was a child not yet 15 . . . [whereas] Alice has had her trials [and is] quite old enough to marry at once.'[51] Alice, though in tears, remained calm as her parents embraced her and, turning to Louis, told him what a treasure they were giving up to him. The young Prince wrote in his diary: 'The Queen led *Her* into my arms. K! [presumably signifying kisses or an embrace] sealed the bond.'[52] Having completed this entry with the words: 'At 12 the bride-to-be took leave of her groom', Louis stayed up late writing to his parents, as well as to his uncle, the Grand Duke of Hesse.

Contrary to what the Queen wrote, however, the couple were not by any means married 'at once'. It was parentally decreed that no ceremony should take place for eighteen months, by which time the shadow of death had fallen across the British royal family. But the early days of being engaged were probably the happiest of Princess Alice's entire life. They were like nothing that had gone before or was to come: carefree and yet exciting; filled with love but free from disillusionment. For Louis and Alice were unquestionably as deeply in love as the limitations of temperament, inexperience and lack of intimate knowledge of each other would allow. Alice, unaware or untroubled by such limitations, let herself go in consequence. For the moment the childlike qualities shut out the serious ones that always lurked not far in the background. 'How happy we were to see each other again for the first time at breakfast,' on the morning after their engagement, Louis records.[53] And how typically 'Victorian' – as we would now call it – was the whole scene that followed. The Prince Consort had gone to London and Louis was for the first time given what was obviously meant to be intimate glimpses into the Queen's and Alice's lives by being shown their bedrooms. After this initiation ceremony Queen Victoria presented him with a lucky horseshoe from Scotland. In his diary he now proudly refers to '*us*' when speaking of Alice and himself.

The newly engaged Princess was meanwhile intoxicated with the moment, oblivious of the fact that her mother was still in reality playing the star part to her complementary supporting role of eldest daughter at home. Alice showered her fiancé with presents on the morrow of the engagement; Louis mentions in particular 'a medallion with her hair, and one with a piece of white heather which she found on September 12, 1860'.[54] And the next day, a Sunday, he received a prayerbook. They snatched as many moments alone together as possible; Louis records the exact hour and duration of such private and much-treasured interludes. The remainder of the time was spent with the rest of the family and guests, and Louis proved himself extremely popular. The Queen herself was delighted with him, having liked him from the very first. Writing years later, Alice's eldest son said his father was Victoria's favourite son-in-law.[55]

According to Lord Clarendon, however, writing soon after the engagement had been announced, 'Nobody seems much to like Princess Alice's marriage and people say that if she is not to be married for 2 years she had better not have engaged herself now as something more desirable might turn up in the meanwhile. I fear that the more the bridegroom is seen the less worthy he will be thought of such a charming little bride.'[56]

But Louis himself was fortunately ignorant of any uncompli-
mentary remarks being made behind his back. If the aristo-
cracy were preparing to be as critical of him as they had been
of the Prince Consort, he was likely to be far enough removed
from English society as to be largely unconscious of it. Little
did the gossips know, moreover, that a more 'worthy' bridegroom would not have suited the master plan behind the whole
match. Princess Frederick William might have been mirroring
her mother's thoughts when writing to her, somewhat smugly,
that Alice's position would not be as fine as hers in Berlin but
that she would have more freedom.[57] Such 'freedom' in fact
meant in the first place greater availability than in her sister's
case for keeping her mother company even after marriage. The
Queen gave serious thought to the implications of all this in
terms of where the engaged couple should live later on. Meanwhile Alice herself was safely lost in a new world of her own,
telling her friend and cousin Princess Mary of Cambridge that
she had difficulty finding words adequate to describe her
happiness. Her main preoccupation was to be worthy of a love
that she felt was more than she deserved.

Louis stayed at Windsor until after Christmas; it was his
first Christmas away from home. He was homesick but still,
in endearingly artless fashion, thrilled and almost unbelieving
about what was happening to him. His Christmas presents
from Alice were a pretty pin, a book and a cast of her hands.
(Casts of hands were very much in vogue at this time.) His last
two hours with Alice were spent, on 28 December, in 'papa-
in-law's' room; that same day they parted, having exchanged
pocket handkerchiefs, which were 'quite in a sop with their
tears'.[58] The last entry in Louis's diary for the year 1860 was
made, after he had arrived back in Darmstadt, in huge letters:
'I WROTE TO ALICE.'[59] Indeed he had been doing virtually
nothing else but write to Alice ever since leaving. He was
rewarded by an immediate reply in the first of a long and
revealing series of letters that streamed out from Alice
over the years to come, were faithfully stowed away in the
Darmstadt Archives and barely looked at by anyone from
that day to this.* As she thinks of nothing and nobody else

* With rare exceptions, the letters exchanged between Alice and Louis
were in German.

than him for whom she longs 'so unutterably', Alice tells him:

> Your picture stood by my bed, and your handkerchief and the paper on which you had written down the stations were under my pillow. God be with you, dear, dear angel . . . I miss you so dreadfully, I see you everywhere and seem to hear your dear voice. . . . When I said goodbye to you yesterday I thought my heart would break; now I think of when we shall see each other again, and of *everything* we talked about and did together, and most of all of when the 18 months are over – and we shall *never* say goodbye again. . . .[60]

'How hard it is to part from someone you love,' was Louis's rejoinder.

> The day before yesterday I was still with you, my darling, and today, at the same time, I am far, far away from you. What my heart felt when I took leave of you I need not tell you, for you know it already, my beloved bride-to-be. When I left for London I felt miserable – first the park disappeared from sight, and then the last tower of the Castle, which I could see for a long time in the bright moonlight. And I felt very sad as the train passed through Staines, for that was the last place where you and I had been together. . . .[61]

In the remainder of a very long letter he constantly reiterates his loneliness and love. As midnight strikes on the following evening he puts pen to paper again to wish Alice '*Prost Neujahr!*'[62] For so, he says, 'the people in the streets are calling out to each other, and so I wish you from the bottom of my heart . . . [Louis here ventures from German into English for the next phrase] A Happy New Year!!!' It is yet another long letter, written as Louis cogitates in the early hours of the morning that 'it is a strange, joyful, proud feeling to be entering on a new year as a bridegroom-to-be, and to be able to think that far away my dear, true bride is thinking of me . . .'. Being up late did not prevent him from rising with the lark to wish Alice a happy new year all over again. Later the same day he wrote yet another letter to tell her he had been dreaming about her the night before, standing in a white dress in the Red Room at Windsor. His parents had not realized that a special photograph had been taken of the fireplace in this room where he had proposed to Alice. But it did not prevent his appreciating the photograph they gave him of the room, including the fireplace; it was yet another of the manifold reminders, all of which he reported in detail to Alice, of how much he longed to be with her. He was very conscious of the exact time at which things happened as well as of the precise number of days or weeks that had elapsed since an important event or would elapse before something else important was due to occur. And in a letter from Potsdam on 10 January 1861 he reflects: 'In *only* [underlined twice] 17 months an L hopes to *marry* an A. . . . Really a very agreeable thought, that!'[63]

The Queen's feelings were summed up in the form of gladness that Alice would '1st of all have a peaceful and happy home without difficulties and 2ndly that she will not be entirely cut off from us and monopolised as poor Vicky is'.[64] But Lord Clarendon was almost certainly wrong in supposing that Alice could hardly wait to escape from England and 'be off to Darmstadt or Potsdam on her own hook'.[65] She was still at this time very much her mother's daughter and willing to relegate her own ideas to second place. The Queen for her part made monumental efforts to secure parliamentary agreement for adequate financial arrangements in her favour. A lengthy request on the subject from her to the Prime Minister, Lord Palmerston (by no means her favourite person), was sent off at the end of July 1861, before any official public announcement of the engagement had been made. The Queen also managed, by her incomparable personal diplomacy with Disraeli, to secure Tory support for a generous settlement. In the event a dowry of £30,000, with an annuity of £6,000, was voted through the House of Commons without a dissentient voice; but the Prince Consort remarked, all too truly: 'She will not be able to do great things with it.' Alongside all her frustrations in later life lack of substantial funds was indeed

an added cross that Alice had to bear. Apart from such gloomy
prognostications about money, what did the Prince Consort
think about all that was now happening? The question is part
of the whole relationship – a very important one – between
Alice and her father.

Chapter Four

14 DECEMBER 1861

A biography of the Prince Consort written with true insight and based on the mass of unpublished material that comparatively few people have even seen has yet to be written. But the myth of his being a stern, unbending Victorian paterfamilias has for some time ceased to hold sway.[1] A quite different picture emerges from a close observance of him in the context of the lives of Alice and her elder sister.

The special relationship between the Prince Consort and his eldest daughter was very striking. Had he lived, however, Alice, though she would not have made her father's love for her sister diminish, might well have become an even more particular object of his interested affection. For she was more like him than was the Princess Royal. She inherited not only his brain and his ideals, but also a sort of compassionate fatalism that had little in common with Queen Victoria's (and the Princess Royal's) dogged (sometimes self-centred) optimism. And had the Prince Consort lived longer he would have provided a stimulus and encouragement to her enterprises that she lacked from other quarters and to which she would have responded in a fashion calculated to delight him. As it was he represented for her, as far as time allowed, an adored father on whose teachings she based her whole life. To the end of her days she adapted her activities and aspirations to what she felt he would have wished. Her dying words were 'dear Papa'; and the Prince Consort, during his own last illness, relied entirely on the one person, Alice, who at that moment was in many ways closer to him than any other person in the world. He told her things about his illness, and his conviction of imminent death, that he did not even like to tell the Queen.[2]

The bond had been forged in the earliest days when the Prince Consort was a frequent visitor to the nursery. It was he who fashioned Alice's first nickname of 'Fatima'; but when she lost her baby roundness she seemed all the more to bring out his most tender and protective feelings. When he spoke of her, as he often did, as 'poor dear little Alice', it was as if he felt the need to take her part.[3] He may well have sensed that, as in his own case, her vulnerability lay in areas other than mere physical health, which in her youth was always good. Tiredness and illness, when it came to both of them later on, came in the same way – through a weariness of the soul. When she was twelve Albert found his second daughter 'still very delicate and nervous',[4] for he was sensitive to a side of her outwardly hardy nature that was largely hidden from others. What he was really spotting was symptoms of her own acute sensitivity – particularly to the feelings and sufferings of others. She was keenly aware, for example, of how much he missed Princess Frederick William after her marriage when she, Alice, took her elder sister's place as a pupil under the direct tuition of her father. She went to his study every evening at six o'clock; but often he was too tired to come. Alice was then fourteen; her father, who had just been made Prince Consort, took on an overpowering volume of work. Alice could see the difference in him, though Queen Victoria, impatient of what she took for lack of physical stamina, could not or would not see the grim writing on the wall. The will to live was slowly draining itself out of this noble servant of his wife, his Queen and his adopted country; his dreams of an enlightened Europe, inspired by a liberal and united Germany, no longer seemed so sure of realization. But Alice all the time learned more from him than he himself was aware of teaching her: above all, perhaps, of how harsh the world can be and how uncomprehending even one's nearest and dearest when a sensitive nature begins to be assailed by frustration. But she also learned much of historical and political reality from both past and present events; her father was a scrupulous tutor and her own reaction was invariably to ally herself mentally with those who suffered rather than with those in search of glory. So it was with the bitter lessons of the Crimean War, which were not lost on Alice even at the age of thirteen; and then, in 1857, came the Indian Mutiny. The rights and wrongs of this tragic and bloody affair do not belong to this story, but Alice's sympathies went out in particular to Lady Canning, the wife of the Governor General, on whom so much responsibility, and some blame, had fallen. Alice's letter to her was, for a girl of fifteen, as mature and understanding as that of any adult.[5]

Alice proved herself to be a true daughter of her father when, in April 1859, she underwent the ordeal of confirmation according to the Coburg ritual. The Prince Consort himself was among those who had instructed her, using the *Manual of Religion and of the History of the Christian Church* by Carl Gottlieb Bretschneider (formerly 'General Superintendent' in Gotha). The Prince's object throughout was to encourage her in serious religious thought and in independent reflections on religious questions.[6] Such preliminaries paved the way for interrogation by the Archbishop of Canterbury. She would never forget, she told the Prince of Wales in a letter, how frightened she was on the day of her examination; but after the first few questions it went quite well.[7]

As Alice at this moment stood on the threshold of woman-hood she was naturally a daughter first of all to her mother. But by the end of the following year, when the Prince Consort stood on the brink of mortal illness she was one of the first to sense what was afoot and became increasingly her father's daughter from that time on. Ironically the first warning signs became visible during Alice's most exciting adventure up to that time: in September 1860 she went with her parents to her father's native Coburg. (This was the occasion when the Queen and the Prince Consort first met her future parents-in-law.) While walking through one of their boyhood haunts with his brother Ernest, the Prince suddenly broke down and said that this would be his last glimpse of his old home.[8] This despairing prophecy followed on a serious carriage accident in which one of the coachmen was seriously hurt and the Prince Consort's nerves were shattered. Though never his former self again, the Prince Consort did not relax in any of his duties, particularly as they touched on Alice in the days immediately following her engagement, which he referred to as the 'great Alician event'.

He was indeed as delighted as the Queen over the match, having formed a highly favourable view of young Louis; among the latter's most precious possessions were the opal studs his 'Papa-in-law' gave him during his first Christmas

stay at Windsor. And it was the Prince Consort who had to do
the hard bargaining on Alice's behalf with regard to her future
in Darmstadt. He showed infinite patience and tact in collabor-
ating with the former Prime Minister, Lord John Russell,*
over the drafting of the necessary marriage treaty with the
Hessian government. Special care had to be exercised over
providing for the probable succession, in due course, of Alice
as Grand Duchess without distress to the present bearer of this
title, Louis's aunt, who was understood by the Prince Consort
still to be hopeful of having children.[9] And the Prince Consort
was insistent that the treaty should be signed in England 'as
was customary'.[10] He was also the intermediary in the protracted discussions between the Queen and her ministers as to
whether, as she wished, Prince Louis could appropriately be
given the title of Royal Highness. After endless legalistic
argument the Queen eventually gave in – for the time being.

Alice and her father became natural and necessary allies in
comforting Queen Victoria during the near-derangement that
overtook her on the death of her mother. The Duchess of Kent
died on 15 March 1861 and the Queen's paroxysms of grief
greatly alarmed the Prince Consort; he knew there was only
one thing to be done, and only one person who could be any
real help. It was to his daughter Alice that he turned with the
words: 'Go and comfort Mama.' The Queen later commented:
'Dear good Alice was full of intense feeling, tenderness and
distress for me.'[11]

The Prince Consort was not only chief mourner at the
funeral that followed but also sole executor of his mother-in-
law's will. His worries and responsibilities were thus, at the
worst possible moment, greatly increased. To add to the strain
Alice and her father had to accompany the Queen at the end
of August on a somewhat macabre pilgrimage. The Duchess
of Kent had lived at Frogmore in Windsor Great Park, not far
from the castle. Characteristically, almost every day during
the previous winter Alice had gone over to see, comfort and
play the piano for her ailing grandmother. Her gift for bringing
solace to the sick was remarkable even then. But now they
were going over to 'keep the birthday' of the Duchess five

* Then, under Palmerston's premiership, Foreign Secretary.

months after she was dead. Though her remains had been removed to the mausoleum in the grounds, the Queen had ordered (shades of things to come) her mother's room to be left exactly as it was at the moment she had died. The Queen's attitude to death has become one of her best-known traits. She indulged in the most morbidly exaggerated demonstrations of mourning and lamentations that can possibly be imagined. She squeezed from them every conceivable atom of the peculiar consolation, verging on a sort of woeful ecstasy, that they provided for her. The August visit to Frogmore was described by her as 'terribly trying' at first,[12] but the next day's placing of birthday garlands on the great granite sarcophagus wrought a wondrous change and she ruminated that this was the 'Brightest Birthday of all to Her who was spending her first in a better world'.[13]

Queen Victoria often spoke in awed and seemingly wistful tones of the beckoning serenity of the hereafter. But kind and good as was her nature its inner depths were far from mystical; she had no desire for a premature glimpse of the next world, preferring what she felt to be the nearest thing to it on earth. And the main source of this was of course the Prince Consort, with whom, as well as Alice and the rest of the family, she now set off for a round of expeditions in the Highlands; everything about it had all the elements, for Queen Victoria, of a visit to an earthly paradise. It never occurred to her that it would be her last round of such expeditions when she wrote, after the third of the three long treks: 'This was the pleasantest and most enjoyable expedition I ever made; and the recollection of it will always be most agreeable to me, and increase my wish to make more! Was so glad dear Louis (who is a charming companion) was with me. Have enjoyed nothing so much, or indeed felt so much cheered by anything, since my great sorrow.' For Alice and Louis (reunited for the first time since their engagement) the idyll was of even greater intensity; despite the pouring rain, the excitement of steering their ponies side by side through the glens and sleeping incognito at tiny inns was positively intoxicating. Lady Augusta Stanley reported that Princess Alice was at one point too excited to be what she called 'getatable';[14] though a few days later she espied symptoms of the melancholy side of love sickness as

Alice hovered about her room: 'I think poor darling that she seeks the sympathy of matrons at present.'[15] Finally the sun shone and on the last expedition of all, through the valley of Cairn Lochan, the Queen wrote: 'Not a cloud was in the bright blue sky.' There seemed nothing to prevent an early announcement of the date for Alice's wedding.

A very big cloud, however, the blackest and most ominous of Victoria's whole life, was lingering just beyond the horizon. Before going to Balmoral and the Highlands that year the royal family had visited the Prince of Wales in Ireland. He was attached to the Grenadier Guards at the Curragh Camp. The Queen and the Prince Consort, anxious about his progress and behaviour, were accompanied by Alice; it was no doubt providential for the young Prince that his favourite sister was there at the time. Their brief moments together made sure – now that they saw each other so seldom – that the special bond between them was unbroken. It was needed at a critical moment some months later when the Prince Consort was dying and it was Alice who sent for him to hurry to the bedside. The Queen refused to do so as she blamed much, if not all, of her precious husband's agony and illness on worry over an isolated incident connected with the Prince of Wales's conduct while at the Curragh.

The first hints of the latter reached Albert on 12 November, by which time negotiations had entered a delicate stage regarding a match between the Prince of Wales and the beautiful young Princess Alexandra of Denmark. The Prince Consort learned, in a letter from Baron Stockmar, of rumours snaking their way round Europe about his son's having had an affair with an actress. Such rumours referred to the smuggling of a pretty young girl called Nellie Clifden into the Prince's sleeping quarters by his brother officers after an evening of merry-making at the Curragh. What happened was thought by many to be inevitable at some point, particularly after the Prince's unnaturally strict and inhibiting upbringing. But it came as a shattering blow to the puritanical Prince Consort, who in his younger days had aroused doubts as to his own virility by his apparent invulnerability to such temptations. The distraught father followed up a long hectoring letter to his son and heir, by that time in Cambridge, with a personal visit two weeks later. All of this came after several other shocks to the already depressed and debilitated Prince Albert: a bad bleeding attack suffered by his haemophiliac son Leopold and the death of young King Pedro of Portugal (once thought of in passing as a possible husband for Alice), on whom such high hopes had been pinned for the liberalizing and reforming of that country. The Prince Consort's visit to Cambridge followed hard on his getting soaked and chilled at Sandhurst while inspecting the new Staff College. Rheumatic pains, insomnia, neurosis and exhaustion gave way to a diagnosis of gastric fever that was thought to have started in the middle of November.[16] The Prince Consort struggled on with his duties, almost his last important official action being to tone down a tendentious Foreign Office dispatch to the United States Government after seizure of the British ship *Trent*. 'He did but show in his masculine princely manner, the same spirit which actuated the Princess Alice, when much later, though thoroughly worn out at thirty-five years of age, she struggled to the last to fulfil the duties of her trying position.'[17] Though refusing at first to believe that her husband was really ill, the Queen ultimately looked upon the trip to Cambridge as the crucial factor in setting the hand of death in motion.

Alice had few illusions about how seriously ill her father was. She sent regular reports to her fiancé as matters became more and more critical. But as early as 3 December she felt that her father's own pessimism meant that he could hardly hope to get any better. Her surprisingly mature grasp of the situation is notable: 'Poor Mama is very unhappy about it – but not worried. But she has no idea how to nurse him, although she would so gladly do everything. One must get used to it when one is young. . . . I have to listen to my dear parents' mutual complaints – I only hope I am really useful to them, for I do want to do everything for them, and I would still more gladly bear everything for them, if it were possible. . . .'[18] Alice, as shown by her further letters to Louis, abandoned all preoccupations alien to her central role, now reaching its climax, as daughter to the Prince Consort. The latter could eat nothing on Sunday, 1 December; as he sat listening to Alice playing the piano after dinner it was plain

that something was badly wrong. The doctors (Dr Jenner and
Sir James Clark) were justifiably worried and a shivering and
wakeful night was followed by deterioration next day. For two
or three days the Prince Consort still tried to go through the
motions of work and normal existence. The Queen was
encouraged when coming in to see him on the evening of the
fifth. Perhaps his improvement was due to the intangible
therapy of the almost constantly present Alice (now sleeping
in the room next to her father), who had been reading to him.
But the improvement was only temporary, a momentary
arresting of the inevitable; and it seemed throughout as if
father and daughter shared an unspoken secret knowledge of
what fate had already decreed.

Such knowledge brought its own kind of reward: a certain
fatalistic peacefulness unattainable by the Queen, whose
feigned optimism was pathetically lost on the dying Consort.
The last Sunday of his life was 8 December, when he asked to
be moved into an airier and more comfortable room. The one
chosen was the Blue Room where, as it happened, both King
George IV and King William IV had died. The patient asked
for a piano to be moved in and one of the two hymns played
on it that day by Alice was 'A strong tower is our God'. She
wrote a very long letter to Louis on 9 December. She was not
put off by the warnings of possible infection and went in and
out of her father's room more than ever. But she confessed
that the preceding week had been the most 'difficult, tense'
one she had ever experienced; she found her father's pathetic
groaning almost unbearable and yet succeeded, unlike her
mother, in appearing calm and happy. Day by day she fought
her private battle against despair. The Princess Royal, and
her specially loved elder brother, were absent; the other
children were too young to be intimately involved in the
drama. Though she was wrapped up only in the agony of the
moment, a terrible shadow lay across the future in a manner
certain to be of particular significance for herself. She meanwhile put on paper thoughts meant only for Louis at this
moment of crisis: 'It always makes me feel so much better,'
she wrote on 12 December, 'to tell you everything, because
you share so much in my feelings and understand my deep
love and reverence for dear Papa, who is so great! so good! in

every respect. . . .' Two spirits, those of father and daughter, were thus at times more intimately linked even than those of the Prince Consort and the Queen herself, as they stood hand in hand on the edge of an eternity in which one had to be swallowed up at any moment. It was as if all other mortals, however important, were momentarily incidental.

It was indeed the quiet dominance of the whole scene by the eighteen-year-old Alice that most struck those round about. Her part in the drama, and in particular in the events of 8 December, were described in detail by a member of the Queen's household a few days after the Prince Consort's death:

The last Sunday Prince Albert passed on earth was a very blessed one for Princess Alice to look back upon. He was very ill, and very weak, and she spent the afternoon alone with him while the others were in church. He begged to have his sofa drawn to the window, that he might see the sky and clouds sailing past. He then asked her to play to him and she went through several of his favourite hymns and chorals. After she had played some time she looked round and saw him lying back, his hands folded as if in prayer, and his eyes shut. He lay so long without moving that she thought he had fallen asleep. Presently he looked up and smiled. She said: 'were you asleep dear Papa?' 'Oh no,' he answered, 'only I have such sweet thoughts.' During his illness his hands were often folded in prayer; and when he did not speak, his serene face showed that the 'happy thoughts' were with him to the end. . . .

The Princess Alice's fortitude has amazed us all. She saw from the first that both her father's and mother's firmness depended on her firmness and she set herself to the duty. She loved to speak openly of his condition and had many wishes to express. He loved to hear hymns and prayers. He could not speak to the Queen of himself, for she could not bear to listen, and shut her eyes to the danger. His daughter saw that she must act differently, and she never let her voice falter, or shed a single tear in his presence. She sat by him, listened to all he said, repeated hymns, and then when she could bear it no longer, would walk calmly to the door,

and rush away to her room, returning with the same calm
and pale face, without any appearance of the agitation she
had gone through.[19]

From now on what the doctors had finally agreed was
typhoid fever gradually took its toll. But the patient's inner
disposition was both reflected in and further conditioned by
the eerie peace of that last Sunday; and of the mortal nature
of his illness he had long been convinced. On the following
Wednesday he asked Alice if she had written to Princess
Frederick William. 'Yes,' she said, 'I told her that you were
very ill.' 'You did wrong,' was his reply. 'You should have
told her that I am dying. Yes, I am dying.' From now on Alice
threw away all hesitation and took unchallenged command of
the whole situation. There was little time to lose and it was
not in Alice's character to let wishful thinking about the
Prince Consort's possible recovery be the cause of an injustice.
For it would have been unjust (and a matter of deep distress
to Alice) had the Prince of Wales, of all people, been prevented from being at Windsor before his father died. But the
Queen still vehemently believed that he was the real cause of
all that was happening and it became evident that she did not
intend to send for him. So Alice did so on her own initiative
and without her mother's knowledge. She 'had tried gently but
firmly to warn her mother of what was coming. But though
by now Queen Victoria realized that he was very ill indeed,
nothing could bring her to believe that she might lose him.'[20]
The telegram to the Prince of Wales went off on the evening
of Friday, 13 December. The young Prince, hitherto in the
dark as to what was going on, took the last train from Cambridge, which arrived at Windsor at three o'clock in the
morning. He was appalled and grief-stricken, and ready to do
anything that might help. 'But the suppression under which
he had been brought up had destroyed his initiative and it was
Princess Alice who took the lead.'[21]

Thus dawned a date – 14 December 1861 – that was never
to be forgotten as long as Queen Victoria lived. The anniversary never came round without grim memories of what had
happened in 1861; and by one of those curious quirks of fate,
it was to be on two subsequent 14 Decembers that no less grim

duels would again be played out between the forces of life and death.

On the morning of the date in question, in 1861, Alice wrote to Louis: 'In another 24 hours everything will be decided.' No one, at certain times, had been closer to her father than Alice throughout the illness; and, at other times, the patient seemed to wish for no one else to be at his bedside. The doctors now wanted to spare her as far as possible, but the dying Prince Consort repeatedly asked for his daughter. Augusta Stanley remained most of the time in an adjoining room with the younger children and the Queen was constantly in and out; but it was Alice who was in the sickroom itself when, at about ten o'clock in the evening, unmistakable signs of the approaching end appeared. In a calm whisper that must have seemed made of steel, Alice told Augusta: 'That is the death rattle'; then she went to her mother, who had rushed from the room in anguish a few moments before.[22] Wife and daughter knelt on either side of the bed, the Queen clasping her husband's already lifeless left hand. It was 10.45 pm.

Alice, as time would show, was to be her father's daughter for the rest of her life. 'In every way open to her, did the Princess try to walk in her father's footsteps and so to honour his memory.'[23] Meanwhile, though the moment was unspeakably terrible for Queen Victoria, even worse moments were to come. How could she survive the loss of him who was her whole life? Only one person, as it turned out, was to stand between her and total derangement; and on this person, an inexperienced eighteen-year-old Princess, the fate of the monarchy would, for the time being, depend. It was as if, in this sense, the whole reign were beginning all over again. A fortnight later, on the first day of the new year, Alice wrote to her future mother-in-law, Princess Charles of Hesse:

My heart is *quite* broken, and my grief is almost more than I can bear. When I think back to the whole dreadful illness, to the Friday and to the last Saturday, that dreadful, difficult time that I went through with Mama seems like a bad dream, and my aching heart bleeds afresh when I remember the last, painful hours. Oh God that it should have been my beloved, adored father lying there dead, his hands so cold

and stiff – I felt as though I had been turned to stone –
when I saw him draw his last breath, and saw the pure,
great noble soul leave its earthly dwelling. That same
evening while I was kneeling alone by his bed, with his
burning hand in mine, I said to myself as I listened to that
painful, difficult breathing, 'Perhaps God will take him, and
then we shall be parted from the dearest thing we have on
earth – it cannot be!' I expected that He would leave us,
but I could not take it in. He was too good, too great for
this wicked world. God has freed him from everything that
still afflicts us. His will be done![24]

Chapter Five

MARRIAGE IN A DEATH CHAMBER

It might have been impossible for the same Alice who had accompanied her father to the very fringe of eternity to be the principal agent for coaxing her mother back with safety to the realities of time. It was not, however, the same Alice but a very different one who now steeled herself for this forbidding task. She was totally transformed by her experiences at her father's bedside. Lord Clarendon showed perspicacity even in under-statement by mentioning her 'strength of mind and judgment, as well as tenderness'.[1] It was indeed the very combination of these qualities that set her apart from so many others. Augusta Stanley was the first to notice how, quite suddenly, she seemed to be 'a different creature'.[2] Her fiancé hurried over from Germany to find an Alice he had never known before. The Queen understandably was not so quickly aware of the change. Even during the Prince Consort's illness much, by design on Alice's part, was hidden from her mother. Her own tears had been poured out in torrential paroxysms only behind closed doors; but the inner effect on her is not difficult to imagine. Indeed she was never quite the same again.

If she had shown during her father's illness 'a fortitude beyond her years',[3] she now displayed all the qualities that a successful nurse most needs. She had 'without suspecting it, passed her first exam in nursing which was to become her destiny'.[4] And Queen Victoria was at this critical juncture in need of the most difficult and important of all types of nursing – that fragile type wherein the patient is not aware of being nursed. Anyone looking after old or infirm relations (and relations are of course even harder to look after than strangers) will confirm the need for an infinitely subtle psychological approach, often exhausting but invariably vital. Alice was providentially gifted in this regard; never were her gifts more needed than during the grim vigil of that first night after her father's death. She wondered afterwards how she and her mother came through the ordeal with their sanity unimpaired. She had her bed moved next to the Queen's in the apartment near the Blue Room. The frail-looking but cast-iron heroine of the hour (whose vital function throughout has ever been blurred by almost exclusive attention to the plight of Queen Victoria) knew not only when to act but when not to. She was careful not to overdo her ministrations. The Queen could find solace neither in sleep nor in tears. Alice sent for Dr Jenner and a mild opiate for her mother served to blunt minutely but sufficiently the razor-like edge of tragedy then threatening to cut entirely through the Queen's powers of resistance. After closing her eyes only fitfully and briefly the relief of tears finally came to the stricken widow; though the worst was not yet over, the solid dam of stark despair had at least been breached. The most tense part of Alice's 'vigil' by her mother's side did not last for that night only but for three bitter days.[5] Few doubt that if her spirit had broken during this crucial triduum, that of the Queen would have done so also. It is interesting, if terrifying, to imagine what might ultimately have happened in such an eventuality. For it is no exaggeration to say that the soundness of the Queen's mind was balanced on a needle point.

Having survived so intense a crisis it is possible to enjoy thereafter a long life that is more vigorous than ever in both mind and body. For just this was the Queen providentially saved (by the instrumentality of Princess Alice). It is equally possible, if things tip the wrong way at the vital moment – perhaps even occasioned by some comparatively trivial circumstance – that meaningful interest in an equally long life thereafter can be provided only by occasional lucid intervals. Such was the cruel fate of the daughter of Queen Victoria's Uncle Leopold, Charlotte, the ill-fated Empress of Mexico. Had the worst happened in the case of Queen Victoria, the Prince of Wales would presumably have taken over the reigns of government, and been virtually sovereign for half a century. As it was, something diametrically opposite came about in that the heir to the throne was ruthlessly excluded from all participation in state affairs. The pattern for this was set in the immediate aftermath of the Prince Consort's death.

The Prince of Wales ran into his mother's arms crying: 'I will be all I can to you.' The Queen kissed him repeatedly, saying: 'I am sure, my dear boy, you will.' But she made quite sure he was not. Hints in the newspapers as to how welcome would be some active collaboration with the sovereign by the Prince of Wales were wholly counter-productive. He was packed off in the following February on a tour of the East. The Queen was unwilling meanwhile to delegate a jot or tittle of her ruling power; but she refused, in the long period of seclusion that followed, to be seen as an effective ruler herself. All the more important therefore, during the first six months of the lugubrious limbo period, was the position of Princess Alice.

Her initial task was two-fold: to clutch back her mother from the abyss of desolation; and to be the agent of the Queen's duties over official matters that could not be shelved. Two days after the Prince Consort's death Granville wrote to Lord Canning:

> The loss to the country is great: To the Queen it is irretrievable. . . . The Prince of Wales has behaved with great affection and feeling. The Princess Alice has shown singular tact and feeling. I own I was afraid that the Queen's nervous system would have given way. Perhaps the grief at the Duchess of Kent's death has been a preparation for her. Still her future is fearful. Having given up [for] 20 years, every year more, the habit of ever deciding anything, either great or small, on her own judgment, the situation is immense for her to conduct the affairs of her family, her Court and of the Country. And who has she upon whom she can lean?[6]

He might more pertinently have asked: 'Who would there have been upon whom she could lean were it not for Princess Alice?' It was only the next day that he began to get some inkling of who was actually in control of affairs in the midst of great confusion and hesitation. For he was 'sent for' to attend to official business at Windsor, and the person who sent for him was Alice herself. Similarly Sir Charles Phipps* now

* Keeper of Her Majesty's Purse, and formerly private secretary to the Prince Consort.

transacted all business through the Queen's daughter, who in returning papers to him would report on her mother's condition.[7] All communications from the ministers and household passed through the Princess's hands to the Queen. She could not have fully realized at the time the magnitude of the burden she was taking on, still less the delayed action it would have on her nervous system in later years.

The Times commented:

> It is impossible to speak too highly of the strength of mind and self sacrifice shown by Princess Alice during these dreadful days. Her Royal Highness has certainly understood that it was her duty to be the help and support of her mother in her great sorrow: and it was in a great measure due to her that the Queen has been able to bear with such wonderful resignation to the loss that so suddenly and terribly befell her.[8]

The destiny of the nation lay at that moment in the slender hands of Princess Alice. 'The knowledge of this fact,' as Sir Theodore Martin puts it, 'and it was a fact – sank deeply into people's minds. It was never forgotten and from that day the name of the Princess Alice has been a cherished household word to all her countrymen and women.'[9]

Knowing what we do of Queen Victoria's extraordinary temperament, it is safe to say that no member of her family at any stage in his or her life was assigned a burden quite like that borne by Alice during this period. Its stifling intensity might have proved too much for a tough and experienced matron, let alone an untried girl of eighteen. The nights were unspeakable, with Queen Victoria sobbing uncontrollably until exhaustion induced a brief and uneasy sleep as dawn approached. And Alice shared every prolonged paroxysm and every renewed outburst. Perhaps only someone who has nursed his or her own mother through a period of acute nervous distress can have some idea of what Princess Alice suffered and of what she achieved. The effect upon the 'nurse' is draining and exhausting beyond all description; the attitude of the patient is wholly demanding and overpowering. And the patient's recovery depends ultimately upon one person only. This person must carry all the strain, though the supreme irony is that the patient must not be allowed to believe that he or she is not doing all the suffering. Thus did Queen Victoria ride out the first, fierce onslaught of the horror, not unmixed with remorse, that assailed her with the approach of Christmas in the year 1861. And thus did Princess Alice act as the channel through which such initial horror worked itself out of her mother's tortured soul. During this twilight three-day interlude, the Queen's pulse could scarcely be felt.[10] It was the most critical moment of her life.

But by 18 December there were unmistakable signs that the nadir of the nightmare and the peak of the crisis had passed. (This was the first vital 'breakthrough'; the second came at the end of January the following year, with Queen Victoria once again re-establishing contact with the official world.) The Queen went out on the day in question and crossed the park to Frogmore to choose a site for her husband's mausoleum. Leaning heavily on the arm of Princess Alice she walked round the gardens until she had found what she thought would be the most suitable spot.[11] Alice's fiancé was a spectator of this melancholy promenade, as well as a chief mourner at the funeral five days later. But Alice had meanwhile gone with her mother to Osborne, King Leopold having insisted (against Alice's better judgement) on the Queen's getting away from Windsor as soon as possible.

Strength began to return to the Queen's shattered spirit as the first days of the new year dragged by on the Isle of Wight. But to Alice it was the most fearsome period of all, even more bitter because it was acted out on the favourite playground of her carefree youth. The painfully simulated calmness needed to succour first her father then her mother was followed by an inevitable reaction. Even so she was still the sole channel for the nation's official business, and still the main prop for her mother. The Queen seems not to have fully realized how great was the toll on her second daughter at this juncture; but others spotted that the beloved Alice (who looked 'wretched') must be afforded some sort of break. The Queen was most reluctant to part with her but at last with great difficulties it was arranged.[12] And Alice enjoyed some much needed relief from the unbelievable tension that she had all too successfully hidden from her mother. She stayed at the Van de Weyerses' house, New Lodge, where the Duke of Cambridge found her obviously in need of the change but not looking as unwell as he had expected. Her recent experiences had in fact made her, he thought, no less 'amiable and affectionate' than she had always been.[13]

The Queen was in no way being consciously possessive or selfish over Alice; and their deep mutual love and understanding were probably never stronger than during this two-month sojourn at Osborne. Any reluctance on the Queen's part that Alice should leave her side was prompted chiefly by terror of what the nights might bring. Alice went on sleeping in the same room with her, and it would seem that the Queen slept better than her daughter.[14] The miracle in fact was that the Queen's health was not materially affected,[15] even if Alice's, for the time being at least, undoubtedly was. Though increasingly the victim of a neurosis – chiefly concerning possible madness brought about by responsibility in the absence of the Prince Consort – the Queen was no hysteric in need of shock treatment but a deeply wounded human animal in need of the most sensitive care:[16] the kind of care that only Alice seemed capable of providing. But it was beyond even Alice's powers to persuade her mother to grasp the main nettle in her path, namely to consent to an official visit from her Prime Minister. It took King Leopold, who came over at the end of January, to manage this. One of the chief difficulties was that the Prime Minister at this time was Lord Palmerston, with whom the Queen and the Prince Consort had had so many unseemly wrangles in the past. But she agreed and Palmerston came, unnerving her more by his humanity and sympathy than by anything else. Thus had the second great breakthrough been accomplished for Queen Victoria by February of that year. The faint outlines of a heroic new beginning were just becoming visible; and it may be said that this very moment marked a new beginning for Alice as well. But there was a sombre difference in the cases of mother and daughter, both of whom, as it happened, had at this very moment reached the halfway-point in their lives. For the Queen, in middle age, the props of her regal world made possible a psychological continuity.

For Alice, in her late teens, there was a radical break with the past. From now on

> ... she felt it to be a sacred duty to foster the recollections of her girlhood and to carry out the principles with which her father had imbued her, whether in the cultivation of art and science, the encouragement of art manufactures, of agriculture and general education, in the tasteful and practical arrangement of her own house, in bettering the condition of the lower and working classes by improving their homes and inculcating principles of health, economy and domestic management. In short in every way open to her, did the Princess try to walk in her father's footsteps and so to honour his memory.[17]

No one noticed the metamorphosis in Alice more than Eleanor Stanley, when she visited Osborne that February to take her leave as maid of honour to Queen Victoria. She was summoned, she records,

> ... to receive Princess Alice in my own room, where she stepped in from the Princess Hohenlohe's next door. She looks thin and worn and speaks very sadly; and this deep sorrow has evidently changed her from a child to a woman very suddenly, but it has also drawn her out and improved, *deepened*, her mind and character. She spoke much of her father's last illness and of his depression and fretfulness, so unlike his usual self, and of the Queen's utter desolation. She told me her own marriage was to be in June next as originally intended here in the house, the Queen to be present at it, in her widow's weeds, and the whole thing to be as private as possible, only the bridesmaids and their mothers to be there beyond the necessary persons.[18]

Few outlooks could have been more sombre for the bride-to-be, though Queen Victoria herself was obviously better and was now sleeping on her own for the first time.[19]

The last day of the previous month had been a particularly

difficult one for Alice, as Louis, whose visit had done so much
to help her, had had to return to Darmstadt.

> Yesterday [she wrote to Louis on 1 February] was a hard
> day for both of us. My poor home seems emptier and sadder
> than ever now that I have not got you here – and every-
> thing seems more difficult. . . . Mama is in a terrible way
> today. She had breakfast in her sitting-room for the first
> time again, and laid her head on my shoulder and clung to
> me as tightly as if she couldn't bear her grief alone any
> more. Oh God – her fate is too sad, too terrible. I took her
> out for a drive yesterday morning. . . . I cannot write too
> much today as I have a headache – but I am *very* sensible
> and do everything you would have wished me to do. God
> bless you my darling – how I should love to put my tired
> head on your shoulder and hold your dear warm hand in
> mine. . . .[20]

And the very next day she wrote again to Louis telling him:
'*What holds me to life – and is the whole focus* of my life – is *you*
– and the longing for our *approaching union*! May we then
never be parted for a *long* time, until God calls one of us to
Him – then the other will follow all the more gladly.'

Meanwhile the time seemed ripe to Queen Victoria for
moving back to Windsor. People were even venturing upon a
'little amusement' with two of three balls being planned,
according to the ever-informative Lord Clarendon. The Queen
felt sufficiently better to complain about her ladies-in-waiting,
the complaint arising over their inadequacy as compared to
the personal attentions of Princess Alice. Lady Churchill in
particular failed to come up to scratch, having never herself
known grief – a grave defect in this context, as far as the
Queen was concerned. Alice was meanwhile reported to be
'better tho' not quite well' by Clarendon, who added that the
Prince Consort's room was left as at the moment of death even
to the open pocket handkerchief on the sofa. 'In the Queen's
place,' he added, 'I should have preferred to inhabit the room
and to have made the changes in it necessary for the purpose
but *there is no reasoning on the modes that grief takes for satisfying itself.*'[21]

In a sense Queen Victoria's grief over the Prince Consort never fully satisfied itself. Over and over again – when she could finally bring herself to mention it on paper – she mourns and bemoans her fate, in her *Journal* and other intimate writings. And she did not, as was generally expected, turn to her children as some sort of replacement for her lost love, her lost 'life'. Rather did her children have to play their part while, as it were, keeping their place: supporting her indeed and falling in with her whims, if only because there could be no substitute for *him*.

The Queen was thus determined that her second daughter's wedding must go ahead, but only in a manner strictly conforming to the required observations of heavily overlaying grief. She had 'intended Prince Albert's mausoleum to be no "Sterbezimmer", no *death chamber*, but a bright monument to his living glory. Not so the room prepared for Princess Alice's marriage seven months after his death. Here was a Sterbezimmer indeed.'[22] It was fortunate that as preparations for the wedding went on meanwhile Alice was obviously made of the stern stuff that earned her golden opinions from alert observers. 'How entirely I agree with you about Princess Alice,' Clarendon could write to the Duchess of Manchester in April 1862.

> There is not such another girl in a thousand. I never met with one who at her age had such sound principles, so great judgment and such knowledge of the world, yet she has been boxed up in a gilt cage all her life and has not had the advantage of interchanging ideas as other girls have. I wish she had better prospects before her but she is going with a dull boy to a dull family in a dull country and I have a presentiment that she won't be happy.[23]

Later that month, the twenty-fourth, was Alice's nineteenth birthday, a birthday, as the Queen wrote to Lord Tennyson, 'which should have been so happy, for the arrangements for her marriage were almost completed, was the saddest I remember'.[24] This was written soon after the first meeting between the Queen and the man who had become Poet Laureate twelve years earlier because of Prince Albert's

admiration for 'In Memoriam'. Tennyson had been asked in
January by Alice to write something about her father. As a
result Emily Tennyson's diary recorded that 16 January 1862
was 'a day to be remembered by us' because of 'a letter of
thanks to Alfred from Princess Alice telling us that his lines
have soothed our Queen, thank God'.[25] The Poet Laureate
never forgot the Princess who was so closely associated with
his first introduction to the Queen; and in the issue of the
Nineteenth Century for April 1879 (four months after Alice's
death) he published, with his famous ballad 'The Siege of
Lucknow', a 'Dedicatory Poem to the Princess Alice'.

The extraordinarily difficult time through which Alice was
now having to pass should, in other circumstances, have been
among the happiest of her life. Being in almost constant
attendance on her mother would have been exacting enough
had they stayed on at Osborne. But after the seclusion of the
first two months she was obliged to follow her now restless
mother to Windsor for March, back to Osborne in April, to
Balmoral in May, and then to Osborne again in June, with
only a few weeks to go before the wedding. Denied to her were
all the trimmings and trappings that assume such importance
for a bride-to-be: no question of seeing dressmakers about
pretty clothes for the bridesmaids; virtually no invitations to
send out; no flower arrangements to be pondered on; in fact
no joy of any kind whatsoever to be derived from the expectation of a ceremony that was normally allowed to mean so
much. The Queen was evidently determined that the whole
event should be as grim as possible; on 26 May she wrote: 'The
Angel of Death still follows us. The Grand Duchess of Hesse
has just died and so now Alice's marriage will be even more
gloomy.'[26] Even the details of Alice's trousseau had been
settled a year before, the total cost having been about £4,000.
This included such items as a £950 pearl and diamond brooch
and other jewelry, the Queen being in constant communication
on the matter with Lady Caroline Barrington.* No single
detail escaped their joint and scrupulous attention, some of
the minor work being farmed out here and there. 'I propose,

* Lady of the Bedchamber to the Queen from 1837 to 1875 and, from
1851 (in succession to Lady Lyttleton), 'Lady Superintendent to their
Royal Highnesses the Princesses'.

if agreeable to your Majesty,' Lady Caroline wrote, 'giving 6 dozen pairs of drawers to be made at the school and the other 6 dozen to my dear sister who is anxious to have some work to do and who I understand works very well.'[27]

With what zest, during that halcyon mid-summer of 1861, had Queen Victoria thrown herself into the plans for her second daughter's wedding! It would have been an intoxicating reminder of her love for the Prince Consort and life with *him*; he in person would dominate all. In the event he was still to dominate the occasion, but from the other side of the grave. And thus did preparations go mournfully ahead for converting the small dining-room at Osborne into a 'death chamber' for the occasion. Princess Alice did not cope with it all with the weapon of sheer goodness, though she possessed plenty of this. Her nature had a tougher side as well, which was often much needed. The Queen's wish, for example, that she and Louis should have a financial adviser after their marriage was resented by the latter; but his opposition was tactfully overcome by Alice.[28] Such toughness seldom revealed itself in outward demeanour or expressions, but was distinctly there in the background. It came quickly into operation when something she felt mattered was at stake; and then just as quickly and unobtrusively it disappeared. She was not for example prepared to let people take advantage of the austerity of her nuptial plans; she must have known how mean people can sometimes be over wedding presents. But the gossipy Lord Clarendon makes too much of a story he had heard third hand that she had intimated to Lord Methuen that the Lords-in-Waiting should make separate presents – 'a dodge of course to get them more valuable'.[29] (Of such titbits do historical legends spring.) A month previously he had berated the Duchess of Buccleuch for presuming to speak for all the bridesmaids' mothers in fixing £50 as an adequate sum for their presents. He also mentioned the bridesmaids who were 'dispensed with', by which he meant only some of those originally asked outside the immediate family, such as Lady Mount Edgecombe and Lady Elgin, adding that these would give £25 and £50 respectively as presents.[30] (At the actual wedding there were four bridesmaids: Alice's younger sisters, the Princesses Helena, Louise and Beatrice, and Princess Anna of

Hesse.) Alice at all events had to call on all her powers of grim determination not to be put out by petty jealousies. They might have been the last straw on top of the nerve-racking ordeal she had suffered as the heroic daughter of the monarch when she needed, more than at any other time, nothing less than heroism of such a kind.

The events on 1 July 1862, Princess Alice's wedding-day, have often been described, but never in the light of the combined reactions of all the main participants, including those recently arrived from Darmstadt. Among these were Alice's newly appointed German lady-in-waiting, Christa Schenck. She was evidently a girl of unusual sensitivity and charm, even if she did not possess radiant good looks by accepted English standards. And her description of the overall scene at Osborne adds an extra dimension to a mere catalogue of who was present (very few), what they wore (half-mourning),[31] the state of the weather (dull and cloudy)[32] and so on. Moreover the English view of their visitors (Christa and her companion Marie von Grancy) has its ironical side. Lady Churchill describes the 'Hessian Ladies' as 'very good natured but oh! – most awful dressers with hats, antiquated, ugly. . . .'[33] Christa, however, was anything but unaware of the curiosity that she and her friend were attracting on this, their first visit to England: 'They probably thought that the two shy German girls in their simple dresses belonged to the class of country cousins or, as they say here that they were "country bumpkins".'[34] She adds plaintively that 'at that time' (just after their arrival in England) 'we were very homesick and many a salty tear fell – we hope unnoticed – into the Royal food with which we were served'.[35] But perhaps the most valuable of Christa's observations concerned the Queen herself. For it was she, the Queen, who dominated the whole sequence of events immediately surrounding the wedding; and Alice, though it would normally have been exclusively *her* day, was content that this should be so. Indeed she was conscious, at this very moment, of being a daughter to the Queen in an intimate sense that would probably never be reproduced in quite the same way again. She had some time before stopped sleeping regularly in the same room as her mother, but they slept together the night before the wedding, during which the Queen 'scarcely got any sleep'.[36] Apart from anything else, the noise of the final preparations in the wedding room (it seems odd that they were not completed before) disturbed her in the early morning. At this point Alice got up and came over to kiss her mother, who gave the bride-to-be her blessing and a prayer-book 'like one dear Mama gave us on *our happy wedding morning*'.[37] After breakfasting alone with Alice the Queen began her rounds of the house. Her first visit was to Princess Charles of Hesse* who now presented 'Alice's two ladies' from Germany. Christa (let us allow her to take up the story) had arrived the night before after three days in London, being

. . . accompanied by General Grey, a witty, highly esteemed private secretary of the Queen with his beautiful daughter Sybil, the future Duchess of St. Albans. We travelled [to the Isle of Wight] on the yacht *Elphin*† and arrived at Osborne House towards 10 o'clock in the evening . . . it may sound improbable, but I can say that from the moment when next day I was presented to the Queen, and her kind, almost motherly words in pure German sounded in my ear, a feeling of home came over me. The illustrious lady has, as long as I knew her, exerted a true charm over me and she has always shown me the most undeserved kindness and appreciation. Some letters written by Her Majesty during the most difficult times of my life – amongst them after my father's death – are a precious proof of her kindness.[38]

This richly deserved tribute serves to put into perspective any attempt to describe the Queen's many-sided temperament. For it is all too easy to overstress her apparent morbidity over death and the selfishness with which she seemed to let this cast a shadow over Alice's wedding. Her contemporaries, above all Alice herself, did not see things in this light; but her extreme emotional reactions (and demands on others) after the Prince Consort's death have been necessarily described to

* Prince Louis's mother.
† The *Elphin* was the tender to the *Victoria and Albert* and was used as second royal yacht.

highlight circumstances that made Alice uniquely important
among all the children of Queen Victoria and the Prince Consort: as the one who best understood both her parents and
stood closest to them in the respective hours of their greatest
loneliness and need. Such hours had now passed in terms of
pure time. But for the Queen it was an hour that defied such
temporal limitation; it went on and on, and she could not help
herself. Alice may well have suffered, now and later, as a direct
result; but she did not mind: she understood – she loved. And
though when the wedding-day came the Queen's almost suffo-
cating grief was painfully obvious to all, Christa attests her
personal anxiety, down to the minutest detail, that others
should be made as happy as possible. Thanks to this solicitude
on the part of the broken-hearted but large-spirited Queen,
Christa and Marie, when they went to their rooms after the
celebrations, 'found beautiful bracelets, a present from the
Queen, and a huge piece of wedding cake'.

Before giving her own description of the actual wedding
Christa Schenck recalls a question she often asked herself at
the very beginning of her friendship with Princess Alice. (It
could have applied even more readily to the initial stages of
a planned royal match from the same period – to that of Alice
and Louis themselves.) It struck her when she first met her
future mistress, only just before the marriage was to take
place.

At that time [she writes] I asked myself, and I still ask
myself the same question today, how is it possible that two
people who had never seen each other before, had hardly
heard anything about each other and were suddenly introduced with the words, 'you now as it were belong to each
other, see to it that you get on with each other' immediately felt attracted to each other and could judge each other
objectively? In later years the Princess and I often spoke
of this first meeting from which a truly intimate relationship
was born.

And Christa, despite having just arrived in England, also came
quickly to the conclusion that Alice at that time was 'probably
the most popular person in her country', still being 'completely

under the influence of her dearly beloved father' while 'every-body talked about the support she gave in those days to her sorrowing mother'.

Meanwhile the matutinal activities of 1 July went ahead, with the Queen continuing her rounds of the house. She inspected the dining-room 'which was very prettily decorated, the altar being placed under our large family picture'.[39] This was the famous family group painted by Winterhalter when Alice was about four, dominated by the seated figure of Prince Albert. It still hangs in the same spot in the same room at Osborne. All the usual furniture had been removed from the room, which was now filled with plants and flowers. The Queen, having inspected the Council Room, where the 'break-fast' table had been set for the royal guests, took a short drive with Princess Helena before going to see the bridegroom. Not surprisingly she found him 'nervous and overcome'. Apart from the grim period just after the Prince Consort's death, and a short visit in June to settle arrangements for the wedding, poor Louis had seen little of his bride. The totally carefree days of the previous autumn in the Highlands seemed infinitely far removed. He could scarcely have failed to notice that since his return to England at the end of June Queen Victoria's gaze suddenly seemed more critical than before. Perhaps, after what had happened, this was inevitable.

Ministers, guests and clergy having arrived by special train and ferry, all was set by the end of the morning for the ceremony to begin. The flavour of what followed is best described by Queen Victoria's own words:

Alice was dressed before 1 o'clock, looking lovely in her bridal attire. She had no train, but the half high dress with a deep flounce of Honiton lace, a veil of the same and a wreath of orange blossoms and myrtle. She had her order on and wore the beautiful opal cross and brooch. There were four bridesmaids, our three girls and Anna of Hesse. . . . The time had come and I, in my 'sad cap' as Baby* calls it, most sad on such a day, went down with our four boys, Bertie and Affie leading me. It was a terrible moment for me. No

---

* The Queen's youngest daughter, Princess Beatrice.

one was in the room but the Archbishop of York (the Archbishop of Canterbury not being well enough to come) the
Dean of Windsor and Mr. Prothero, who were in their places
near the altar. Then all the guests came in, and the different
Households. I sat all the time in an armchair, Bertie and
Affie close to me. The Hessian family stood opposite,
Clementine, Augustus and Nemours, next to them. After a
short pause Louis came in conducted by Lord Sydney and
followed by his two brothers William and Henry. After
another pause came the dear, dear Bride on her Uncle's
arm, followed by the bridesmaids, a touching sight. The
service then commenced, the Archbishop performing it
beautifully. Alice answered so distinctly and was full of
dignity and self possession. Louis also answered very distinctly. I restrained my tears, and had a great struggle all
through but remained calm. The service over, dear Alice,
who was wonderfully composed, embraced me, as I did
also Louis, after which they left the room, followed by
us all.

A little while after the couple, Prince and Princess
Charles, very overcome and most kind, and dear good Fritz
came into the Horn Room, and the Dean brought in the
Register, which we all signed, the rest of the family coming
in, in succession. When that was over I took leave of all the
guests and went upstairs, where Alice and Louis joined me,
and we lunched together, all the others lunching below.
Mr. Thomas made a slight sketch of Alice and then she went
into her dear Father's room to change her dress, putting on
a white 'Mousseline de soie' with a tulle bonnet trimmed
with orange blossoms. Her calmness and composure continued. They both went to wish Prince and Princess Charles
good-bye, who then came with their sons and daughter to
take leave of me. Ernest C. [Coburg] went to Town with
them, but returned in two days. Dear Alice and Louis sat
with me for a short while and at 5 o'clock I parted with
them, blessing them both and saw them drive off (I standing
on the stairs.)[40]

The Queen had indeed restrained herself with courage
throughout the ceremony, over which a heavy pall of melan-

choly had hung. But in writing afterwards to her eldest daughter, the Crown Princess of Prussia (as she had become in 1861) she described the whole wedding as having been more like a funeral. As far as the guests were concerned the whole cheerless occasion – the saddest royal marriage in modern times – was over by 4 pm and they all returned to London. It was not until 6.15, according to Louis,[41] that they finally set off for their honeymoon. The description 'no confetti, or old shoes, no cake and no fun'[42] is not strictly accurate, since the Hessian ladies found the cake supply most abundant. According to Christa, moreover, the parting couple looked 'radiant' and, 'according to English custom', a tattered old shoe *was* in fact thrown into the carriage by one of the young Princes.

They had not far to go for their extremely unsecluded honeymoon, for by 7.30 they had reached the house called St Claire (lent by the Vernon Harcourts) near Ryde. This (by English standards) 'vast, castellated mansion'[43] was described by Louis as 'a pretty little castle'.[44] They walked in its delightful garden after dining *à deux*; and apart from the unobtrusive presence of Lady Churchill, General Seymour and Herr Westerweller* – who formed their 'suite' – they enjoyed their three days alone together, uninterrupted except for a visit for tea by Queen Victoria on the second day.

The Queen was meanwhile pouring her heart out to the one person, the Crown Princess, who, she thought, would best understand her feelings. Her letter of 2 July speaks volumes:

Poor Alice's wedding (more like a funeral than a wedding) is over and she is a wife! I say God bless her – though a dagger is plunged in my bleeding, desolate heart when I hear from her this morning that she is 'proud and happy' to be Louis' wife! I feel what I had, what I hoped to have for at least 20 years more and what I can only have in another world again. All that has passed since December 14 seems gone – forgotten. What I shall not forget is Alice herself, and her own forbearing – such calmness self-possession and dignity, and how really beautiful she looked, so tall, and graceful, and her voice so sweet. The Archbishop of York

* Equerry from the Hessian Court.

read that fine service (purified from its worse coarsenesses)
admirably, and himself had tears running down his cheeks
– for he too lost his dear partner not long ago. I sat the
whole time in an armchair with our four boys near me;
Bertie and Affie led me downstairs. The latter sobbed all
through and afterwards – dreadfully. Dear Uncle Ernest is
very low and sad and was much affected. It was a comfort
to me that he, darling Papa's only brother, led her and gave
her away! I had rather he than anyone else should do it. He
was so affectionate at our marriage. Prince and Princess
Charles were much affected – but we none of us liked her,
and Alice not at all. She was very cold, very grand and not
at all affectionate to Alice and most unamiable (and I must
call it 'de mauvaise foi') about Alice's living a good deal here
and about what is right and proper. But she has nothing to
say and Louis is all right about it and most amiable. Alice
is very determined and from the first has taken her position
vis-à-vis the 'mother-in-law'.[45]

There could hardly be a better example of how much of
reality was missed by Queen Victoria. This comes out nowhere more clearly than in hitherto unpublished data relating
to Princess Alice, part of whose technique for helping and
consoling her mother was to conceal much from her. Added
to this is the consistent element of wishful thinking in the
Queen's outlook; even her pessimism and self-pity were a sort
of obverse form of wishful thinking, as Alice well knew. On the
occasion of Victoria's tea-time visit to St Claire she was careful
not to let her mother think that she was too happy; she knew
that the wedding was a sad affair for the Queen, not only
because of the awakened memories about the Prince Consort
but equally because of the tinges of jealousy that her mother
experienced when made too conscious of any romantic bliss
experienced by her daughters. As regards Princess Charles,
moreover, the facts were quite different from what Queen
Victoria imagined. Alice and her future mother-in-law had
long been exchanging the most cordial of letters.[46] Within
days of her engagement she was being referred to by the
Princess as a 'second daughter'; Alice wrote to say how moved
she was by such a title and how 'truly and lovingly devoted'

Princess Alice on her wedding day, 1 July 1862

The wedding of Princess Alice and Prince Louis of Hesse, Osborne, 1 July 1862

she was to Louis, whom she treasured more as each day went by.[47] Largely to please Louis's mother, but also to satisfy her own studious bent, she had begun to make a close study of Hessian history. She responded warmly to the very strong and natural piety that came out in many of the letters from the Princess Charles; and on the anniversary of the engagement the latter sent Alice a devotional book with thoughts for every day, which she hoped Alice and Louis could read together later on. And it was to her 'dear Mama' – and not just to 'dear future Mama' as hitherto – that Alice unburdened herself so candidly soon after the Prince Consort's death. Even Queen Victoria, in her grief and mental solitude, seemed less aware than Princess Charles of the dangers to Alice's health when she was wearing herself out in the cause of supporting her mother. And perhaps the most significant letter from Princess Alice to her future mother-in-law had been written during that excessively trying period. Alice thanked Princess Charles for her kind letter and said how glad she was that she and the Prince of Wales had met each other. But she hoped that he had not alarmed her 'about my *tiresome* health. I have been better for the past few days but the doctors insist that I have a change of air – and get away from home altogether. I refused for a long time – but now they say I would not be well by June otherwise, and would not be strong enough to undertake the 22 hour journey to Balmoral with Mama at the end of April, which I long to do. So I told Mama I would have to go away for a short time, and she gave her consent unwillingly.'[48] The understanding of all relevant factors, and of Victoria's as well as Alice's feelings, is strikingly apparent in the reply received by Alice from Darmstadt.

I do so much sympathise [Princess Charles wrote] with everything that you say about your grief for your beloved Papa, but I don't want to go back to that day, because I am so glad to think that you are away from all the sadness round about you, and in quite different surroundings. If you were 25 or older, I should say nothing, but at 19 the strain and the stress which you have been going through does you no good, and can have a very dangerous effect on you physically! I had so hoped that King Leopold would have

D

pointed this out to your dear Mama. But it is so under-
standable that *she* should *not* think of it, in her terrible
grief. . . .[49]

Alice throughout remained a faithful and indeed deeply
loving daughter to her own mother, notwithstanding her
growing *rapport* with her mother-in-law-to-be. The best indication of her dual, but not conflicting, loyalties appears in
what she wrote to Princess Charles just after her nineteenth
birthday. Grateful for the 'dear letter and charming pin', she
goes on to report:

> . . . my birthday was a very sad day, which we spent
> quietly together. The weather was warm and heavenly, the
> sea blue and smooth as a mirror, the birds were singing –
> everything was as always, only the ray of light which filled
> everything with joy was missing. . . . I missed *his kiss* which
> was always the first, *his* loving words. He always used to
> take me to Mama and then to my birthday table. . . . Our
> home has been laid waste as it were by this terrible loss, and
> my poor Mama's heart and health are broken. I have seldom
> seen her crying so much, so weak and so unhappy as she
> was on the 25th. I am more sorry for her than I can say, for
> I know *how* she suffers, although she does not always show
> it, and can be cheerful at times. How I longed on that day
> for Louis, my dear good Louis, – you will understand,
> Mama, how I depend on him more than ever now, and how
> the time seemed to me to pass so slowly until we are *at last*
> united, never more to part until death, if God wills. . . .[50]

Queen Victoria was thus mistaken in supposing that Alice
did not like Princess Charles 'at all'. The Queen was writing
this under the stress of annoyance that Louis's parents (not
surprisingly) were opposed to their son and daughter-in-law
living so much away from their new matrimonial home. The
Queen probably did not realize how much more 'unamiable'
would have been a prospective mother-in-law less endowed
with pious longanimity than Princess Charles. Alice's well-
developed tact was severely strained in avoiding a festering
feud within days of her wedding. In the event she spent most

of the first year of her marriage – and many subsequent long periods – in England; but the love and affection between Princess Charles and herself, far from being diminished, grew deeper and more touching with the passing of the years.

Louis and Alice returned from St Claire to Osborne on 4 July, with plans to leave finally, for Germany, four days later. For Queen Victoria it was a very different and very much more terrible moment than when her first daughter had got married. And to her she now wrote:

> We visited the 'Honey-Couple' on Thursday evening with Aunt, your two sisters, and Bertie and found dear Alice and Louis quiet and happy – but Oh! it all seemed so sad. And she looks so serious, so unlike the excited bride of '58! But then all is so dreadfully sad! All steeped in mourning and poor dear Alice has gone through so much – the sight of my dreadful grief not being the least of it all – that no wonder she should be melancholy and serious. Louis is very kind and very affectionate but here also to me, things are different to what they were with adored Papa and Fritz. You know what I mean. But he is so good and kind, so discreet and affectionate, that Alice will be happy. Here, Alice seems far the oldest though he is 6 years older than her![51]

Alice, however, as mentioned, did not feel nearly so melancholy as she evidently appeared to her mother. Her technique was in fact working extremely well and though the Queen woke early and felt wretched on the day of the couple's intended departure, her *Journal* begins to show a strong rallying of that basic goodness mixed with sound sense that was so often an anchor for herself and others.[52] All self-pity vanished in the 'absolute satisfaction' as to Alice's happiness. Her only real anxiety about Alice was as for her health ('she has grown again very thin'). She had therefore got together, while the young couple were at St Claire, with the family doctor, Sir James Clark. He thereupon produced a twelve-page letter – for delivery to the Princess before her departure – that might have been written as a caricature of the 'Victorian' view of medicine, morals and the dangers of living in foreign parts.[53] Well-ventilated rooms and 'steady perseverance in the use of

the cold bath every morning' were prominent recommenda-
tions. (It is hardly surprising that Alice soon became a chronic
victim of excruciating rheumatic pains.) Sir James also advised
plenty of walking, as he gathered that 'abroad' no other
exercise, such as riding, was likely to be available. Though the
Prince Consort had instructed Alice on the basic facts of life[54]
Sir James presumed she might have difficulty in knowing
whether or not she was pregnant. He accordingly gave her,
with due delicacy, the kind of information that the Queen
always found so distasteful. Having no confidence in foreign
doctors, he advocated returning home if at all possible in any
real emergency. He rounded off his epistle by commenting on
the necessity for extra special care, courtesy and consideration
in her general conduct now that she was 'going among a
strange people'.*

The 8 July was the day of departure. The *Victoria and
Albert,* the royal yacht launched on the day when Alice had
been born, lay off Osborne, dressed overall. She stood ready
to take the newly-weds to Antwerp on the first leg of their
roundabout journey to a new home and a new life. The next
day it seemed almost as if the Queen had been widowed for a
second time, as she took up her dogged pen to write once more
to the Crown Princess:

> Yesterday was a sad day. Alice, dear, excellent child is an
> immense loss for she has been a support, a comfort, which
> no one can sufficiently estimate and in my very reduced
> state I could not have allowed her marriage for another
> year – if she were not to return at the end of October or
> beginning of November. I am quite easy and happy about
> the young ménage. They are quietly, really happy – and
> Louis dear boy, is so nice, and very sensible about Alice's
> health and so unselfish, so affectionate towards me, so little
> playing the husband or taking possession of her. I wish I
> felt so easy about darling Alice's health as I do about her
> happiness! She looks very delicate, and very frail since the
> last ten days. We all anxiously hope she may not begin
> having a family so soon and the doctors think it is unlikely.

* Full text of letter appears as Appendix I.

However all is in God's hands as dearest Papa used always to say – that we must take what comes with resignation and with satisfaction and gratitude.[55]

The Queen, at last, had lost her precious second daughter. But not for long.

Part Three

WOMAN

Chapter Six

A WIFE AMONG 'STRANGE PEOPLE'

Who were these 'strange people' to whom Alice, as wife to Prince Louis of Hesse, was now also wedded? The Hesse-Darmstadt of 1862 was hidebound and old-fashioned, and Alice's knowledge of 'the world' up to that date was virtually limited to her royal homes in England. But an instinct for adventure and reform was already stirring strongly in her breast; and among the 'strange people' with whom she was to live such instincts were conspicuous by their absence. In a world untouched by the somewhat smug superiority of the jet age, peoples' lives were circumscribed by the boundaries of their own small and self-contained compartments; and many a small national or political entity was content with a minute cosmos within which to evolve. One such entity, centrally placed within what was then merely known geographically as 'Germany', was Hesse.

Not unnaturally, every history of Hesse begins with the ancestress of its royal house, namely St Elizabeth of Hungary, 'an ideal embodiment of Christian neighbourly love which was to be handed down over and over again in the Princely House of Hesse down to the mother of the last Grand Duke, Alice . . .'.[1] This famous Elizabeth – 'of Hungary' because she was the daughter of that country's king – was born in 1207. Almost immediately strange legends began to surround her name and her tiny hand was credited with healing a blind man in Pressburg. Married at thirteen* to the heir of Thuringia's mighty Count Herman, she was widowed at twenty when her husband, Louis, died during a crusade to the Holy Land. Her life thereafter – what there was of it – was a battle against intrigue and adversity. Notable memorials survived her, including the hospitals she founded and in some of which she

---

* One of the most ancient and valued Hessian relics is a small piece of the wedding dress worn by St Elizabeth in 1220. It is now kept by Lord Mountbatten at Broadlands.

herself acted as a nurse. Few women, given less than a quarter
of a century of life, have managed to bequeath so much to
posterity, the Hessians being her principal beneficiaries.
'Through the centuries her spirit again came alive in the
charitable women of her House. Through her this sex seemed
to be favoured by fate but also, through her example hardened
to bear suffering and distress.'[2]

Elizabeth's daughter Sophia married Henry II of Brabant,
which in the time of their son – another Henry – was united
with the Thuringian *Land* of Hesse. Elizabeth's grandson was
thus the first of a long line of sovereign counts (or 'landgraves')
of Hesse, of whom Philip the Magnanimous (1518–67) was one
of the most important and popular. He brought the Protestant
Reformation to Hesse, but weakened his landgraviate by
dividing it up territorially between his four sons. Only two
survived him, however, the younger being George, founder of
Hesse-Darmstadt. Territorial increases and intermittent pros-
perity were climaxed by the reign (starting in 1790) of Louis x,
an energetic reformer who brought Hesse-Darmstadt into the
Rhine Federation under the enlarged name of Hesse and the
Rhine and became – as Napoleon's protégé – its first Grand
Duke. The impetus of reform faltered under the next two
Grand Dukes, Louis II and Louis III, the latter being the uncle
of Alice's husband. And it was to a vulnerable and heavily
retrenched oligarchy that Alice was brought in 1862 as bride
of the heir presumptive. The great unanswered question at this
time was whether Austria or Prussia would preside over an
inevitable regrouping of the central European states, leading
ultimately to the unification of 'Germany'.

But politics were far from the minds of Louis and Alice as
they made their first triumphal entry into Darmstadt. The
atmosphere was fairly overpowering as far as Alice was concerned, from the moment when they arrived at Bingen on the
Hessian frontier on 12 July. The bridal pair were greeted by
pouring rain and large crowds, and were introduced to the
town officials before boarding a special train for Mainz. There
they were received by the Governor and Commandant at the
Palace. Then, after they had finally had breakfast and Louis
had changed into uniform, they went on by a gaily decorated
steamer across the Rhine to Gustavsburg, and finally by

another special train for the last bit of the journey. 'The rain stopped when we got to Grossgerau,' Louis recorded and from here – the last station before the capital – 'Uncle Louis, Mama and Papa, sister and brothers, Uncle Alexander and his wife accompanied us the rest of the way. A guard of honour here in Darmstadt. An address from the town council, girls in white. We 2 drove in a carriage and six preceded and followed by men of Darmstadt on horseback. The Rheinstrasse and Wilhelminestrasse were bursting with people and school-children, clubs and guilds lined the route. . . . *Such a warm welcome.*'[3] Alice's impression tallied with her husband's: 'I believe the people never gave so hearty a welcome,' she wrote to her mother.[4] And her sister, Princess Helena, relayed to the Duchess of Manchester the scenes of exuberance: 'Nothing could have been more enthusiastic than her [Alice's] entry into Darmstadt was. The town was decorated and there were triumphal arches, and flags; there were bands. All the school children, 1500, lined the streets; the girls were all dressed in white with flowers in their heads and baskets with flowers which they showered upon Alice.'[5]

Alice, however, who had hardly ever been away from her family before, was homesick and bewildered, even though her letters to her mother were bravely cheerful. She was inevitably 'touched by the kindness and enthusiasm shown by the people, which is said to be quite unusual. They wait near the house to see us and cheer constantly – even the soldiers.'[6] But whenever she thought of home, which was frequently, her heart grew heavy, not so much because she missed her mother acutely, though she did, but because she suddenly could not believe, now that she was far away, that Papa was not still safely alive comforting and caring for the Queen. She could not get out of her mind the emptiness of Osborne without her father, as it must have appeared to Queen Victoria. This represented an almost psychic piece of insight, for the Queen, though she said nothing to Alice, was at this time filling her most private *Journal* with lamentations of unprecedented mournfulness.[7] Alice's departure had occasioned a new and almost overpowering sense of loss, loneliness and privation in Queen Victoria not, however, on account of her daughter's departure, as such, but through a sudden flooding back of her

longing for the Prince Consort. Foreknowledge of this overriding emotion takes away some of the shock of seeing her
write (on 20 July): 'Already nearly a fortnight since our dear
Alice has left and strange to say – much as she has been to me
– and dear and precious as a comfort and an assistance, I
hardly miss her at all, or felt her going – so utterly alone am
I – by that one dreadful loss – that one thought, that everything passed by unheeded!'

In Darmstadt, meanwhile, if the ordinary people were
warmly demonstrative this was scarcely true of the professional and political personalities with whom Alice gradually
came into contact. Their stiff and stand-offish attitude was a
cold douche to the first excitement. Within a week of arrival
she had met all the members of the government and found
them almost impossible to talk to.[8] They stood waiting to be
spoken to and were wholly unresponsive to her desperate
efforts to make polite and suitable conversation. (Alice was,
of course, bilingual in German and English.) It was an
extremely unnerving experience for the newly married Princess, not yet twenty. The inner depth of ministerial feeling
against her was even greater than outward displays of passive
resistance portended. The Grand Duke's principal minister,
Dalwigk – whom Alice came to detest and distrust later on –
was intent on proving that the young Princess could do
nothing more than imitate her sister's example in Berlin. By
this he was implying that Alice was and should remain a
mere cypher. This development was reported back to England
by General Seymour,[9] who had accompanied Alice and Louis
to Darmstadt and had stayed on for a short time.

Alice was forced to bide her time and she contented herself
in these initial months with trying to make something of their
first home. This was a small and unpretentious house in a
quiet quarter of the town near Prince and Princess Charles,
in fact virtually an annexe of their palace.

> People say we may still have the Palais but I doubt it
> [Alice wrote to her mother]. I am going to tell the Grand
> Duke that we return to England in the autumn (not only
> for your sake but principally because I do not wish to in-
> commode our parents any longer, and because in the winter

we could not even receive people here.) The only thing I shall regret in our not remaining here is that the people feel it so much and they are most kind; but they will see and understand that it cannot be otherwise, and it does not arise from ill-will on our part.[10]

This first period in Darmstadt was thus little more than a long preliminary visit. The question of a final and proper home was postponed. But Alice was not yet dismayed by any of the pettier side of married life in her new surroundings. She was thrilled to be Louis's wife and her consequent state of bliss was the main theme of all her letters at this time. She could not praise her husband highly enough, even down to the way in which he had arranged that the tiny rooms in which they were living should 'look quite English'. If her own taste in such matters was more subtle, she continued the work of rearrangement with unobtrusive tact. All in all, in fact, 'the young couple were content to be left alone in their new found happiness'. The remark is made by Christa Schenck, who sums up the interaction between Alice and the people of Darmstadt during that first summer and autumn of 1862 better than anyone. Not all the time was actually spent in Darmstadt; there were visits to Coburg, Heidelberg and Carlsruhe and a longer one in a country house lent by the Grand Duke in Auerbach. This was the well-known Fürstenlager, where the fresh air was a great relief after the heat of the town and the only discomfort was caused by a plague of Rhine gnats. It was here that Christa Schenck got to know Alice much better; and, in the course of those same personal memoirs already quoted, was able to be far ahead of her own compatriots in taking the measure of Hesse's new Princess:

> Living together in the country and our mutual love for music brought us closer together. The Princess, who was very musical and had studied music, often asked me to play duets with her. We understood each other very well and I came to know and understand the qualities of my young mistress. 'She is like a young wine', a young critic said of her; 'one must wait and see how the wine matures'! That it should turn out to be of such a precious quality he himself

would not have believed. At first the Princess was something quite new, to the people of Darmstadt, something that they had never come across, something which was offensive to the old ingrained customs of royal personages. At these small Royal Courts much importance was given to etiquette. The Princess no longer considered this appropriate and tried to change this. Whoever saw her in the early morning in a short, simple costume – during those days still an unusual dress – walking with the Prince or one of the ladies-in-waiting through the streets, was astonished to see that this was a Royal Princess, because people had imagined that she would wear long flowing dresses and a feather hat. Often she was not acknowledged because people did not recognise her and generally speaking she aroused little interest. Only much later did they understand what the Grand Duchy of Hesse owed her. Therefore the relationship with Darmstadt was rather strange when at the beginning of November we returned to England, this time to stay for eight months.

The final decision to spend the winter and spring in England was confirmed when in September Alice and Louis went to see Queen Victoria while she was on a visit to Rheinhartsbrunn (near Gotha) in Thuringia. Augusta Stanley was accompanying the Queen and thought that Alice was 'most delightfully happy, so quietly peacefully so, finding Prince Louis so pleasant and companionable a companion and so willing to share his pursuits and to let him share hers'.[11] The trouble was that there were not all that many pursuits to share, and so far Alice and Louis had done little more than play at having a home in Darmstadt. By the time they returned from England it was hoped that work would have started on a new palace of their own. As an interim measure the Grand Duke was restoring the magnificent old castle of Kranichstein for the young couple to use in the summer months to come. Meanwhile Louis – whose military duties were in any case light at this time – was granted leave from his post as commander of the Cavalry Brigade. But the big news that Alice had for her mother was that she was pregnant; and in accordance with the plans now settled her first baby would be born in England.

The tremendous contrast between England and Darmstadt

is highlighted by the reaction on Christa Schenck's part to the seven months now spent in the former. A new world opened up to her – the world that was familiar and exciting to Alice – but of which Christa would have had no inkling in the sleepy routine of life in Darmstadt. The winter and spring of 1862–3 were thus the 'most interesting and instructive period' of her life. She met the most distinguished men of the day, such as Kingsley, Stanley, Tennyson, Dickens and many leading scientists.

Every weekend these gentlemen and also statesmen – often with their wives – were invited to spend the weekends at Windsor Castle. Since the death of the Prince Consort Her Majesty dined alone with her children and her guests dined with the Court Household. From time to time the guests or somebody from the Court Circle were summoned to dine with the Queen. 'You are asked to dine with her Majesty at 8.30 p.m. tonight' one of the gentlemen-in-waiting whispered in the morning and in the evening punctually one went to the so-called 'Council Room'. Then slowly the Princes and Princesses came in – mostly they were young people with children – and then after a long interval Her Majesty appeared (followed by two beautiful dachshunds, her constant companions) carrying newspapers and letters in her hand and upon her fingers wearing many old-fashioned rings. A peculiarity of the Queen . . . was that according to ancient custom she always carried a hand-kerchief in her hands, folded in a square and in the middle gathered on top. I do not remember ever having seen her without this handkerchief. The conversation was muffled and quiet but the Queen also loved to hear a happy conver-sation and could laugh heartily about something funny that was being said.[12]

After Christmas Louis received many invitations to different parts of England. Some were for shooting, but he also visited places of military and industrial interest. Hardly had he left Alice's side than she would sit down and write to him. A new phase in their married life began, with side-effects on Alice's relationship with her mother. The more assertive and wilful

side of her nature started coming to the surface in her letters
to Louis during January and February 1863; but at the same
time she showed herself determined to be his wife in priority
to any claims attendant on being Queen Victoria's daughter.
She was both demanding and loving in what she wrote to her
husband, with hints – only very slight at this stage – that
Louis's response was not always what she would have quite
liked it to be. Within hours of their first parting Alice wrote
(from Osborne) to protest how 'unutterably' she missed her
adored husband and to apologize for her obstinacy and
thoughtlessness: '. . . be patient with me, my darling husband
– and I will truly strive to overcome these faults, so that you
cannot be angry with me any more. It makes me sad when I
think about it now – that I have so often given in to my wilful-
ness, instead of obeying you at once. But now while you are
away I will respect all your wishes.'[13]

Unfortunately, however, the very next day Alice received a
letter from her mother-in-law about godparents for the coming
baby and the need for Louis to be at home in Darmstadt – in
the same way as the Prince of Wales was in England – in view
of future plans. Alice was furious and wrote off immediately
to Louis, who was at Sandringham:

> . . . When I awoke I received this letter from your Mama,
> which as you can imagine did not cheer me up. As for the
> first point your Mama mentions, concerning godparents one
> *never* decides them in advance; it brings bad luck – besides,
> it is decided by the parents of the child *alone*. Then, as
> regards the building of the house, we have decided on the
> place, and you are not needed for the foundations etc, and
> you have only to give the order to start work from here and
> it will be done. As for the comparison with Bertie, I see no
> similarity – because he has [more important] and heavy
> duties here – with two residences and a home of his own –
> while we are only just building one. If I know the people in
> Darmstadt, they will think it not only understandable, but
> quite *natural* that under present circumstances you should
> stay with me. Your Mama told me that she and your Papa
> would *never* have stayed apart at such a time, and least of
> all the first time – and she told me they were never so

affectionate and never needed each other as much as *we* both do. The *first* time (when one can't know from experience that everything will happen at the right time and all will go well) Fritz W. did not leave Vicky. The only difference is that we are at *my* home instead of at *yours*, where we should be, – but *others* are responsible for that and it is unjust that we poor creatures should have to suffer for it. God knows that I don't want another separation from you, my darling husbandchen – and for a considerable time, with the sea between us – but if you think it absolutely *necessary* and *important* I don't want to stand in your way. I shall wait until I hear from you before I answer this letter, and I will give your Mama the same reasons as I have given you here.[14]

A spirited correspondence was meanwhile being exchanged between Alice and her mother-in-law, and frankness seemed to have paid off, with honour saved and more or less general agreement achieved on all sides. In any event Alice's bark was often worse than her bite and her mood had soon changed back to total benignity. She was delighted with the plans for the house, full of news that she thought would interest her husband and uninhibited in her expressions of love for the absent Louis: '*How I miss you!* – day and night, I *cannot* tell you, darling husband – and *how* I wish I could talk to you!! I kiss your dear picture when I get up, and wish it could speak. It is so lonely in bed when you are not with me – and in this frightful storm it is quite eerie and so cold.'[15] In subsequent letters she again pleaded piteously with him not to go back to Darmstadt, begging him, with many words heavily underlined, to stay and keep her company at this time of special need. Apart from anything else, she claimed, the Queen would try and take over her life in his absence; and by the time February had come round friction was indeed evident between Alice and her mother, the latter insisting that her daughter should get her permission for everything she did and accusing her of disrespect for not doing so.[16]

The truth of the matter was that Alice was the victim of a system. She felt its harshness more than many of those of its victims who were less restless and less determined to do something really worth while. For the time being there was no ready-made position for herself and her husband in the latter's country; and living partly in England and partly in Darmstadt was obviously going to cause increasing strain to all concerned. Once more she wanted to escape from the cage she was in, the cage that had formerly been called 'gilded'. But this had always been something of a misnomer and certainly did not apply, except in an outward and empty sense, to her first year of marriage. It was more from a cage of pettiness and elaborate inactivity that she now longed to escape, first of all to lead a natural life in the company of her husband and secondly to prove her mettle as a woman. Neither of these was possible in the early part of 1863. And the result was that all the pains and exhaustion associated with Alice's condition assumed exaggerated and alarming proportions. Unless she could talk about them to Louis she felt worse, as her mother didn't seem to understand. The psychological atmosphere depressed her terribly; each new kind of pain, of strange feeling, filled her with fear; and the thought that Louis might leave her made her positively desperate. All such feelings were perhaps natural enough in a young and relatively inexperienced woman expecting her first baby in the circumstances then facing Alice. But there are certain hints of her later neurosis involving ill-health, over-anxiety and a sense of lonely frustration.

For the moment, however, all attention was diverted by the marriage on 10 March of Alice's beloved brother the Prince of Wales – who meant more to her 'than all the others put together'[17]– to the beautiful Princess Alexandra of Denmark. The marriage did not break the lifelong bond between Alice and her brother. In some ways it was strengthened, particularly as regards natural problems *vis-à-vis* Queen Victoria. Less than three months after his marriage the Prince of Wales added a postscript to one of his letters to Alice saying: 'I am sure you will agree that it is *most* important that while you are absent we should always pull together – and *never* have any estrangement. Do think of this dear Alice.'[18] Even the difficult Schleswig-Holstein question of the following year – and other political differences – did not disrupt their close mutual affection. Neither, moreover, did the latter prevent a true friendship growing up between Alice and the Princess of Wales, a friendship that had interesting undertones later on – particularly when the Prince of Wales was dangerously ill – but which survived all attempts to undermine it from without.

Then at last, after what had been a painful and troubled winter for Alice, her first child was born on 5 April. 'The pains were very severe,' wrote Louis in his diary, 'because A[lice] has such strong muscles, until she was safely delivered at a $\frac{1}{4}$ to 5 of a girl. May her birthday on Sunday and at Easter bring blessing upon her. . . .'[19] Then the Easter bells rang out over Windsor as Christa Schenck and others were called to see the child. The Queen herself led them to the cot, which was decorated with white lace and red satin, to represent the Hessian colours; and next to the cot stood the beaming father.[20] When the baby was baptized – by the Darmstadt court chaplain, who came to Windsor for the occasion – she was given the names Victoria Alberta (after the Prince Consort) Elizabeth Matilda Marie. She was to become Princess Louis of Battenberg and, in 1917, Marchioness of Milford Haven (mother of Earl Mountbatten of Burma).

Motherhood, meanwhile, brought a new zest and freshness into the married life of Alice and Louis; and this they were at last able to enjoy – having returned to Darmstadt in May – during the uninterrupted bliss of a family summer at Kranichstein. Alice was free to bathe, ride and enjoy those precious, unrepeatable early months of wonder and contentment after the birth of a first baby. The tiredness brought on by pain and continuing even after the birth – and identified by Queen Victoria with the same 'natural indolence' she mistakenly ascribed to Prince Albert[21] – began to be forgotten.

The Queen received happy reports from Alice and herself visited them at Kranichstein in August. Louis, taking up his duties again, was able for the first time to introduce his wife properly to the people and the ways of Darmstadt and Hesse in general. 'Now' in fact, as Christa Schenck put it, 'the real life in the new homes started for the Princess.' (She spoke of the 'new homes' because the New Palace might not be ready for nearly three years.) They would have to divide their time meanwhile between the tiny house next to Louis's parents and their summers at Kranichstein. Few places in the vicinity of

modern Darmstadt – most of the old town having been destroyed by bombing in the Second World War – are more
evocative than Kranichstein of the time of Alice and Louis.
Its magnificent park and woodland setting made it ideal for
the endless sporting activities that were such a passion with
Louis. It is now part-hotel and part-museum, the latter being
devoted to an extraordinary and extensive collection of every
conceivable kind of object connected with hunting and shooting from that period.* Visiting Alice and Louis in August 1863,
the Duke of Cambridge recounts how he 'drove with them to
their country house in the Park a very nice old place which
they have managed to make very comfortable. We dined at
once, at 4, and then they showed me their present town house,
which is very small, and the one they are building which will
be a large and good building. Afterwards we drove in the
Forest, or Park, till it was dark. The Forest is beautiful, full
of wild Boar and Red Deer of both of which we saw a good
many.'[22] *À propos* the Duke's remark about their 'dining' at
4, this was in fact a Hessian habit that the English Princess
disliked and eventually managed to change.

Alice's main preoccupation in 1863–4 was to get to know –
and be known by – her husband's compatriots, and somehow
to solve the problem of Queen Victoria's demanding that they
should still spend so much of their time with her. They visited
England briefly in the autumn of 1863 and the Queen was
deeply gratified that Alice consented to come 'when everyone
else failed'.[23] And they were there again the following summer;
but at the end of that year (1864) John Brown became
Queen Victoria's personal servant, and she became considerably less *exigeante* towards her second daughter from that time
onwards. This was providential for Alice, who by now had a
second daughter of her own, Elizabeth (Ella) born on 1
November 1864. She derived particular satisfaction from
nursing her new baby herself (which she had not in the case
of the first). The Queen, however, heartily disapproved and it
was at this time that the first serious rift between them
occurred. The Queen, furthermore, felt that she had been

* The head of the famous 'Battenberg stag', with the world record of
23 points, hangs here. The collection of sporting guns and rifles is the
greatest known collection belonging to a single family.

'thrown overboard' by Alice and could in future 'place no reliance on her visits or at least the time or duration of them'.[24] Thus 1865 ushered in a new phase in the relationship between Alice and the Queen. The mother, still a deeply grieving widow, seemed to be jealous of the happiness enjoyed by the daughter so intimately associated with the last days of the Prince Consort and the macabre aftermath of his death. But Queen Victoria was not fundamentally selfish and her outspoken complaints need not always be taken at their face value. If she spoke her mind much of what she said was at her own expense, or at least exhibited disarming evidence of astute self-knowledge. 'Her [Alice's] happiness,' she wrote a month after Ella was born, '(dreadfully trying as it is to me to hear of it *now* when I have lost all) is so true and reasonable.'[25] Unfortunately a month or so later she concluded that happiness had made Alice selfish,[26] and that she should not be consulted over the question – which was to cause more friction later on – of Princess Helena's marriage.

The question of breast-feeding was important enough for Alice to be a minor turning-point in her life. She became from this time onwards more and more interested in all aspects of child care. Nor was she so self-centred as to be concerned, in this respect, only for her own family; she was concerned – more and more so as time went on – for the families of others, and in fields not confined only to the welfare of children. And as she got to know her adopted country better she became increasingly aware of a particular contribution she might be able to make to its improvement and enlightenment. But she would have to move with great caution. She was well aware that her advanced liberal views would be anathema to the Hessian bourgeoisie unless they were put into operation with ingenuity and tact. She would have, as time went by, to plant ideas and help them to grow as if they were primarily the innovations of others. Throughout 1865 she began sowing the seeds. She had by then become the acknowledged centre of social life in Darmstadt, with a particular talent for finding the right people to whom to communicate appropriate ideas. People found it difficult to resist her requests and there was a sudden awareness of her exceptional talents and considerable organizing ability.[27] She had already reported to her mother at the end of 1863 that she was 'going to visit the hospital in the town [of Darmstadt] which is said not to be good or well looked after. I want to be able to succeed, for the people have plenty of money, but not the will.' She had furthermore 'called into life what did not exist, that is linen to be lent for the poor women in their confinements, and which I hope will be of use to them, for the dirt and discomfort is very great in those classes'.[28]

Of such discomfort Alice was soon to gain some personal knowledge. In 1864 she became patroness of the Heidenreich Stiftung, whose members brought linen and other help to such Wöchnerinnen ('women in childbed') as claimed their assistance. Alice received reports of all such cases, one of which she decided to investigate for herself. She thus set off incognito with Christa Schenck to find the address in the old part of the town. This they finally did, with great difficulty. They made their way across a dirty courtyard and up a 'dark ladder' into one little room. There they found the woman in bed with her baby and, in the same room, four other children, the out-of-work husband, two further beds and a stove. Alice sent Christa down below with the children, then with the husband cooked something for his wife, arranged her bed, bathed the baby's eyes and did some other odd jobs. She went a second time, again unrecognized, and was particularly struck by the people's sterling qualities and solidarity, despite their extreme penury. 'If one never sees any poverty,' she wrote to her mother, 'and always lives in that cold circle of Court people, one's good feelings dry up, and I feel the want of going about and doing the little good that is in my power. I am sure you will understand this.'[29]

From such glimpses behind the scenes Alice never looked back; but it took the tragedy of war, in 1866, to break the crust of Hessian resistance to social change along the rather revolutionary lines envisaged by their English Princess. And there were other reasons why, during 1865, Alice could do little more than plan theoretically for a future campaign. She took great personal interest in the care of her two small children. They had not yet moved into their permanent home; and above all 1865 was a year when steadily worsening relations with Queen Victoria were a distressful preoccupation. It had all started with what the Queen called 'that stupid quarrel about that still more stupid nursing'.[30] It was exacerbated by Alice's refusal to help her sister-in-law, the Princess of Wales, and her sister, Princess Helena, to entertain at 'Drawing Rooms' in England that the Queen declined to attend.[31] And it was climaxed by Alice's opposition to the choice of a certain Danish Prince as a prospective bridegroom for Princess Helena. The bond between Alice and her brother was not only preserved but even further strengthened throughout this episode. The Drawing Room question was of minor importance; and in April the Prince of Wales was able to write reassuringly to Alice that their mother had been 'quite appeased' by Alice's letters over the nursing issue.[32] (Soon after this the Princess of Wales's second son – the future King George v – was born and Alice was asked to be godmother.) But controversy over Princess Helena's marriage caused deep divisions in the family that took a long time to heal. The basic problem once more was that of providing companionship for Queen Victoria. 'I must solemnly declare,' the Queen had written to King Leopold at the end of 1864, 'that I cannot do without Helena except when Alice is here.'[33] For her third daughter the Queen wanted a 'tame' husband who could be relied on not to take the Princess away from 'home'. The royal choice fell upon Prince Christian of Schleswig-Holstein-Sondenburg-Augustenburg, an almost middle-aged nonentity whom Princess Helena did not even know. Alice was convinced that the marriage was designed to serve her mother's needs rather than her sister's happiness. The Prince of Wales was even more strongly opposed to the match. He was backed up to the hilt by his wife, largely for political reasons. In the previous year Prince Christian's elder brother Frederick had been a claimant to the key Baltic duchies of Schleswig and Holstein, against the Princess of Wales's father, King Christian ix of Denmark. The question was highly complicated but was settled in practice through annexation of the duchies by Prussia, who dragged in Austria as an ally. The whole affair was to have significant repercussions for Europe in terms of the coming power struggle. For the time being, and at personal levels, Prince Christian was, from the Princess of Wales's point of view, an 'enemy'. He was, on the other hand, a great friend of the Prussian Crown Prince and Princess, who strongly backed him as a suitor for Princess Helena.

The Queen was extremely bitter about Alice's opposition to her plans and ill-feeling rankled under the surface for a long time to come. 'In strict confidence,' she wrote to King Leopold, 'I grieve to tell you that Alice cannot conceal her extreme dislike to her sister's settlement in England which is mere jealousy and pains me.'[34] A further blast reached the Belgian King from his aggrieved niece three weeks later: 'Alice (to my great sorrow for she used to be such a comfort to me) is very unamiable and altogether not changed to her advantage. But the contrary in many ways – sharp and grand and wanting to have everything her own way. I hope however that this will in time wear off.'[35] But the rift was deep enough to colour the Queen's view of Alice when, much later on, other disagreements occurred. Even as late as 1871 she was deploring her second daughter's 'principles of mischief and intrigue',[36] and referring to her as a 'mischief-maker and untruth teller'[37] and even as 'a real Devil in the family'.[38]

Little did the Queen know how much of a peacemaker Alice was behind the scenes – and in a very important direction. For when it became clear that Princess Helena was going to marry Prince Christian come what may, the Prince of Wales threatened not to turn up at the wedding. Once again Alice decided to use some of her well-tried magic on her brother, to whom she wrote:

> Oh, darling Bertie, don't let you be the one who cannot sacrifice his *own feelings* for the welfare of Mother and Sister. Mama knows and deeply regrets what you feel, but, nowhere would she find another, and she almost broke with Papa's only brother and all her other relations and friends for you and Alix, saying never should political feelings stand between her and her son's happiness do you both dear ones repress your feelings for a Mother's sake and let not political feelings toward Alix's relations stand between you and your own sister's happiness.[39]

Things thereafter were rapidly patched up and all was, outwardly at least, forgiven and forgotten. But it took longest of all for the Queen and the Princess of Wales to become real friends once more. And when they did Alice again played a significant, if ironical, part in the accompanying drama.

The psychology behind the whole situation is interesting. Alice almost certainly understood her mother better than any of the other children. She and the Queen had after all been almost as one person during the ordeal following the Prince Consort's death. None of Alice's brothers or sisters had experienced or would ever experience – not even Beatrice, Queen Victoria's companion in the twilight years – such intense intimacy with their mother. But the overpowering and all-pervading loss of the Prince Consort had paradoxical effects on the Queen's troubled psyche. Did she somehow resent what she craved – the support and companionship of Alice – because this might have filled a vacuum that she was determined to preserve? Did this, in turn, inject some kind of love–hate element into her feelings towards Alice, the once 'wounded warrior' and willing martyr now desiring to be independent? Or was it rather that the tough side of Alice's nature was capable of some hardness towards her mother in areas touching on the loss of one whom *she* also adored? Was there even a hint of what later came to be known as an Oedipus complex in Alice's life, in the form of a strong attachment to the memory of her father, coupled with the possible suspicion, however unfounded, that some blind spot in the Queen had contributed to the Prince Consort's lack of grim resistance to death?

Many might instantly dismiss such suppositions as grotesquely fanciful. But to reject them completely – or something very like them – makes the known facts even more puzzling. For on the surface Alice and the Queen remained on excellent terms. They seldom, if ever, quarrelled openly with one another. Not a single one of Alice's letters to her mother during this unpleasant and contentious period betrays any sign of acrimony between them. And she kept up a stream of frequent and detailed reports to the Queen about all the events of her life. This circumstance, even allowing for considerable editing in the published edition of her letters and monumental tact on Alice's part, is a remarkable one. It thus appears that, though willing on occasion to say harsh things about one another to third parties, neither Alice nor her mother could bring herself to inflict any really deep direct wounds. That they had a tender fundamental love for each other is quite apparent; and though there was a distinct cooling off on the Queen's side in the late sixties and early seventies (realistically, if almost cynically, accepted by a somewhat disillusioned Alice), she was outshone by none in sympathy and generosity when tragedy seemed to haunt Alice in the last years of her short life.

Two other events – two particularly sad deaths – cast heavy shadows over 1865. The first was, as far as Alice was concerned, poignant and penetrating in its impact. For on 16 April Anna, Louis's only sister and a bridesmaid at their wedding, died a few days after giving birth to a daughter. It was a great blow to the Hessian royal family, who had recently and with joy celebrated Anna's marriage to the Grand Duke of Mecklenburg-Schwerin. The effect on Alice was devastating, as was shown by her letters both to Queen Victoria and to her husband, who left immediately for Schwerin. 'Oh, it is sad, very sad!' she wrote to her mother. 'Life indeed is but a short journey, on which we have our duty to do, and in which joy and sorrow alternatively prevail.'[40] No less fatalistic were her words to her husband: 'When one of us dies,' she ruminated, 'it will be terribly hard for the other, when all contact is cut off – and when the fearful silence of the grave intervenes. May the dear Lord preserve us for each other – and let us die together.'[41] (Her last phrase was to be given an unconscious but eerie echo in something said by her son years later.) She wrote each day to Louis while he was in Schwerin during the week following Anna's death. She hated his being away, but it was to be the first of many sad – and disruptive – partings during their life in Darmstadt. The Queen, meanwhile, sent a very sympathetic letter, part of which Alice quoted when writing to Louis. She spoke of 'the anxiety it is to a mother to have married daughters with these events happening often – it is always such a risk and such an uncertain thing'. 'As for this last sentence,' was Alice's comment, 'I don't think it is any more uncertain than the whole of life – and women do after all exist for that one purpose – and one resigns one's self to one's fate, trusts God, and hopes for the best, – don't you think so, my darling? I am sure you think as I do.'[42] Such occasions made Alice speak very much from the heart, despite her practical and sometimes very demanding personality. She wrote things she might not always have said. 'How I shall thank the dear Lord!' she wrote to Louis on the eve of his return from Schwerin, 'when I have you with me again – how I have thanked Him morning and evening ever since we belonged to one another, that I was permitted to be your wife. . . .'[43] From Schwerin Louis wrote: 'My parents and brothers send you much love and are so touched by your sympathy which you express so beautifully in your letters.'[44]

Death, which had come to the young Anna in the spring, turned its attentions in the depths of winter to the ageing King of the Belgians, that 'Uncle Leopold' whose loving wisdom seemed to have been there since time immemorial and whose life seemed almost to have acquired the tinge of immortality. His leaving this world was something impossible for Queen Victoria to take in at first. 'Alas!' Alice wrote to her, 'beloved Uncle Leopold is no more! How much for you, for us, for all, goes with him to the grave!'[45] No one was a better judge than King Leopold of which things and which people were most deeply pleasing and beneficial to the niece whom he loved. And it was for this reason that of all Queen Victoria's children Alice had always been King Leopold's favourite.

Chapter Seven

'THE HESSIANS FOUGHT LIKE LIONS'

The fact that Princess Alice's life was so short may make it seem unrealistic to speak too often of 'turning-points'. But 1866 was a particularly important year of transition: it was a year that would see the map of Europe changed by a short but decisive war. This war was to occasion the longest separation ever in the married life of Alice and Louis. It was also to dictate to a significant degree the form taken by that life work of Alice's which, despite the paucity of time allowed for its execution, was nevertheless her most distinctive legacy. And it was in this year that such work began in earnest.

Indeed for many people apart from Alice 1866 marked the inception of a clearly defined period that was very different from all that had gone before. King Leopold's death was a final milestone of obvious significance. Its very finality helped Queen Victoria, still a repining recluse as far as her subjects were concerned, to realize that now she must face the outside world alone, or leave it for ever. It was thus that her first official public appearance since the Prince Consort's death occurred when she opened Parliament in early February. 'The emotion and all other feelings recalled by such an event must have been very powerful and have tried you much,' wrote Alice. 'It was noble of you, my darling Mama, and the great effort will bring compensation.'[1] This breakthrough on Victoria's part was a great relief to her second daughter. For when, in the following month, she and Louis moved into the now completed New Palace, it was with a feeling that at long last Darmstadt was truly 'home' and that future visits to England need be neither as long nor as frequent. Not that reminders of Alice's original home were banished; rather the opposite. 'We are comfortably established here,' she reported from the New Palace, 'and I can't fancy I am in Germany, the house and all its arrangements being so English.'[2] The New Palace was unfortunately one of the main factors contributing to her increasingly acute financial worries. Such worries – on top of everything else – were to torment and frustrate her in the years to come. But in 1866 the new home was not only an immense thrill, it also provided a permanent base for her philanthropic and kindred activities.

Such activities were to prove revolutionary as to their method and underlying inspiration. Their first major outlet provided an example of Alice's reasoning processes, which were rather more analytical than those generally in vogue at the time. This involved an honesty about the practical limits of purely 'religious' endeavour that was to lead her into hazardous and much criticized paths later on. But in 1866 she was still trying to find a tangible formula for the new approach that she instinctively felt was desperately needed if deserving people were to be helped with no detriment to their dignity as human beings. She hit on the secret that many to this day have not fully grasped; and she thereby produced a synthesis between charity and 'welfare' that often seems sadly lacking in modern times.

Princess Alice's thoughts on the subject began to take shape during this particular year. She had attended some lectures on the need for special asylums for 'poor idiots', the expression then used for such men and women. The lectures, which fascinated her, were given by a very able clergyman from the Odenwald; but in his basic approach he was, unlike Alice, highly conventional. As a result of the lectures Alice became determined to found a pioneering home for the mentally handicapped. But she found herself faced straight away with a dilemma that for her was more than a merely theoretical one. The lecturer and his supporters could envisage only an institution bearing a strictly religious stamp. Alice did not agree with this approach, believing it vital to separate the religious-cum-amateur elements of the work from the practical and therapeutic ones. She wanted – and here she was many decades ahead of her time – to establish the principle that the alleviation of suffering was a civic and public as well as a pious and private duty. And she wished any institution such as the one now envisaged to be run with maximum professional efficiency. She felt sure that this could never be achieved by a purely paternalistic, charitable body, however

well meaning; but she felt equally sure – thus clearly differen-
tiating her concept from many a soulless modern counterpart
– that committed love must be not only the original but also
the continuing motive for the whole enterprise. And few
realized better than she that the latter demanded a high
degree of selfless devotion, often in the most unglamorous,
inauspicious and discouraging circumstances.

As already mentioned, Alice was adept at what we should
now call making the 'right contacts'. She sought out those
sympathetic to her somewhat novel views. Her mother-in-law,
Princess Charles, agreed to be the 'Protectress' of this particular enterprise; and the recruiting of a suitable committee
was undertaken with skill and diplomacy. It consisted, in its
final form, of three doctors and four ladies. Of the latter one
was a doctor's and one a parson's wife; and as it was felt that
a Roman Catholic should also serve, a certain Frau von
Riedesel* joined the committee at Princess Alice's suggestion.
No time was lost in producing outline plans. But it was Alice
who had to shoulder the main initial burden – the inevitable
one of raising the necessary funds. She decided to organize
something that at that time had never been heard of before in
Germany: a 'Bazaar', which was intended to be something like
a massive sale-of-work. Its very novelty was well calculated to
attract good custom. And so indeed it turned out, the four-day
event being held at Alice's and Louis's new home from 6 to 10
April. It was a sensational success. Apart from anything else
the citizens of Darmstadt were delighted with this first opportunity to see inside the gay Renaissance-style 'New Palace'
that had just been built (at such crippling expense, as it
turned out) in their midst. The financial success – far greater
than anything that had been expected – was a tremendous
personal triumph for Alice. 'Nobody could resist her personal
charm which here for the first time could make its influence
felt on the great mass of the population consisting of all classes
of the people.'[3] The total sum realized (16,000 florins) was
enormous; but the occasion was no mere glorified jumble sale.
Many of the objects purchased had originally been beautiful

* Probably the wife, or a relation, of the Master of the Horse at the
Grand Duke's court.

and valuable gifts to Alice. But such a bazaar was never repeated. Alice's continual insistence on separating the idealistic from the practical made her treat it – however successful – as a once-for-all expedient rather than as a normal way of raising money for such undertakings.

The home for the mentally handicapped was Alice's first major project. But its completion and success were delayed by the political events that overshadowed the rest of the year 1866. The war over the Schleswig and Holstein duchies two years before proved to have been an ominous curtain raiser, though such implications were not realized at the time. Bismarck had successfully gambled on Britain's not intervening actively as Denmark's ally. The whole exercise had thus served, for Prussia, an object similar to certain key events preceding the Second World War: the German occupation of the Rhineland; the Italian invasion of Abyssinia; and even the Spanish Civil War. The political climate having been thus effectively, if brutally, tested, the stage was set for the big attempt to seize power. Bismarck's search for a *casus belli* was soon over. Prussia and Austria, the principal aspirants for leadership, were now the administrators of Schleswig and Holstein respectively. The attempt by Austria, forced on her by grave financial difficulties, to reinstate the duchies as an independent state was supported by the Frankfurt Diet on behalf of the Germanic Confederation. But it was an empty gesture by an already weakened conglomerate and this belated attempt to check Prussia boomeranged badly. Bismarck declared that the whole manoeuvre was a violation of the Gastein Convention – regulating the situation of Schleswig and Holstein – and accused Austria of trying to provoke a war. As a 'defensive' measure he marched into Holstein; Austrian-inspired mobilization by the Diet made general hostilities inevitable. Prussia, militarily and politically the upstart underdog, led by a Chancellor lacking public enthusiasm for war, had to win rapidly or not at all.

In fact all was quite quickly over. For so decisive a struggle as the Austro-Prussian War of 1866 to last only seven weeks was comparable in modern times to a military showdown between Israel and Egypt lasting only seven days. But another future cataclysm was even more eerily portended by the events of 1866. The Crown Princess in Berlin, though she hated Bismarck, vacillated in her views on Prussia's national aspirations and the means to achieve them. A counter-irritant to her political preoccupations was her concern over her seven-year-old son with the maimed left arm, the future Emperor Wilhelm II ('Kaiser Bill'). Alice in Darmstadt was unvacillating in her support of Hesse as Austria's ally, but hated the thought that her country and her sister's would be enemies. Little did either of them know that their own children would be on opposite sides in a far more devastating conflict, the most deadly the world had ever seen. And this conflict, the First World War, was occasioned by circumstances uncannily paralleled in 1866, when Bismarck was able to use a decision for general mobilization as a pretext for war. In 1914 a similarly fateful decision to mobilize was made by Czar Nicolas II of Russia. The German Kaiser of that time, though hopeful of avoiding war, was obsessed with the fear of encirclement; Russian mobilization proved to be a final determinant in his decision to march. And the ill-fated wife of Russia's tormented and tragic Czar was none other than Alice's daughter, the Empress Alexandra Fedorovna. This daughter – known as Alix in her girlhood days – was not yet born during the 1866 rehearsal for a future and supposed final struggle for the mastery of Europe.

To such horrendous lengths, involving millions of innocent people, was taken the basic conflict that began in the 1860s between democratic and authoritarian ideologies, between patriotic balance and nationalist obsession, between progress and reaction. The germs of it all were just beginning their insidious process of self-propagation in 1866; and at the very heart of the process were two sisters who loved each other dearly. Sharing their father's liberal dream for a Europe based on the Coburg theory of constitutional monarchy, they were spared from witnessing the spectacle of its brutal frustration when the Hohenzollern conception of the divine right of kings overreached itself. It is sadly ironical to unravel the human threads in the one-time dynastic maze that ran through European power politics, for we know that Alice and her elder sister would have wished nothing more for their respective

Louis IV, Grand Duke of Hesse

Princess Alice

children than to live in peace as loving and united cousins, rather than as implacable enemies.

The events of 1866 had considerable immediate and personal implications for Princess Alice. She dreaded the possibility of war – 'civil war' – with an intensity inseparable from the 'anxious nature'[4] she had inherited. But it was a possibility she had squarely to face within weeks of the elating success of the 'Alice Bazaar'. It made her reflect that life was a pilgrimage in which 'a little more or a little less sorrow falls to one's lot' and that 'the anticipation of all evil is almost as great as the evil itself'.[5] And then in the middle of June, a week before another baby was due, the blow struck. Hessian troops made up part of the 'federal army' opposing Prussia and Alice's husband, as a Major-General, commanded his country's Cavalry Brigade. On 1 July he took his leave of a wife ill-prepared at this juncture for what, to her, was an intensely painful parting. Apart from anything else it was their fourth wedding anniversary. She could not help thinking – mindful perhaps of her spiritual ancestress Elizabeth – that she might never see her husband again. Next morning she wrote her husband the first of a series of letters that poured out almost daily and sometimes two or three times in one day during their seven weeks' separation. 'Good bye my dear, adored husband,' she wrote; 'You are never out of my thoughts and I see your dear loving face before me always.'[6] To add to everyone's burden the heat was overpowering. Within a week what was in fact the decisive battle of the war had already been fought, the Prussians inflicting a crushing defeat on the Austrians at Sadowa. The fate of Louis and his army became more uncertain than ever; Alice, expecting almost hourly that her confinement would begin, hoped he might get a few days' leave during the apparent lull, when there was even talk of an armistice. She meanwhile sent him a copy of a letter from her friend Florence Nightingale about field hospitals. Alice's main concern was with practical aspects of the war, in which even women could be involved; but apart from such tasks as making bandages out of sheets before hostilities had begun, one would have thought that her condition would debar her from further participation for the time being. In fact, despite wild rumours of panic sweeping Darmstadt, she remained

restlessly active and grimly realistic. 'I feel so heavy and
tired,' she told Louis, 'and my time must be coming at any
moment – and I am still dragging on – nevertheless I never
stop working on bandages and stockings etc., for the soldiers.'[7] Earlier than most people, moreover, she sensed a
Prussian victory, but contented herself for the time being with
the thought that 'we shall have in any case to [live] with
Prussia again afterwards and blood spilt for nothing is *so*
terrible'.[8] Then, providentially, Louis was able to get back
briefly to Darmstadt on leave; and while he was there (on 11
July) another daughter – the third of their 'three graces' –
was born. But soon the guns of battle could be heard from
Darmstadt itself; he hurried back to the front and was immediately engaged in the fighting. 'Our people had a bloody
battle with the Prussians before Aschaffenburg,' he reported
in his next letter. 'Our people fought splendidly but we had to
retreat, although in perfect order. . . . I did not expose myself
to danger because there was no need to, I am being careful for
your sake. . . .'[9] From then on the couple did their best to keep
one another informed as to events within their own respective
areas. Alice reiterated her almost frantic hope that Louis
would not endanger himself in a cause that was 'already
lost'.[10]

Then, on 17 July, the Prussians entered Frankfurt, a town
of such symbolic and geographical importance for the *Bund*,
which it seemed Austria might now be forced to abandon.* If
this happened 'the first stone of German Unity will be laid',
Alice told Louis.[11] 'You cannot imagine,' she continued, 'how
many people here are now showing different attitudes from
before, and how the present mood inclines toward peace and
agreement with Prussia, and acceptance of her reform proposal, etc.' The last phrase is significant, since Alice no less
than her sister – despite the imposed differences of the moment
– still cherished her father's dream of what German unity
could and should mean for the rest of Europe. She could only

* Austria was the leader in the alliance with the South German Confederation (*Bund*). The decision to abandon Frankfurt had to be made
by Prince Alexander of Hesse (the brother of Grand Duke Louis III and
uncle of Prince Louis) in his capacity as Commander of the Confederate
Army Corps.

be amazed and disgusted meanwhile by evidence of the insta-
bility of certain individual Hessians under strain. A false
alarm that the Prussians were entering Darmstadt caused most
of the youth corps to flee from their posts, though the Palace
sentries – under her very windows – stayed on guard. But she
was particularly incensed by the hysterical behaviour of a
certain Colonel Laue, who was in charge of the military hospital. Losing his head completely, he rushed into the hospital
at 1 o'clock in the morning, shouting, 'The Prussians are
coming, every man for himself.' Those of the unfortunate
wounded who could walk struggled outside, only to find the
streets calm and deserted, with no sign of Prussians anywhere.
Returning in the dark to the hospital, many got back into the
wrong beds. When Dr Weber – Alice's friend and collaborator,
who was also an eye specialist – came round next morning he
found the whole place in a state of hopeless confusion.[12] Alice
was to make it her business to ensure that in no future emergency would nursing and hospital affairs be prone to such
infantile panic or instant chaos.

Everywhere 'federal' resistance to the Prussians was crack-
ing, and her enemies were sueing separately for peace. The
Austrians forfeited more and more sympathy on the part of
Alice, who even felt it right to pray that defeat should not, at
this late hour, still somehow overtake the Prussians.[13] The
latter admitted that 'the Hessians fought like lions', and the
military honour of Louis's people as a whole remained intact.[14]
Alice could only hope, as days of anxiety dragged by, for a
speedy end to 'this horrible bloodshed, which is so pointless
for our people'.[15] Another argument of hers against Louis's
taking military risks – his bravery was reported to her – was
that they had no son.[16] The succumbing of the small states
and the growing conviction that Austria would desert her
allies made her courage begin to falter badly for the first time
as July neared its end. She was furious, above all, with such
ministers as Pfordten in Bavaria, Benst in Saxony and the
Hessian Dalwigk. Innately reactionary, they harboured illusions that 'foreign' intervention was still possible, and that
Germany could and should be split up again. 'Since these bad
Ministers make their Princes so stubborn, Prussia must of
course continue the war,' was Alice's bitter complaint.[17] Since

the Prussian terms as then offered seemed favourable she felt it shameful that the troops should be expected to make more sacrifices. 'I consider it murder – these gentlemen will have to answer for it.' The last days of July were the most critical, with the Prussians, having ceased hostilities with Austria but not yet with Hesse, advancing on the Hessian troops from three sides. Thus did the sterile and nerve-racking conflict drag on; the 'odious frivolous Dalwigk' stuck like a leech to his post, while Alice felt that her uncle (the Grand Duke) had 'also been greatly at fault through cowardice, indolence and egotism'.[18]

Louis, for his part, answered Alice as fully and frequently as possible.[19] He repeatedly pleaded with her to be 'sensible', to keep up her strength and to try not to worry. He basically agreed with her thesis of the uselessness of continued fighting, especially after an armistice had been arranged between Austria and Prussia. He was less critical at this time of Dalwigk and felt that the minister, as well as the Grand Duke, in fact agreed with the general desire for a close union with Prussia. 'But,' he wrote to his wife, 'we want to keep our old Oberhessen and not to be given Bavarian territory near Aschaffenburg in compensation for it. Bismarck is unwilling to agree because of France. We would gladly give up Rhein-hessen for it, if that would make things easier; talk to Becker about it, and write and tell the Queen and Vicky our side of the question, and give them both my love. . . .'[20] Louis's most important piece of information for Alice, however, was that an armistice had been concluded as far as Hesse was concerned. They were now 'safe' and he would be seeing her soon, he hoped. A few days later Alice was on the way home from visiting her parents-in-law when quite unexpectedly she met Louis in the street. Her relief and delight were naturally intense; together they visited the wounded and two days later Louis was appointed by his uncle, the Grand Duke, to the command of the Hessian division then in the field. But the end was now in sight; the Prussians entered Darmstadt and Alice – despite a cholera epidemic in the area – shared Louis's quarters after he had rejoined his troops in Rhenish Hesse. Before leaving Darmstadt she made a last tour of visits to wounded soldiers, accompanied by Louis. She was by now becoming a familiar sight in the wards of the town's hospitals, and many a wounded soldier had experienced the therapeutic effect of her tenderness and comforting powers.

On this particular visit even her powers failed in the case of one soldier. He had had an operation since Alice had last seen him; she now found him very low and crying like a child. It was barely possible, even for Alice, to bring him any real comfort; he just held her hand and kept moaning, '*Es brennt so*' ('It burns so').[21] The secret of Alice's success with such patients – apart from her instinctive nursing ability and past experience – was that she loved them dearly. They were so young, attractive and potentially strong; and to her they seemed, 'for that class', particularly well educated. Her heart bled for them, as she herself wrote in a letter to Florence Nightingale soon after the war had officially ended.[22] The letter shows what a close friend and major influence on Alice's life and work the famous Crimean War heroine had by this time become. Miss Nightingale had been able to send, on behalf of certain generous benefactors in England, a sum of money that came at a providential moment. Alice made it clear how appreciative were all in Darmstadt and elsewhere; money was to be added to a fund for the support of those irreparably injured or maimed by the war. These were men who, the Princess reported, had suffered greatly but with 'touching cheerfulness'. As a faithful disciple of Miss Nightingale, she was now constantly vigilant about such matters as cleanliness, ventilation and water supply in the hospitals. One of her greatest consolations was the progress that had been made in these respects by the time the Austro-Prussian War had come to an end.

Care of the sick, disabled and needy became from now on almost an obsession with her. She had thought about it constantly during the seven-week war, and despite the birth of a child had missed as few opportunities as possible for hospital visiting, study and general work connected with the subject. The advent of peace she hailed as heralding a distinctly new chapter in her life; and the date on which this new chapter can be said to have begun is clearly identifiable as 12 September 1866. There was every reason to think of it as the harbinger of new hopes. It was Louis's birthday and the date on which peace was officially ratified in Berlin. But it was above all the day on which their baby was christened – with the names Irene Marie Louisa Anna. The last was in memory of Louis's sister, whom Alice had loved so much. Among the child's sponsors was the Cavalry Brigade that Louis had commanded, and the name Irene was chosen for a very special reason: it was derived from the Greek word for 'peace'.

Chapter Eight

ALICE THE WONDERNAME

The peace that followed the Austro-Prussian War left Prussia by far the strongest state in central Europe, and possessed of the most formidable army that continent had ever seen. Austria lost none of her territory but almost all of her prestige; her pretensions toward mastery of Germany were extinguished for ever. With the dissolution of the old *Deutscher Bund* all the states north of Frankfurt and the River Main – such as Saxony, the Thuringian states, Hesse-Cassel, Oldenburg and Hanover – were incorporated into a Prussian-controlled North German Confederation.

Hesse-Darmstadt was one of only four German states to remain independent – the others being Baden, Württemberg and Bavaria. But Hesse lost its territory north of the Main – Hesse-Homburg – which even before the war had been separated from the rest of the country by a small strip of land belonging to Hesse-Cassel. The heaviest burden laid upon Hesse was that of financial reparations to Prussia. This meant that the tiny state, by far the smallest of those remaining independent, had to face a penurious future at a time when finance became an increasing personal worry to Alice and Louis. The former, whose allowance was meagre, often had to ask her mother for help. Unfortunately such requests produced 'horror'[1] and Queen Victoria had, by 1871, formed the opinion that Alice's 'greediness for money' was terrible. The intervening years were thus lean ones for Prince and Princess Louis. The irony was that the main recipients of any spare cash Alice might have obtained would have been needy cases. But in this respect lack of money had one providential effect. It made it all the more imperative for Alice's projects to be eminently practical and therefore self-supporting, as indeed her inclinations already dictated. And this was to be a guiding principle in launching and maintaining the various societies linked with Alice's name that came to flourish in the years following the Austro-Prussian War. Constituting as they did Alice's life work and most lasting legacy, they represent an aspect of her life that somehow transcended its other events and their chronology; they supplied that extra dimension that raised her life far above the ordinary. And they made such things as petty squabbles with the Queen and run-of-the-mill social occasions seem of small significance by comparison.

In embarking on the course that was to end up with a string of associations bearing her name – and intimately involved with herself – Alice faced particularly formidable difficulties. Apart from financial worries, which were to be with her to the grave, her health from 1866–7 onwards became the cause of increasing concern. More and more of her letters to Louis mentioned the worsening pains of neuralgia and rheumatism, of excessive tiredness, strain and headaches. She had even reported once during the war that 'because of my eyes I do *nothing at all* the whole day'.[2] Complaints about bad eyesight became more frequent in the years that followed. There is something of a mystery about all this, since Alice had never been considered particularly delicate in her younger days. Indeed in times of very severe trial she had shown signs of exceptional physical and mental stamina. And in later years the symptoms of serious ailments, at least physical ones, seemed least apparent when she was busiest or dealing with challenging problems. When she had nothing special to take her mind off life at its most ordinary the aches and pains appeared to be at their worst. Were they caused, at least partly – or at any rate made worse – by boredom and frustration? Was the occasionally poor eyesight conceivably an hysterical symptom – if only in a mild form – as is medically known to be possible? Was her married life, though superficially happy, fundamentally unsatisfying? Was this a contributory cause, through subconscious channels, of some of her infirmities and of the increasing frequency with which she mentioned them as time went by?

These questions are easier to ask than to answer, and their fuller consideration belongs to that period when her soul seemed to be struggling through a dark night in the wilderness. Bad health was at all events an additional adverse factor at the moment when her most important work was beginning.

The period between the Austro-Prussian and the Franco-Prussian Wars (1866–70) was one of immense activity and achievement. Alice had already shown special concern for women 'in childbed', for the blind and for the mentally handicapped. Such interests were kept up, and the concrete plans for the mental care project went steadily ahead from 1867 onwards. But Alice's sights were now set much higher; above all she wished to be personally and actively involved – rather than just charitably or nominally associated – with a systematic programme to bring help – *as of right* – to those in greatest need. From such ambitions sprang the famous '*Alice-Frauenverein*'. The concept of this Women's Guild or Union grew directly out of Alice's observations during the recent war. Help for the troops, whether wounded or on active service, had indeed been provided, but only by private individuals in a haphazard fashion. Lack of organization had made it impossible for shortages occurring in some areas to be rectified from surpluses piling up in others. So Alice's scheme – 'no small undertaking', as she described it[3]– was for a Women's Union serving the whole country through a network of committees, with a co-ordinating committee in Darmstadt under her personal direction. The object was two-fold, depending on whether wartime or peacetime conditions prevailed: to assist (in wartime) the Geneva International Convention, to which Hesse belonged, in nursing and providing for troops; and (in time of peace) to have nurses trained and ready for the task of nursing when and where they might be most urgently required in times of emergency. An appeal dated 1 June 1867 set out the plan and invited all the women of Hesse, married or unmarried, to join. The proposed statutes were published and the formation of subsidiary organizations was envisaged.[4] What thus emerged, once it had been officially founded early in 1867, was a flourishing sisterhood with active (qualified nursing) and auxiliary (non-nursing) members. In introducing its aims Alice expressly mentioned the *Frauenverein* that had been formed in 1859 by the Grand-Duchess Louise of Baden, as well as the inspiration and practical advice she had received from Florence Nightingale.[5] The sisterhood went from strength to strength over the years – exactly seventy in fact – until it was merged with the German Red Cross in 1937.

But it is difficult, especially in the early days, to separate the Alice Societies one from the other. Their aims constantly overlapped, and they also gave rise to subsidiary societies later on for the extension and continuation of the work. One of Alice's principal collaborators was Sophie von Follenius, who has given a valuable account of the work and its development.[6] Though initial prejudice against Alice was very strong, she disarmed her critics by encouraging them to speak their minds as freely as possible. Her faithful band of co-workers grew all the more quickly. She was readily receptive to suggestions, as well as being full of ideas of her own. It was thus that 1867 saw a dual foundation: not only the *Alice-Frauenverein* for nursing and training nurses, but also the *Alice-Verein für Frauenbildung und Erwerb*. The latter was extremely important, both as to its underlying principle – the proper education of women – and its practical objective, enabling women to earn their own living. As a pioneer effort in 'Women's Lib' it may well seem tame by contemporary standards; but it seemed revolutionary at a time and in a place where the notion of women working for money was thought to be virtually immoral.

These societies, the first to bear Alice's name, complemented each other in the eyes of their creator. They existed side by side, with their founder showing equal and constant interest in them both. The first two nurses were trained in Bethanien, Berlin, and completed their training on 6 January 1868. They left with diplomas certifying excellence in ability and knowledge. They were therefore the first two active members of the *Alice-Frauenverein* who had been properly trained in nursing and had been given a certificate by the Central Committee; before all the assembled members of this committee they took an oath, whose wording seems worth quoting:

I promise that as long as I am an active member of the Association I will carry out nursing in accordance with the provisions of the Statutes and the conditions laid down by the Central Committee; in particular I promise punctually to carry out the instructions and orders of the doctors. I also promise at all times to observe an inviolable silence in respect of everything I may see or hear whilst nursing in the family of the patient, whether these be unimportant or important matters.

The above was read out, with the words 'I promise' alone being spoken by the adjuring sister. Further nurses were trained in the Municipal Hospital in Darmstadt and in the Rochus Hospital in Mainz, with the result that after the first two years the sisterhood already had ten nurses at its disposal. Some were employed in private nursing and others in military hospitals, where they worked under the supervision of experienced doctors.

The first task of the *Alice-Verein für Frauenbildung und Erwerb* was to form a sales outlet for needlework. The aim was nothing less than, by sheer force of an efficient organization of its own, to guarantee a proper wage for female workers, who were at that time shamelessly exploited. After deducting only what was necessary to carry on the business properly, the Union devoted all profits to this purpose. The women were also trained to do highly proficient work, and the finished articles were carefully checked by a committee of women, who rejected anything defective or imperfect. It was admittedly a small and insignificant beginning, carried on at first in an old lending library. The experiment was successful, however, and the premises became the permanent site of the sales outlet for work passed as perfect. It represented a notable breakthrough, despite seemingly endless difficulties, for similar sales organizations had been tried all over Germany and all had failed. Now at last a practical demonstration of success was there for all to see, and in various towns, such as Dresden, Schwerin, Stuttgart and Stettin, similar branches were opened. Quite soon the whole concept had changed, fewer gifts being given for sale and more work being carried out on commission and to individual specifications. A much-needed eye-opener was also provided for the women on the committee. They gained for the first time an insight into the very inadequate training hitherto received by women in a field that was obviously of great potential use to them. For nowhere in Germany was needlework obligatory as part of girls' primary education. The association, on the personal initiative of Alice, succeeded in persuading the powers-that-be to remedy this defect by means of new legislation. A key helper and ally was Alice's vice-president, Louise Buchner. She was an authority on almost every aspect of the occupations suitable for women, and soon a point had been reached where even in the poorest village every girl could learn how to make clothes and look after them. This marked a minor revolution in rural life, since it was no longer necessary for a tailor (male) to make a summer visit to each village in order to patch and make good the wear and tear of winter.

Another accomplishment of the new association was that women and girls now came to be employed at the County's Central Statistics Office. At first twelve women worked there, alternately in longer or shorter shifts. During the three peaceful years of 1867, 1868 and 1869 the Alice Societies consolidated their early achievements and successes. The political and other consequences of the Franco-Prussian War belong to another part of the story; but naturally the Alice Societies were heavily involved from the start. Though the *Alice-Verein* for nursing by now had branches all over the country, it had only sixteen fully trained nurses at its disposal when war broke out in 1870. It was necessary to increase this number with all possible speed and here Alice's own personality played a crucial part. Inspiration and organization, bearing her unmistakable stamp, worked a sort of miracle, thanks to the corresponding self-sacrifice of women and young girls and the help given by doctors. In only a few weeks an encouraging number of sufficiently trained nurses from all walks of life became available through the association. A hundred and sixty-four nurses could be sent to as many as thirty-six posts, and they found themselves working in hospitals of the *Hilfs-verein** in reserve military hospitals and also in some field hospitals.

This war, for Alice, was very different from anything that had happened in 1866. She was not only able, most of the time, to be more active but she had herself made sure that there would be a pre-existing framework within which such activity could bear maximum fruit. She thus remained 'at her post' in Darmstadt – a post involving almost incessant work – while

* Voluntary organization for helping servicemen.

her husband went on active service at the head of the 25th Division. And once more war brought another turning-point: Alice was now a *German*, proud to be the wife of a German officer and gratified to be accepted as such. She was more successful in this respect than her sister in Berlin, and yet she was not disloyal to that part of herself that was still very English. The *Hilfsverein* had meanwhile received permission to work in her palace, where she herself was available every day for anybody to talk to and from where she visited the various hospitals and railway dressing-stations. She also built up a storeroom to supply all requisites for the nursing and transport of the sick and wounded. This storeroom was later transferred to the palace on the Luisenplatz, where an enlarged Ladies' Committee, formed by Alice, was doing its work.

The name Alice was thus quickly becoming a sort of 'wondername' throughout Hesse-Darmstadt. Previously unknown (and awkward to pronounce) in German, it could only indicate one person; it literally worked wonders in certain cases, and the transformation of the spirit of the whole country within five years was a remarkable one. In 1953, in Darmstadt, Alice's grandson, also a Prince Louis of Hesse, gave a lecture on the famous Alice Hospital, founded seventy years earlier. He well understood the approach of his grandmother, for whom 'the point of departure always remained a human being who was ill and needed help, and his needs in war and peace. At his side stood the person willing to give help, wishing to ameliorate his needs and for this purpose could make use of an organization (the Alice Sisterhood) which was becoming more and more streamlined.'[7] The main topic of this lecture was that famous Alice Hospital that was not founded in its permanent form until five years after its inspirer's death. But it was not the first hospital to be called by this name, for during the Franco-Prussian War the original *Alice-Verein* went a stage further than merely sending nursing staff to existing military hospitals: it took over in addition the complete running and administration of three reserve military hospitals in Darmstadt, one being in the Riedselstrasse and another in the Pioneer Barracks. But the third and most important was the military hospital opened with the gifts of

English doctors and specializing from the outset in internal ailments. It consisted originally of four barracks with 120 beds and its excellence and special usefulness did not escape the attention of the higher military authorities. It was an extremely proud moment for the determined but often frustrated Alice when concrete recognition came from usually conservative and sometimes hostile quarters. And the military authorities now became responsible for the building of four further barracks with 450 beds and appointed English doctors as medical officers. But most important of all they made a contract with the *Alice-Frauenverein* for the permanent management and supplying of nurses for this and the other two military hospitals. This was perhaps the most notable vindication of its kind for Alice's initiative; and at the head of the new organization needed to cope with these widening responsibilities she appointed one of her close associates in the *Alice-Frauenverein*, Frau Minna Strecker. It was now (in 1871) that the term Alice Hospital was first used. It foreshadowed that more elaborate and illustrious establishment that was to be Alice's most outstanding single posthumous memorial among the people of her adopted country.

A veritable social revolution accompanied all these developments. Less than twenty years had passed since Florence Nightingale's epic struggle that had initially involved a very difficult task – that of establishing nursing as a 'respectable' profession that was no longer immediately associated in people's minds with drunkenness and prostitution. Consequent changes were specially slow to find their way into German hospitals. 'What was endured by the German wounded at the beginning of the [1870] war equalled in horror and far exceeded in scale anything in the Crimea.'[8] Such suffering, as far as the Hessians were concerned, would have been infinitely worse – would indeed have been unspeakable – but for the Florence Nightingale of Darmstadt, Princess Alice. And long before the war was over the effects of this particular social revolution were visible everywhere. It was entirely due to Alice, for example, that women became 'accepted' in places and positions where they would formerly not have been tolerated, though such acceptance was of course occasioned by the exigencies of war. Women, invariably members of the *Alice-*

Frauenverein, were seen without embarrassment or detriment to their dignity not only in hospital wards – stench and squalor notwithstanding – but also in such places as railway stations dispensing refreshments, hospital trains, hospital steamers and the like. One of the reasons for the breakdown of prejudice and embarrassment was the frontal attack made by Alice in the realm of hitherto unmentionable subjects. Personal hygiene had been much neglected, even by doctors. The *Alice-Frauenverein* organized public lectures on the subject. Alice was well acquainted with Lister's pioneering work in England in the field of antiseptics. She tried, through the lectures and at council and other meetings, to put similar ideas across in Darmstadt. One of the means she favoured for the promotion of bodily hygiene was the installation of baths in private homes. This would involve a whole new drainage system, for which Alice fought tooth and nail, her only ally being the family doctor, Dr Eigenbrodt. One of the delegates at a meeting on the subject – a member of a well-known local family – turned furiously on Alice and said, 'We do not want such ideas Your Highness. It is a luxury if everybody can have a bath. I have never bathed in my life and yet I am clean. These are new fangled English ideas.'[9] Though Alice's ideas won in the end, it was an uphill and sometimes even an unpleasant task. But there were compensations and an amusing incident occurred with regard to the first general meeting of the *Alice-Frauenverein*. This was held on 7 September 1869 and a report of it was sent to Florence Nightingale. The envelope was addressed to 'Miss Florence Nightingale, London'. It was delivered to Buckingham Palace, having already been opened once. Presumably the Post Office, seeing that the signature on the communication was that of Princess Alice, thought that the letter should go to the Palace. There it was resealed and sent on to Florence Nightingale. The envelope and its contents are now preserved in the British Museum.

It has been suggested that Alice was what we would call a socialist,[10] but the description seems to call for some qualification. She favoured the increasing use of public funds for the alleviation of private distress, but preferred needy cases to be cared for where possible by individuals rather than institutions. It was thus, for example, that a 'hybrid' system came into operation for the care of destitute orphans: they were looked after in private homes at public expense rather than being relegated to orphanages. This was done on Alice's advice, though she was well aware of the personal and human difficulties that would inevitably arise. The *Alice-Frauenverein* therefore acted as a go-between for orphans and foster-parents, a special committee being set up for the placing and supervision of children in appropriate homes. This voluntary supervision was extended in years to come so that orphans leaving school but not supported by public funds came under the committee's care for as long as necessary.[11]

Another indication of Alice's viewpoint can be seen in the mental home that had been her first main project. No provision at all had existed for the care or treatment of the mentally defective when Alice first came to Darmstadt. But her practical mind dictated that what had been started with private donations, and by means of the famous Bazaar, could be maintained on a permanent basis only if it was a national responsibility. Fortunately she was able to persuade the State to take it over, and the official inauguration of this successful foundation finally came about in 1869. Perhaps Alice should be called a liberal with a small 'l'.* If she was far in advance of her time as regards the hitherto neglected rights of politically unrepresented and economically exploited members of the public, she was convinced that a redressing of the balance was as much an individual as a corporate responsibility. Her ideology had much more in common with Mazzini than with Karl Marx, but she might well have sympathized with much in the gospel of John Burns.

Modern socialists, moreover, would not have seen eye to eye with the motives behind what came to be called the Alice Lyceum. This was primarily intended to help upper-class young women who had outgrown formal education but who wished to continue 'improving their minds'. Courses were made available in German and English literature, art and German

---

* Alice's eldest daughter, Victoria (Marchioness of Milford Haven), always denied that her mother was either a socialist or a liberal. She referred to her as 'progressive' and pursued similar ideals for herself and her children. It is not difficult to observe traces of such ideology in the most illustrious of Alice's descendants.

history, as well as the natural sciences. The 'upper-class' element was diluted somewhat as time went on and the association in charge of the Lyceum broadened its horizon considerably. It became increasingly concerned with the whole field of female education, anxious to cure existing defects and blaze new trails, particularly in the realm of improved teacher-training courses. Its most revolutionary suggestion was for the opening of technical, industrial and trade schools for women.

September 1872 saw a particularly important high-spot when a general meeting took place of the various associations existing in Germany for the improvement of education and the social position of women, especially the middle classes, in respect of trade and commerce. It was held at the New Palace in Darmstadt and naturally no one was more interested than Princess Alice, who was present at all meetings. The occasion was particularly memorable because of the moderation with which purely practical ways and means as to how women could better earn their own living were examined. Special training for women was discussed in equally concrete terms. Mrs Marie Simon, the founder of the Institute of Nurses at Dresden, was a delegate and Miss Mary Carpenter, Miss Florence Hill and Miss Winkworth represented England. Discussion ranged far and wide; it concerned women joining the postal, railway and telegraph services, the effects of the educational principles of Friedrich Froebel on the expansion of women's professions, kindergarten teaching, exhibitions and shops for the sale of needlework, nursing as a recognized profession and not just a praiseworthy vocation, higher education for girls, the English Women's Guild and the education of women in England. In the evening Princess Alice issued a private invitation to all those taking part. In the course of numerous conversations she was reported as 'not being content merely to show interest in a matter which was dear to her (which the person to whom she was speaking considered an honour and encouragement) but she listened patiently, made suggestions and gave practical help'.[12]

As the conference acknowledged what the people of Darmstadt had accomplished so it encouraged them to make further efforts. It even planted the germ of yet more adventurous plans in Alice's fertile mind, though she was already beginning to show signs of taking on too much. As well as attending official functions at the Palace she often entertained committee members at five o'clock tea, or they spent the evening in the library alone with her or with one or two others; they brought their needlework and could speak of anything they liked, either concerning the work of the association or of a personal nature. The Princess seemed endlessly interested and understanding, the late sixties and early seventies being the years when her influence was still at its most dynamic and direct. Thereafter it became increasingly indirect, as what her grandson called 'the great exhaustion' began to take its toll. But Alice had already contributed a monumental share; what was important was that her work not only went on but bore, as it were, compound interest year by year. Legislation to extend the scope of primary education for girls in more practical directions meant that, thereafter, one development led to another. After the new School Act came into force in 1874, the first course in training eighteen pupils to be needlework teachers started in May 1875. In a few years' time Darmstadt became a recognized German centre for such training. And in glancing at the list of Alice's social achievements, far too numerous to warrant further detailed description, one gains the impression that she would have found the modern expressions 'liberal' or 'socialist' meaningless in the context of her work.

The year 1872 saw the climax of her most important achievements and attitudes. The former assume more impressive proportions when one takes into consideration the mental strain she was then under. But she was intensely gratified that in this particular year the *Alice-Verein* for nursing was able to acquire its own home – the 17 Mauerstrasse Nursing Home – where a nurses' training school was opened. She was able to take special advantage of her friendship with Florence Nightingale at this time and the two women exchanged several important letters throughout that year.*[13] The letters display not only a very deep *rapport* between these two women but also a mutual sense of professionalism, realism and, of course, humanity. As a result of these negotiations the first

* See Appendix II.

matron to be appointed by Princess Alice to the new hospital was the gifted Charlotte Helmsdorfer and Alice herself paid, at no little personal sacrifice, for her training at the Johannis Hospital in Leipzig and also at a hospital in Liverpool. But her most important period of training was spent at the Florence Nightingale School in London. During the autumn, as already mentioned, the big general meeting of the Women's Associations took place in the New Palace; and it was in this year that Alice took the opportunity to summarize the true concept of the nurse's vocation when she handed some of them their diplomas. On 8 December 1872 seven nurses of the *Alice-Verein* for nursing received a handwritten letter from Princess Alice saying: 'You should be dedicated, friendly to the highest degree, discreet, always remembering your very difficult task but not thinking of yourself.' She also wrote and reminded them of their duty of faith and obedience. But she spoke in no merely regal, remote or abstract sense; she included herself in her own admonition: 'We work together to reach a human goal, and neither of us can do without the other.'

She unquestionably seems to have worked wonders, which to this day are associated with her name and with her memory. Though these should not be underestimated, neither should they be exaggerated. For she was not of course the only woman in Europe trying to shake fellow mortals out of their apathy and apparent indifference to the needs of others. But it might well be asked what would have happened to Hesse had Alice never come to live there. Something equivalent to the Alice Societies, and all that they implied, might perhaps have been inspired by some other person. What is extraordinary is that their establishment, and all the thought and work they demanded, represented only one aspect, albeit an important one, of a life as short and filled with other pressures as that of Queen Victoria's 'forgotten' daughter.

Chapter Nine

EVENING SHADOWS

Despite all the thought and work demanded by the launching of the Alice Societies, the Princess herself was far from having a one-track mind. Another kind of woman, just as altruistic and dedicated but less intelligent and practical, might at this stage have become immersed in do-gooding activities to the exclusion of almost everything else. But Alice was preoccupied in the early months of 1867 with Hesse's political future and she became engaged behind the scenes on some telling personal diplomacy. Her uncle-in-law, the Grand Duke, was still relying on Dalwigk as his principal adviser. Her husband was meanwhile in an invidious position. He had been appointed to top military command the previous August and was of course heir-presumptive to his childless uncle. But he lacked any political power. And ever since the Convention with Prussia (concluded soon after he had taken command) he had found himself opposed by his uncle and the War Department in carrying out the commitments regarding military reform and reorganization made to Prussia. He felt that his country's government was playing false toward Prussia, and his friends were anxious that he should 'not be implicated in the present sad and desperate state of affairs'.[1] It is not difficult to guess that Alice was one of the most important of the hidden persuaders influencing him at this delicate juncture. For she still shared with the Crown Princess the Coburg dream of a German-inspired liberal Europe; and an increasingly influential Prussia, the ugly side of whose military ascendancy had not yet become apparent, still seemed the best means of making this dream come true. The petty-mindedness of the Grand Duke and his *Umgebung* – the people round him – were thus anathema to her. They were jealous of every concession to Prussia, even relatively small ones, and were oblivious of the much greater dangers involved in alienating their former enemies.

Alice and Louis had meanwhile – in February – paid an important visit to Berlin. Their relations with the Prussian royal family were very friendly and the King persuaded them to prolong their stay. In an hour-long session with him the young couple acted as their uncle's advocate. The Prussian King asserted that he had the Grand Duke's wishes very much at heart; and the result of the conversation was a mutual feeling that all outstanding differences between their countries could be settled if intelligence and good sense prevailed. Obviously, however, the two sovereigns were more at the mercy of devious and ambitious ministers than they would have cared to admit. Alice nevertheless felt justified in sending an optimistic report of their Berlin visit when writing to her mother-in-law, Princess Charles: 'Although many people at home were against our coming here, I believe it has nevertheless done some good, particularly for later – and one cannot please everyone. But I hope that we have acted rightly towards you all, and towards our dear sister and brother here, on whom, after all, everything will depend later. . . .'[2] Alice was now looking well ahead, to the days even when she and her sister would be consorts of the sovereigns of Hesse and Prussia respectively. She could not know that such periods, when they came, would be so short and so frustrating for both of them.

Uncertainty about future relations between Darmstadt and Berlin continued throughout the spring. By that time Louis – thanks, almost certainly, to the influence of Alice – realized he must make a definite stand, at whatever personal risk. He asked his uncle to accept his resignation from all his military responsibilities if the commitments to Prussia that were within his competence were not carried out. Things hung in the balance for about a week in the middle of May and the suspense was tantalizing for Alice and Louis. Fortunately Louis made certain conditions under which he would stay on, though one of the most important – and the one that stuck most firmly in his uncle's gullet – was that he should in future have a Prussian officer as a collaborator. Largely because he could find no one – except perhaps a Prussian general – capable of replacing Louis, he gave in to the conditions. It was a great triumph for Louis, though possibly an even greater one for Alice. Certainly she was immensely relieved and having, at the end of May, chaired two important committee meetings concerning the embryonic Alice Societies, could look forward with a relieved mind to the coming visits to Paris and London.

In the former a great exhibition had been mounted, to which the Emperor Napoleon III and Empress Eugénie had invited all Europe's sovereigns and princes. Louis and Alice accepted the invitation and a glittering concourse of crowned heads turned up. This Paris of the Second Empire was then at the zenith of its power. That such power would soon be successfully challenged by Prussia was a possibility that entered few heads. One of the most important monarchs to be made welcome was Prussia's Kaiser Wilhelm himself. Another was Louis's uncle-by-marriage, Emperor Alexander II,* on whose life an attempt was made at Longchamp during the Paris Exhibition festivities. Among the modest Hessian entourage was Christa Schenck, who felt that the most memorable moments of the Parisian visit occurred after the big 'stars' such as Alexander and Wilhelm had left. For then 'only a few lesser princes still remained in Paris and were shown great kindness by the Royal Family'. The Empress Eugénie had always been particularly fond of Alice, whom she had known since childhood. She invited the Hessian party to travel with her down the Seine to Saint-Cloud. The guests were intoxicated by the beauty of the countryside on a cloudless June afternoon suffused with the scent of roses and new-mown grass. Carriages then took them, led by the Emperor and Princess Alice, from Saint-Cloud to the Grand Trianon, where a little boy broke away from the group of officers and ran up to the leading carriage. 'He must have been about eleven or twelve years old,' according to Christa, 'had short-cut dark brown hair and kind blue eyes with long black eye lashes; he was not especially tall but well built. He was dressed in knickerbockers and a jacket made of black velvet, red silk stockings and a small black hat which he took off as the Royal coach approached.'[3] It was the heir to the throne of France. 'Embrace me, Loulou,' said the Empress to her son; the boy

* Married to the Hessian Grand-Duke's sister Marie, and Emperor of Russia from 1855 to 1881. His son Serge and grandson Nicholas (Czar Nicholas II) married two of Alice's daughters, Ella and Alix respectively.

did so and then kissed Princess Alice's hand. It was the first time she had ever seen the luckless young Prince Imperial, destined never to sit on his father's throne. While in Paris Alice and Louis were looked after by the British ambassador, Lord Cowley, who sent a résumé of events to Lord Clarendon.[4] Apparently the Prussian King created a better general impression than the abrupt and haughty Czar, who was saved from public opprobrium only by sympathy over the attempt on his life. Alice's elder sister 'was thought stiff', the ambassador added; but 'Princess Alice made a better impression'.

Alice and Louis, joined by their three children, then went on to visit London, staying first at Clarence House, according to arrangements made by the Prince of Wales. Under the surface there was still some friction between Alice and her mother. The eldest son manfully tried to act as peacemaker, having written more than once to Alice regarding arrangements being made for her visit.[5] He felt that if the Queen wanted Alice to help her out with 'Drawing Rooms' she might at least let her stay in comfort at St James's Palace, rather than be crowded with her children into Buckingham Palace. But a 'separate' establishment was apparently impossible. 'How low the Royal funds must be just now!!' the Prince of Wales commented in parenthesis, concluding: 'What cannot be cured must be endured.' Alice was equally philosophical about such comparatively trivial matters, her stay in London being made worth while by something quite different. 'I visited the two great hospitals, St. Bartholomew's and St. George's,' she wrote to her mother-in-law. 'I think they are magnificent, and perfect down to the smallest detail in nursing, food-supply, ventilation etc! I asked a lot of questions about the duties of the sisters and nurses and learnt a great deal.'[6] She appended a postscript to this letter, saying, 'You tell me not to forget you for my Mama – you spoil me too much for that ever to be possible!'

The return to Darmstadt at the end of July was very sad for Alice: her seventeen-year-old Malay servant boy had suddenly died before her return. He had come into her service four years previously, becoming almost like an adopted son whom she educated and had christened. She was more upset than she would have been even for a relation with whom she had not been intimate. 'Were it not for a strong faith in a future,' she reflected, 'it would indeed be cruel to bear.'⁷

The following month presented a particularly important opportunity for further personal diplomacy on Alice's part. The general *détente* between Prussia and the other powers, as hoped for by Alice, was obviously not helped by stiffness between Prussia and Britain. And no one in the latter country was more anti-Prussian than Alice's sister-in-law, the Princess of Wales. Memories of Prussian aggression towards Denmark over Schleswig-Holstein still rankled. But it so happened that almost all that year of 1867 the young Princess of Wales had been suffering from a painful rheumatic ailment; she already had it when her daughter Louise was born in February, and Alice could see how much it was still bothering her during her summer visit to London. The illness became localized in the knee, being treated with splints, bandages and lying-up; as a result her whole leg became rigid and she had to walk with sticks. A slight improvement towards the autumn prompted the idea of a visit to the famous spa of Wiesbaden (a few miles from the Hessian border) in September. The King of Prussia was to be visiting Frankfurt and Darmstadt (for talks with the Hessian Grand Duke) and it seemed an auspicious moment for his meeting the Prince and Princess of Wales in nearby Wiesbaden. Alice went to visit her brother and her sister-in-law soon after their arrival; but the Princess of Wales's health was at this stage everyone's chief concern, rather than politics. Alice reported to Louis, who had stayed behind in Darmstadt: 'Alix is to go out today for the first time in a wheel-chair. A great event which the doctors had urged her to try in vain – I am very proud of having persuaded her to do it, but only by agreeing to accompany her in another. She has walked a little on crutches too, and was delighted – but it makes me terribly sad to see the lovely creature like that.'⁸ In the same letter she relayed her brother's and sister-in-law's invitation that on Louis's forthcoming birthday they should all dine together at Wiesbaden. The short distance from Darmstadt caused no great travelling problem. But there was still no certainty of any meeting with the Prussian King. Nobody was more hopeful that this would happen than the Queen of Prussia, who had long since succumbed to Alice's intelligence and charm, writing to her on occasion, in somewhat stilted English, as 'Dearest Lady Proctectress'.[9] Now she wrote most urgently to her in the hopes that she could pave the way for a meeting between her husband and the Prince and Princess of Wales.[10] But the latter was reluctant and the Prince wrote to Alice – the old bond still being in operation – that while he was not against such a meeting (and indeed had made a point of going to see the Kaiser in Frankfurt), his wife's health and deep mourning should be borne in mind.[11] Finally, however, the meeting did take place, though in Darmstadt rather than Wiesbaden. Alice reported: 'The visit of the King went off very well, and Alix was pleased with the kindness and civility of the King. I hear that the meeting was satisfactory to both parties, which I am heartily glad of. Bearing ill-will is always a mistake, besides its not being right.'[12] (Perhaps conscious of how Queen Victoria's affection for the Princess of Wales was not at that moment as lively as it had been, Alice was careful to tell her mother about the wonderful improvement in her health, and how she found her 'a most lovable creature'.) The Prussian Queen meanwhile wrote delightedly to Alice as the successful go-between in the happy reconciliation between the Prince and Princess of Wales and her husband.[13] Was this in fact a result of Alice's combined charm, tact and persuasive powers? Or was the Princess of Wales the heroine of the hour?

It is possible, no doubt, to credit Alice at this stage with greater maturity and wisdom than her years would normally warrant. She certainly exhibited such characteristics in much of what she said, did and wrote; but she was still only twenty-four. For most married women of this age the long, seemingly endless 'summer afternoon' of happy family life is barely beginning. But for Alice this halcyon interlude was over almost as soon as it had begun. Though she was fortunately spared any definite foreknowledge of the future, certain vespertine shadows began crossing her path as early as 1868. After a winter of non-stop activity – mostly concerned with her newly launched societies – she went to spend two or three weeks in Gotha with her Coburg uncle and aunt and the Crown Princess. As usual when parted from Louis, she immediately sent off the first of her almost daily letters. And whereas when writing to her mother she gave few clues as to her inner self and well-being, she gave quite a few – some of them probably unconscious – when writing to Louis. When one reads through these numerous letters it is difficult at times not to imagine the writer being in her late forties rather than her twenties. She misses a husband for whom she obviously has a deep and tender affection. But one assumes that he never aroused her most passionate instincts and desires when she could talk of sharing his bed, instead of sleeping alone, as being 'comfortable' rather than exciting.[14] If too much can be made of such speculations, their omission would leave the portrait incomplete. Alice moreover now begins to complain more than ever of feeling almost continually unwell; even so one senses that this is not the main reason for her being so thoroughly out of sorts. Her ailments were irritants rather than causes for grave concern: headaches, tiredness and an apparently everlasting cold. The romantic circumstances of occupying the identical rooms as on her first visit to Gotha's Schloss Friedrichstein – when the Queen and Prince Consort had had their decisive initial meeting with Alice's future parents-in-law – did not work any special wonders. And even Alice's maternal instincts seemed to have deserted her in the bitter comment (to Louis): 'I see you have the children with you a lot. That noise is music to you? But it usually gives your poor little wife a headache, this music.'[15] In a week it would be her twenty-fifth birthday, by which time Louis should have arrived in Gotha. Might her melancholy have melted with some promise of their being carried away – if only in a momentary ecstasy – by transports of love? There is no way of telling for sure.

There may have been a prosaic explanation for Alice's depression. She was expecting another baby in seven months' time and the hard work, plus bouts of illness, during the previous winter had unquestionably pulled her down. She was terrified, in fact, of a miscarriage, telling Louis that she did not feel justified in doing anything that could harm '*your* child'.[16] Dutifully and fairly promptly Louis would answer all his wife's letters; but his affection and sympathy seemed tinged somewhat with an emotion akin almost to awe. The suspicion is irresistible that he was affected at times by Alice in the same way as she sometimes had been in the past by Queen Victoria.

And he found it difficult to deal with her irritability, being too good-natured ever to move away from a purely defensive position. His apologies that his visit to Gotha would have to be delayed and curtailed[17] brought a sharp retort from Alice about 'the old donkeys who want to shorten your visit here. Really it is Uncle Louis, who is so weak, and that odious Schnacke who are to blame for everything, as usual. In fact I should be only too glad if you would have nothing more to do with the whole disagreeable pack of them! – I had better leave with you on Monday, instead of Tuesday. . . .'[18] Not for the first time, conflicting ideas about the Hessian establishment were thus the cause of friction. Poor Louis writes revealingly that he was glad not to have been present when Alice had fired her last broadside: 'I can really hear you talking and getting angry, so we should certainly have quarrelled.'[19] The rest of the letter tries to be cheerful and comforting, but could almost have been written by an over-anxious, somewhat innocent son to a lovable but formidable mother.

Another complication was that Louis, good, kind and courageous though he was, was no match for Alice intellectually. She was impatient of his unimaginative forbearance toward the bungling and corrupt ministers surrounding his uncle and running the country. And for her life in Darmstadt was almost suffocatingly dull compared with what could be savoured in London, Paris or Berlin. Constant lack of sufficient funds obviously did not help. Few if any of Louis's tastes lay in a cultural direction, his recreational activities being mostly outdoor ones. So the visits to England, one of which occurred again this summer, at least provided a mental oasis that Alice sorely needed. And then in the autumn an entirely new figure loomed up on her horizon; this was the philosopher David Strauss. Alice's intense intellectual *rapport* with this remarkable man was to have both a stimulating and a depressing effect on a mind so receptive and inquiring as hers.* But she did not get to know him really well until nearly two years later, for apart from anything else two important events occurred in the latter part of 1868 to absorb most of Alice's attention.

* See Part iii, Chapter 11.

The first was the birth on 25 November of a son and heir –
christened Ernest-Louis. His godparents were the Queen of
England and the King of Prussia. This son, in giving an
account of his early days, has provided an important impression of Alice as a mother, as well as an extremely interesting
glimpse of his father and other members of the family.*

The other event was to have profound effects on British
history that no one could possibly have foreseen in 1868. Not
generally known is the provision by Alice of a key link in the
important chain of events. Louis's uncle, the Grand Duke, had
a younger brother, Alexander, who with his cultured Polish
wife Julia, Countess von Hauke, brought a whiff of intellectual
fresh air to Darmstadt that was deeply treasured by Alice.
Alexander's wife was created Princess of Battenberg in 1858,
and ten years later found that her fourteen-year-old son Louis
was bent on making the navy his career. This meant entering
the service of some 'foreign' country, Britain being one possible choice. As a result of a long talk with the ambitious young
man, Alice made soundings in London, to which she got a
favourable reaction.[20] The upshot of it all was that Prince
Louis of Battenberg took the oath of allegiance as a subject of
Queen Victoria. On that date of such fateful associations, 14
December – in the year 1868 – Louis passed his examination
and was accepted into the British navy. Thus began the
career of one of Britain's greatest peacetime sailors, foreshadowing an even more spectacular wartime sequel in the
life of Prince Louis's son, and Princess Alice's grandson (also
christened Louis), Admiral of the Fleet Earl Mountbatten of
Burma.

The year 1869 was a comparatively peaceful interlude before
the convulsion of the Franco-Prussian War. Louis and Alice
did not visit England but travelled more than usual elsewhere.
Such travel did not unduly interrupt Alice's work, which was
a constant preoccupation; the end-product of her original
scheme – the opening of the lunatic asylum, as it was then
called – took place this year on 15 October. Another 'opening'
of more spectacular proportions also occurred in the latter

* See Part iv, Chapter 12.

part of the same year – that of the Suez Canal. The Crown Prince of Prussia – whom she called 'Fritz' – and her husband were present at the opening, after making a long roundabout journey on their way there. Having met in Venice, they continued by way of Corfu and were ceremonially received in Athens and Constantinople. They then went on to Jaffa, Jerusalem, Hebron, Damascus and Baalbec, arriving at Port Said on 15 November. After the canal formalities were over they journeyed up part of the Nile before returning via Naples and up through the rest of Italy. Louis accompanied Prince Frederick William on this trip at Alice's suggestion and with her encouragement, as she felt that the value to him of such a journey would be 'very great'.[21]

Their respective wives meanwhile visited Cannes together. It was a very unusual sort of break for Alice, lasting seven weeks; and despite missing Louis she found it enjoyable and beneficial. Her rheumatism, which had been extremely bad before she set off in mid-October, had 'completely disappeared' by early December. This represented the notable shrinking of one particularly unpleasant 'shadow', and it may well have been something more than mere sea, warm sea-baths and some sunshine that effected the change. She had not spent so much time with her sister since the latter had married over ten years before. Of the numerous letters written to Louis during this period that of 31 October was probably the most significant. She had just received her latest accounts from Darmstadt, showing a deficit for the year, whereas if she had not come to Cannes there would have been a 'small saving'. Though this worried her (money was always a worry) it prompted her to write to Louis:

> It does me more good while you are away to have Vicky's stimulating company and to get right away from the narrow, stifling atmosphere of Darmstadt, than to make a small saving. When I am so happy with you and our family, heaven knows I have no right at all to complain – but you know what really oppresses me mentally in our life together!! I long so much for England and for a society completely different from what we can *ever* have. Vicky learns and hears so much, and she makes really good progress each year,

which I certainly cannot say of myself, and I feel dis-
couraged, for in some respects I have more difficulties to
contend with than Vicky, and have to seek out everything
for myself, without any help. . . . *Enfin* [echoing a phrase
used by the Prince of Wales before her last visit to London]
what cannot be cured must be endured.[22]

Apart from wishing to be reunited with Louis she might
well have wished never to see Darmstadt again with all its
pettiness and frustration. In Cannes she was free of all such
shadows; and despite occasional mishaps, such as being thrown
from her horse for the first time ever, she revelled in the conversation, the adventures, lack of inhibitions and above all the
company of her year-old son Ernie. She wrote less frequently
to her mother and when doing so stuck to superficial descrip-
tions of events. She thus committed the same fault – but for
very different reasons – as that with which she upbraided
Louis, whose letters she found too full of empty facts and not
sufficiently enlivened with his impressions. Louis did his best,
though writing less frequently than her. The unerring eye of
the sporting and military man dominated his impressions of
Venice, where his attention was drawn to a collection of
weapons in the Palazzo Morosini, including a prayer-book
with a built-in pistol.[23] Alice resigned herself to getting more
interesting information out of him when they met. She meanwhile continued to bombard him with news, including a
reminder, even now, of how her mother had not forgotten
Alice's opposition to Princess Helena's unsuitable wedding.
The Queen must have had an uneasy conscience over this to
go on harping on it so long afterwards. 'I had an unpleasant
letter from Mama,' Alice wrote. 'The same old story – you
know what it is – and I can tell from it how little she thinks
about seeing us again, and how little she really cares about our
affairs. It is very hard! and I am sometimes *so* homesick!!'[24]
Even if Louis was not the ideal and dynamic fulfiller of her
deepest needs, no one ever replaced him as her 'best friend',
closest confidant and the person for whom she had unlimited
affection. She seldom failed to tell him how much she longed
to be with him again. By New Year's Eve they were reunited
in Darmstadt – exactly nine years since Louis had wished his

fiancée a '*Prost Neujahr*' from there a month after their engagement. Was 1870 to be a happy new year for Alice? It was certainly a strange one; the first, in fact, of several that can only be described as having been lived by Alice at two levels. One of these rested on the external events of 1870 and 1871; the other concerned a more private world of spiritual struggle.

Chapter Ten

14 DECEMBER 1871

The Spain of the late 1860s, rendered decadent and impoverished by the Carlist Wars, found itself a prey to bitterly opposed factions. A liberal military revolt put Marshal Prim at the head of a provisional government, favouring a constitutional monarchy; but in 1869 there was no monarch. Prim felt that a Hohenzollern prince, Prince Leopold, who was also a Catholic and related to Napoleon III, would be acceptable to all the Powers. Though the King of Prussia was agreeable, France was not. Leopold renounced his candidature and France demanded that the Prussian King should on no future occasion champion any renewed attempts to press his claims. The Kaiser, taking the waters at Ems, received the French ambassador and, though with much conciliatory politeness, declined to give such an undertaking. Bismarck saw his chance and made the Kaiser's courteous refusal seem like an insult to the government of Napoleon III. France swallowed the bait and in July 1870 declared the war that Bismarck badly wanted. But the French government was, in reality, equally eager for a showdown to decide who would be masters of Europe.

Princess Alice was convinced that France had provoked the war and was thus guilty of a 'crime that will have to be answered for'.[1] Her feelings were torn between pride in 'the name of Germany' and heartbreak at having to part with Louis whose division formed part of Prussia's Second Army (commanded by the Crown Prince). War for Alice and Louis came as a cruel interruption to their happy family summer at Kranichstein. This new war involving Hesse, though spared the internecine elements of 1866, could well be bitter and protracted; and Alice was once more expecting a baby. She feared a long separation when parting with Louis on the highroad outside the village where he had been quartered for the night. They looked back in the late light of the long summer evening until neither could see anything more of the other.

Princess Alice's drawings of her children

Princess Victoria of Hesse

This moment was one of several in Alice's married life that can be described as distinctly emotional rather than sentimental; for Louis it was, as in all such cases, sentimental rather than emotional. Such was ever the difference between them when strain or separation affected their innermost feeling. In other words Alice, basically tougher than her husband, tended to express her feelings in nervous, sensitive and more intellectual fashion. The generally easy-going Louis, slower to perceive the hidden nuances of a situation, was more easily led by a generous but childlike heart. Alice tended to be temperamental where Louis was taciturn; demanding where he was docile; critical where he was phlegmatic; demonstrative where he was reserved. But it was he rather than she – and nowhere is the difference between them more striking – who had to keep a handkerchief by him while writing to her, as he so often cried while composing his letter and had to wipe away his tears.[2] One can never imagine this happening to Alice, despite the high tension that so often accompanied what she wrote to her husband.

This and much else is revealed in the voluminous correspondence that flowed between the pair during the long separation caused by this war. Barely a week after parting they were briefly united. 'I must tell you,' wrote Louis immediately afterwards, 'what great joy our meeting in Worms gave me, even if perhaps I did not show it; I was really happier than I can say to have seen you again for a few days.'[3] This pleasing statement was followed by the less welcome admonition that Alice should be 'very sensible' – a favourite and oft-recurring expression of his – 'and keep up your strength, so that you keep healthy for me and we meet again safe and sound'. Alice would probably have preferred such advice to be couched as an order or not proffered at all; and the sad fact is that the unimaginative Louis often irritated the quick and impetuous Alice. As a result they quarrelled when together, even though they missed each other touchingly when separated. The Queen urged Alice to seek refuge from the war for herself and her family in Berlin with her sister. But she replied: 'Now is the moment when a panic might overcome the people; and I think it my duty to remain at my post, as it gives the people courage and confidence.'[4] And to Louis she wrote: 'You know

I prefer to stay here! And I believe it is what *you* prefer my
darling – is it not?'[5] Though she felt the war to be a crime, she
at least did not feel it to be as futile and possibly self-destruc-
tive as that of 1866. But unlike some women she was never a
'warlike wife'. Though she felt the German cause to be a just
one in 1870, she dreaded the bloodshed and the danger to
Louis and longed for it all to be over quickly. She felt that 'a
poor woman was not so far from the truth when she said "it is
wonderful, the Princess has asked for our troops to be put in
the Reserve"! Such an amusing idea, but still. . . .'[6] The
'distressing' early news however was soon replaced by reports
of German success: first at Saarbrücken in August and then
at Sedan the next month. The French Empire was defeated;
the German one was conceived. But France was determined to
fight on even after her Emperor had surrendered to the King
of Prussia; and a new French government held out for another
six months, while scattered but bitter fighting continued and
Paris was subjected to a lengthy siege.

Alice's war in Darmstadt consisted of worry and work.
There was constant and abundant cause for both. Huge numbers of wounded and later many French prisoners poured into
Darmstadt. She made an almost endless round of hospital
visits but was shocked by evidence among the wounded of
what a '*terrible*, bloody war'[7] was being fought. The Chassepot
was a needle-gun adopted by the French army in 1866. Only
now were its effects becoming visible, and Alice noticed that
the wounds inflicted, though comparatively small, shattered
the bones more than any bullet previously known. An even
more stringent test was thus presented for the greatly improved, widened and more expert nursing system set up in
Princess Alice's name between the wars for dealing with such
emergencies. All the more despairing was her reaction to War
Department inefficiency in their side of the arrangements. She
found that three weeks after the war had started none of the
military hospitals that the minister was supposed to be setting
up was making any progress. The hospitals had nothing they
needed and Alice had a fierce quarrel with Dornsieff, the relevant minister, over War Department negligence and inefficiency. Nothing was more calculated than such bureaucratic
flabbiness to make her completely lose her patience. She was

powerless to prevent two major field hospitals going off without instruments; and in the absence of all the young doctors old Dr Wernher was left to cope with a clinic overflowing with sick and seriously wounded men. There were only two of Alice's very young nurses to help him. Alice, fearing that 'dreadful things could happen' in the badly ventilated and overcrowded building, sent, apart from supplies and staff reinforcements, wooden partitions for a new hospital hut to be built. Her 'hard struggle' against officialdom and other adversities was more than ever reminiscent of Florence Nightingale. By dint of determined application on her part the situation gradually improved; and though the struggle tired her it also invigorated her, as she was frequently able to report to Louis, 'I am well.' When frustration was held at bay so, it seemed, were the worst of her aches and pains.

Unfortunately, however, she could not banish certain baleful thoughts about the future, especially as her pregnancy advanced and 'only you' – as she told Louis – 'can comfort me'.[8] Paradoxically – but in accordance with her 'two-level' existence at this period – she could also report: 'I am well and I can do a great deal', even though she saw and dreamt of nothing but suffering and could not sleep without an opiate.[9] More and more, from now on, such conflicts and contradictions were to appear in her nature. And her chief physical complaint at this time was the recurrent one of bad eyesight. This appeared to increase alarmingly during September; that the cause was at least partly psychological seems an inescapable conclusion. Though Louis's strongly sentimental feelings about their separation continued unabated, emotions of a very different kind appeared to be almost constantly on the boil in Alice's mind and nervous system. More melodramatic and fatalistic were her modes of expressing their mutual dependence. In this sense she proved herself to be more her mother's than (as she predominantly was) her father's daughter. The pen might have been that of Queen Victoria as she wrote a letter to Louis containing some curious phraseology: 'The long-famed military renown of the Hessians has been revived under your command – and you must be very proud! I am for you – but it is dearly bought. We know how heavily the present time weighs on the other – I keep my spirits up – every piece of news of you gives me fresh heart – but sometimes the struggle against despair (in my condition) is very hard!'[10] Perhaps it annoyed her that despair never seemed to enter Louis's head; his main needs seemed to be for plenty to drink, as they were always thirsty, and Alice was only too willing to send as copious supplies as were possible. But surprisingly Louis and his brother officers seemed chiefly to slake their thirst on wines and spirits. 'We consume a great deal of liquid,' Louis recounted. 'No water, but wine instead, and spirits after every meal. Ten bottles with differing contents are set out before me, some bought, some supplied, some from food parcels.'[11] Thus for the easy-going Louis life was, in the many lulls between the fighting, far less harassing than for the constantly tormented Alice. Tension built up to a climax – with correspondingly ill-effects on her side – towards the end of September. Louis wrote somewhat matter-of-factly that they would probably have to resign themselves to not being reunited for some time. 'I am very glad,' he then said – perhaps a shade too complacently for Alice's taste – 'that you are with Vicky . . . she will cheer you up and restore your spirits.' With touching – or irritating? – artlessness he added:

> I should so much like to dash over to you one day, and be able to hold you in my arms for at least one day, and kiss you, perhaps even in front of other people, which I don't usually like doing, and for which you have often scolded me!! It seems so strange to me that we have sometimes quarrelled quite violently with each other – I had forgotten all about it, and I shall forget it again and I think only of all the nice loving things you have said to me, which I am afraid I have repaid so badly.[12]

To this Alice replied with a letter she afterwards regretted, evidently berating Louis for his lack of sensitivity. By a very rare exception to an otherwise virtually unbroken custom, this letter does not seem to have been preserved in the Darmstadt archives. As Alice later on personally put in order all the letters she had written to Louis since they had got married, this particular one must have been destroyed by her, unless it was lost or destroyed by Louis at the time of receipt.

Ironically enough it crossed with a letter from Louis looking back – with inevitable sentimentality – on their married life, during which his 'heart was always full of love . . . but I am simply not a communicative person and I understand only too well how you often felt this, and were displeased that I of all people who should feel most called upon to give you affection, praise and recognition for your dear fine qualities, gave you so little of these things.'[13]

Alice meanwhile wrote again to say that she was sorry that she had written the day before, when she had been feeling particularly unhappy, fearing that her letter might have been misunderstood.[14] Louis, however, defended himself in spirited fashion by saying:

You complain of my being so dry and unsympathetic, but I am not at all like that: on the contrary I am always very pleased to hear from you, and as I think you also want to hear from me, I write to you pretty often, but I really can't spend all my time complaining about not being with you and not being able to come to you – it doesn't alter the situation at all and it makes one feel unhappy, which is the last thing either of us needs at the moment. My dear sweet darling, don't be cross that I am writing to you like this, you know I mean it well, and you must be patient with me. My dearest, sweet darling, you know I love you so much that I just can't go on repeating it to you all the time, I am so proud of you and of everything I hear about you. I wish I could come to you and tell you all this myself, and kiss you and press you to my heart, but I cannot leave here. . . . Goodbye my angel. . . .[15]

Alice was grateful for the affection but 'hurt' by the praise, for reasons that she said Louis already knew. This was connected with her efforts to bolster up his confidence and decisiveness, and not to let him get a complex about her being more competent than he was. She also reported not only that her eyes were worse than ever but also that she had given up all hope of recovery.[16] She had lost faith in Weber as a suitable doctor for her confinement.[17] The air, she said, was 'poisoned' in Darmstadt.[18] Indeed virtually everything and everybody seemed to get on her nerves.[19] But with the arrival of Queen Victoria's doctor, Dr Hoffmeister – who had looked after Alice as a child – her confidence returned. And the high tensions subsided after the safe arrival of a baby boy, their fifth child, on 7 October 1870. This was Frederick William ('Frittie'), whom Alice was ardently to adore. This 'new proof of our love' prompted a very cheerful letter to Louis. But continued bad eyesight prevented her from writing so frequently for the next two months. On the following New Year's Day the ever faithful Christa Schenck was able to send glad tidings to Louis. 'The Princess and all the children have begun the New Year in very good health; altogether I believe that her Royal Highnesses health is now better than before her visit to Berlin; even the eyes are better and the Princess's looks leave nothing to be desired.'[20] Her ups and downs, however, were far from being over.

Did either Louis or Alice regret what they had said to each other at the fireplace just over ten years before? Louis's answer to this question, posed by himself, was definitely 'No'.[21] And he would always be grateful to Alice for saying 'Yes' then and for making him so happy. 'I am not blind to my faults,' he confessed. 'But I think I can say that we did not choose badly then, and that we have been a very happy couple.' But he was worried about Alice, who had changed and aged such a lot – so much more than he had – during the intervening years. He needed no extraordinary powers of perception to notice the psycho-physical nature of his wife's condition at this time. 'What worries me particularly is that you still have not recovered your health and strength, for one's state of mind is more closely linked with one's physical condition than is commonly thought.'[22] Louis may well have guessed that anxiety had brought on much of Alice's illnesses; but he was probably even more apprehensive that continued physical debility would occasion increased depressive tendencies as time went on. And this was a situation that she knew he was powerless to cope with. Herein lay the principal difference between them; and the long separation of the Franco-Prussian War seemed to have made it more marked, particularly as to the respective ways in which they had missed each other.

On Louis's side the feeling was uncomplicated, just as it was

when they were together. His straightforward affection for
Alice made him miss her independently of whether he felt a
definite need for her by his side; it was the same affection that
made him happy when they were together. Alice's loneliness
in his absence, though also based on affection, had an exigent
element in it as well; yet when they were together she found
his company less satisfying than he hers. One might almost
say that she missed him for more selfish reasons than he missed
her. And yet – another paradox – his sentimentality in personal feelings did not spur him to as much compassion for
strangers as a restless social conscience spurred on his wife.
She upbraided him severely on hearing that he took no personal interest in the sick and wounded during the long wait at
Orléans; but she then added a soothing postscript for fear she
had been too harsh, as she knew how 'dear and good and unselfish' he was at heart.²³ But Louis, it must be admitted, did
not always feel at ease when comforting or conversing with
strangers. Alice, the introvert–extrovert of old, had to a great
extent overcome this difficulty; but the basic conflict in her
nature remained, and was becoming more and more apparent
in the rapid changes of mood that began to characterize her
outlook in the early seventies. Perhaps it would have been
impossible for her not to inherit much of her mother's *pen-
chant* for the kind of melancholy whose chief antidote was a
tendency to dominate others when there was no one capable
of satisfying her own latent desire to be dominated. To this
must be added the fatalism allied to intelligence inherited
from the Prince Consul. Alice may well have been unconsciously expressing something of such mixed feelings when
writing to Louis: 'In your last letter I see you're still the same
old simpleton, for you write quite a lot of nonsense. But every
letter is a joy for me, and I feel something is missing every
day when I do not hear from you.'²⁴

Furthermore the war had unquestionably toughened Alice
mentally. During the last two months of its duration, in
January and February 1871, she did not slacken – in fact she
redoubled – her efforts on the much-needed nursing and organizing front, working at one particular hospital every day
while also visiting the soldiers' mothers, wives and widows and
personally looking after certain patients at the New Palace

itself. But she had become disillusioned over human nature as conditioned by war and was particularly bitter about the French. Smarting against British criticism of German military conduct, she reminded her mother that 'such a long and bloody war must demoralize the best army', and added that 'the French peasants, often women, murder our soldiers in their beds, and the wounded they have used too horribly many a time'.[25] She was appalled, on the other hand, at the extreme expedients to which the French had been forced toward the end of the war: 'Hospitals are filling up again . . . some French wounded mere boys sixteen years of age who do nothing but cry and lament. It is a shame to make such untrained children fight. . . . Gambetta will have something to answer for in deceiving the country and sending all men to fight when it avails their country nothing . . . the Republic, which the English are so enchanted with, is a far worse despotism than that of the Empire. . . .'[26] And when Germans told her – 'with such a look' – that some of their wounded had been killed with English bullets, she wrote with bitter understatement: 'It is not pleasant.' As regards the Hessian political situation, hope flickered in the breasts of both Louis and Alice in early April, only to be immediately extinguished. 'Minister von Dalwigk, the destroyer of our country and government, has retired at last . . .,' wrote Louis in his diary. 'Bechtold is President in charge of Internal Affairs, while Lindeloff takes over Foreign Affairs. So the corrupt system stays!!!'[27]

'This past year has been so unhappy,' Alice lamented a few weeks later;[28] and to crown everything Louis's final return had to be delayed until June. So they were actually separated, with only a few short breaks, for nearly a year. As for the peace terms Alice, with all her animosity against France, thought them unduly harsh. Louis, his restricted imagination not letting sentimentality extend far beyond his own private world, did not agree. But as far as Hesse was concerned the only political change was the expected one of being wholly absorbed into the German Empire that now replaced the North German Federation; but independent grand-ducal powers continued until 1918 and Hesse qualified for two votes in imperial German affairs. Prince and Princess Louis – more at his wish than hers – attended the triumphal entry of the

German troops into Berlin on 16 June after the official conclusion of the peace. And later that month the Prince entered
Darmstadt at the head of his Hessian division. But exhaustion
was barely hidden by the proud trappings of the moment and
the couple could hardly wait to get away on their own. They
were off to London as soon as possible, spending three seaside
weeks on the way at Blankenberghe in Belgium, and were at
Balmoral by mid-September.

A comparison with the autumn of ten years before was
inevitable. But that happiness of those last Highland expeditions was, by its very nature and intensity, unrepeatable.
With the intoxicating feeling of liberation from all possible
cares – and a sense that even time and space were momentarily meaningless – Queen Victoria with her husband, and
Alice with her Louis, had savoured every second of that unforgettable interlude. The intervening decade had dealt harshly
with the Queen and played some strange tricks on her second
daughter. For Alice in 1861 life had meant pure romance; for
the Queen it had meant only the Prince Consort. But in 1866
Alice had written to her mother: 'Life is meant for work, and
not for pleasure.'[29] And in 1871 the British public at large had
hardly set eyes on their sovereign for ten long years. The
damage being done to the nation, and potentially to the
monarchy itself, was totally lost on Queen Victoria. It was
thus that her children now felt impelled to beg her to break her
unseemly and dangerous seclusion. They wrote her a letter on
the subject, but in the autumn of 1871 she was not well
enough to be given it; and in fact she never saw it. The coming
of Alice to Balmoral meant not just the arrival of a daughter
but the arrival of a nurse as well – and a providential arrival,
for the Queen was very low both in body and mind; and Alice
the nurse took charge. After a fortnight she wrote to her
mother-in-law:

Mama was weak and unwell when I arrived, as she was
getting over two serious illnesses – a very bad throat infection, and then the abscess . . . on her arm which had to be
operated on. Four days after our arrival a third illness
appeared, by far the most painful – rheumatoid arthritis
. . . she was confined to the sofa and could not move at all

without help. She was able to stand for the first time yesterday. . . . I often sat with her, and the children too – they are in great favour and amuse Mama very much. I play to her every evening,* either alone or with Leopold. The latter is well at the moment.[30]

The Leopold referred to was Alice's youngest brother. He had a wilful nature and was endowed, like Alice, with their father's brain; but he was cursed with haemophilia. Little did Alice then know that the same curse was germinating in the delicate little body of her own young Frittie, born the previous year.

The Queen's recovery was very slow. When the worst was over Alice, though she had helped save yet another day, could not help feeling that her continued presence was unwanted by her mother. Thus she and Louis moved on to stay with the Prince and Princess of Wales at Sandringham in Norfolk. Here Louis was in his element as a participant in England's grandest shoot; but just as they were due to leave Alice's brother suddenly became seriously ill. His complaint was diagnosed as typhoid fever. Instead of going home with Louis, Alice stayed on and 'became the moral hope and stay of the house taking charge of her sister-in-law, quiet and confident and responsible, and serving in the sick-room as a trained nurse'.[31] Alice's key part in the drama that followed emerges clearly from the seventeen letters she wrote to Louis during the three critical weeks that followed. There was a nightmarish quality about it all from the very beginning. Her experiences of exactly ten years before gave an ominous *déjà vu* element to the scene, on which were now superimposed the reactions of a virtually 'self-trained' nurse.

Alice has been accused of being too actively involved, even domineering, in the care of her brother while she was the guest of her sister-in-law the Princess of Wales, and her part in the whole affair was subsequently played down by the Queen. But even while she was at Sandringham Alice was aware of much pettiness and jealousy all round her; the Princess of Wales, on the other hand, showed from the beginning how indebted she was to her sister-in-law, who loved the Prince of Wales so

* Alice had never lost her skill and love for the piano.

deeply. The sister, from previous experience, was naturally more worried than the wife when the diagnosis was given. 'It was a hard blow that it turned out to be typhoid fever after all – Papa's dreadful illness, which I know so well,' she said in her first letter to Louis. 'I get very worried sometimes – and Dr. Clayton is by no means the right doctor to have, and is not at all decisive or careful.'[32] How fortunate it was that Alice came to this conclusion may never have been fully realized; but had she not done so Princess Alexandra would almost certainly never have sent for Dr Gull* to take over. Greater confidence was henceforth observable all round and in asking Louis to write to her every day – 'better nonsense than nothing at all' – Alice reported with respect the views and opinions of the principal doctor now in charge of the case. After a few days the Queen announced that she intended to visit Sandringham and Alice, though not favouring the idea, was expected to arrange it. This had to be done without telling the Prince of Wales who, they knew, would not want his mother to see the house for the first time under the conditions then prevailing.[33] Queen Victoria meanwhile disapproved of the Hesse children joining their mother at Sandringham. ('She is always making one's life difficult,' Alice commented to Louis.)[34] Alice showed particular skill in calming her brother as the fever began to get a worse hold of him, a development that frightened the Princess of Wales, 'who knows nothing of such illnesses'.[35] And neither did the Princess, fortunately for her, realize that her husband was 'hovering on the brink of an abyss'. The crisis was now beginning and this was the tenth day of an illness that had about twenty-eight days to run. Alice was probably one of the first to realize the date on which death – or the first signs of recovery – could occur: 14 December. In a couple of days she sensed that the first corner had been turned. She was extremely tired but told Louis not to worry, as 'one has twice as much strength in difficult times and mine seldom deserts me'.[36] In 'the midst of the storm' telegrams and letters would 'rain down'. The Princess of Wales's lady-in-waiting, Lady Macclesfield, was appreciative at first of the fruits of Alice's experience; but she later came to be somewhat resentful of

* Sir William Gull, one of Queen Victoria's own doctors, well known and trusted by Alice.

what she considered to be her possessive attitude. This was
hardly surprising, since Alice and her sister-in-law spent so
much time together at the bedside and elsewhere and Lady
Macclesfield inevitably felt a bit out of things. The point is
important, as it affects the credibility of her later evidence
concerning Alice. 'We are all furious at seeing the Princess sat
upon [by Alice] and spoken of as if she had not sense enough
to act for herself,' was Lady Macclesfield's complaint.[37] To
make matters worse, Alice was admitted to the sickroom when
others, even the Princess of Wales herself, were not. The
doctors felt that it was in the Princess's own interests to
arrange things thus. Lady Macclesfield heard that the Prince
of Wales's fevered ravings were dreadful and for this reason –
with 'all sorts of revelations and names of people mentioned' –
his wife was kept away from him. This, at least, was the
account written on 29 November by Lady Macclesfield to her
husband.[38] Alice, on the other hand, who could read the
symptoms of the illness and the course it was taking with
uncanny accuracy, could afford to be objective to the point
even of seeing a funny side to it all.

> When Bertie was delirious the other day [she recounted to
> Louis (also on 29 November)] he said to Alix 'I have had a
> terrible scene *but I gave it one of them well*' – whereupon he
> hit Mrs. Jones – then he said 'that mad woman, I can't
> stand her any longer . . .' today he said to Mrs. Jones . . .
> 'Do you know who that is – he is a Swedish gentleman I
> know.' Then he gives orders that all gentlemen are to come
> in tights 'because I'm very particular about dress – and
> Gen. Knollys must kneel down and give me a glass of water,
> it was always done in former days.' Sometimes we can't
> help laughing to see him like that in spite of all our worry
> and distress. This morning he asked me – 'What does Louis
> do without you? Does he know you are here – he'll never
> see you any more – sad state of affairs.' He doesn't know
> Alix he calls her 'waiter,' and says to her 'You were my
> wife you are no more – you have broken your vows'.

A week of torture followed, during which Alice and her
sister-in-law were virtually never out of each other's company.

'I feel encouraged and comforted to know that it does her so much good to have me here, and that it is reassuring for everyone in the house,' Alice wrote, presumably oblivious of the thoughts seething in Lady Macclesfield's mind.[39] The latter's main desire, with an apparent improvement in the illness on 7 December, seemed to be that Alice should leave Sandringham as soon as possible. 'But how Princess Alice is to be rooted out it is not easy to see,' she wrote to her husband. 'I shall have a great deal to tell you on that subject. Suffice it to say for the moment that she's the most awful story-teller I have ever encountered, meddling, jealous, and mischief-making. For a short time she is everything that is charming but the less one knows of her the better.'[40] It is clear that poor Lady Macclesfield's nose was being put thoroughly out of joint by the presence of Alice. It is not quite clear what 'awful' stories the latter was supposed to be telling, unless perhaps they concerned some of the delirious sayings of the Prince of Wales, to which neither the Princess of Wales nor Lady Macclesfield was privy.

The suspense for the onlookers – by now becoming almost unbearable – was to last another week. Then, quite suddenly, it became clear that the worst was over. Danger of death receded on the very day when, ten years before, the Prince Consort had died. An immensely relieved Britain – which had been agonizingly holding its collective breath – broke into unrestrained rejoicing. The decisive date was 14 December 1871. All the venom until recently directed against a seemingly selfish and invisible Queen, who had seemed to be neglecting her subjects, came to an abrupt end. The republican movement, which so nearly succeeded, was checked decisively. Would all this have happened if the Prince of Wales had died? Would he have died if Alice had not happened to be at Sandringham when he fell ill? Most would say 'No' to the first question. Many might not be prepared to give 'Yes' as the answer to the second. It remains one of the imponderables in the life of Queen Victoria's 'forgotten' daughter.

The Queen's immediate reaction was naturally one of overpowering relief. It looked as if Alice, the daughter who had dared to oppose her over the choice of a husband for Princess Helena, was now likely to become a popular heroine. But the

Queen, still mindful of such opposition, was anxious that her
daughter-in-law rather than Alice should be given the main
credit – in the eyes of the public – for the successful nursing
of her son and heir. And to her daughter-in-law all former cool-
ness disappeared; from now on they became better friends
than ever before. Alice, who stayed on for the first part of the
Prince of Wales's convalescence, went to Windsor for a few
days in the New Year before returning home. She felt more
exhausted in mind and body than at any previous time in her
life. But all that now mattered was that her brother had been
delivered from the hands of death. She had played a key role,
possibly a decisive one, in the drama during which his fate
and that of the British monarchy had hung in the balance. 'I
still do not like leaving England before Bertie's convalescence
is more firmly established,' she wrote to Louis from Windsor.
'But his condition improves so slowly that I shall just have to
go. And of course Mama would be pleased to be rid of me. . . .'[41]
Whether or not this last statement was an exaggeration,
arising out of frustration or bitterness, there was no doubt
that at least one other person would be gratified by Alice's
departure, and this was Lady Macclesfield. The climax of her
antipathy toward Alice appears to have been reached as the
result of a conversation at Sandringham during the illness.
'Talking of Providence,' she reported, 'Princess Alice burst
out *"Providence, there is no Providence, no nothing, and I
can't think how anyone can talk such rubbish"*.'[42] This
alleged statement provoked from the Princess of Wales's
outraged lady-in-waiting the somewhat prim comment:
'Imagine having struggled through all this without any trust
in God to support one! Our dear Princess does believe and
pray and she finds comfort in so doing.' How does this recon-
cile itself with Alice's writing to her mother about a month
earlier, on the Prince of Wales's birthday, 'I pray earnestly
that God's blessing may rest on him'?[43] Had Alice really abandoned all 'trust in God'? And if she had, what uncharacteristic
and drastic convulsion had taken possession of her soul? The
answer can be sought only by retracing our steps slightly to
explore that part of Alice's life that, as already mentioned,
had begun to exist on a different 'level'.

Chapter Eleven

DARK NIGHT OF THE SOUL

In autumn 1871 – about three months before the 'outburst'
on Providence reported by Lady Macclesfield – Alice's sixth
child was conceived. This conception was to change the whole
course of the world's history, for the embryonic being in
question was the future Empress Alexandra of Russia. 'It has
been suggested,' as David Duff has written, 'that the mysti-
cism in the future Empress of Russia was due to her being
conceived at a time when her mother was in a state of tension
over her religious convictions.'[1] It is certainly true that Alice
was undergoing a period of unusual tension that continued
during the time of agony over her brother's illness. And on 12
December, when anxiety over the Prince of Wales was at its
highest point, she wrote to Louis: 'I think the child is coming
to life; if only this does not harm it.' Despite her appearances
of calmness in fact (her composure was rock-like compared to
that of her sister-in-law) Alice was at this time groping her
way through what was probably the emotional nadir of her
life. If, however, she had been cursed with a depressive nature
she was also equipped with a resilient temperament. And what
she suffered at this time was saved from turning into a recog-
nizable nervous breakdown as a result. Had such a thing
happened, however, perhaps the Empress Alexandra would
never have been born. And the Russian Revolution would
have come, if at all, for very different immediate causes and
in a vastly different dynastic setting: no Empress Alexandra
Feodorovna; no haemophiliac only son and heir; and no
Rasputin.

As it was, Alice's suffering was perhaps akin to a nervous
breakdown, but one whose outward appearances had been
ruthlessly suppressed. But her mental sufferings had been for
some time considerable and her letters both to her mother and
to Louis had contained numerous references to worry, anxiety,
pain and distress. During the respite of the visit to England in

the late summer of 1871 there was obviously the danger of an emotional reaction. And it is quite possible for a person physically to go through the motions of an apparently normal life while the spirit passes through a 'dark night of the soul'. The expression was originally used by St John of the Cross in the sixteenth century. He too had been through a punishing ordeal before he composed the work of that name. He had even been to prison in the cause of reforming the Church from within by trying to re-equip the Carmelite Order to which he belonged with something of its pristine purity. He had begun his 'Ascent of Mount Carmel' with the verse: 'In A Dark Night With Anxious Love Enflamed . . .'. His subsequent search for God is described in a mystic language that is really a long paraphrase of this verse.

It is thus that a comparison suggests itself with Princess Alice, 'that woman of more than ordinary gifts' who 'was slightly clairvoyant and psychic'.[2] The opinion was that of a famous woman of advanced views for her day, Frances, Countess of Warwick. How far must one follow her view, for which she gives no evidence or examples? Alice's many references in her letters at this time to physical health are obviously indicative of a state of mind as well. She had already voiced a foreboding of premature death. From about 1867 onwards she refers quite often to the toll being taken on her health by the strain of life. 'I am not up to much,' she wrote to the Queen in May of that year. 'I don't always feel quite strong; but the change [she was looking forward to a visit to England] will do me good.'[3] But apart from the rheumatic pains she displayed no notable symptoms of any organic illness at this time. She was, nevertheless, suffering an observable deterioration in her general health. The gradual downward path had begun with her sister-in-law Anna's death in 1865, on which she dwelt sadly and introspectively: 'Oh, it is sad, very sad. Life indeed is but a short journey, on which we have our duty to do, and in which joy and sorrow alternatively prevail.' This was written in April 1865. At the end of May she spoke of the 'serious books' she had been reading, especially one containing a sermon called 'the Irreperable Past'. It reminded her of Anna: 'A short life indeed, and it makes one feel the uncertainty of life. . . .'[4] It is in this letter that she mentions how much she has been suffering from rheumatism.

Less than two months later she received news from her mother of the death of an old friend and contemporary, a certain Victoria Brand. In a letter to her mother she was moved to quote the scriptural passage 'In the midst of life we are in death', and to comment: 'The uncertainty of all earthly things makes life a real earnest, and no dream. Our whole life should be a preparation and expectation for eternity.'[5] Then comes a most striking passage, written on the last day of the year but one, when (at the age of only twenty-three) she wrote to Queen Victoria: 'Each year brings us nearer to the *Wiedersehen* [by which she meant reunion with the dead], though it is sad to think how one's glass is running out and how little good goes with it, compared to the numberless blessings we receive. Time goes incredibly fast.'[6] Life had become a beautiful pilgrimage, during which 'a little more or a little less sorrow falls to one's lot'.[7] Ostensibly she was referring to her mother's grief in a letter she wrote in March 1866. But she must have been reflecting much of her own feeling when, referring to the death of her grandmother, the Duchess of Kent, she wrote: 'That was the commencement of all the grief; but with darling Papa, so full of tenderness, sympathy and delicate feeling for you, how comparatively easy to bear, compared to all that followed!'[8]

The twilight years of the 'evening shadows' had brought an astonishing change in Alice. It was as if the morbid aftermath of her grandmother's and her father's deaths had produced a delayed but prolonged emotional hangover. The headaches and insomnia increased, almost certainly symptoms of a growing nervous disability. 'I am very sleepless and never without headache,' she wrote in 1870. 'But one has neither time nor wish to think of oneself.'[9] Finally her eyes became affected; and she mentions being 'still forbidden' to use them in September 1870.[10] From this entry, taken by itself, it could be concluded that this was a temporary condition due entirely to physical causes; but the complaint appears to continue and is referred to a month later and again in February of the following year.[11] That the prime cause of such deterioration was more psychological than physical seems a fair deduction if one remembers how often during 1870–1 she refers to the same disability in her letters to Louis. Quite obviously she was not consciously 'closing her eyes' to the horrors of certain realities around her. Indeed her efforts on behalf of the suffering and injured were, as has been seen, heroic and tireless. But was there a subconscious 'closing of the eyes' to certain things? A form of self-induced mental myopia with physical symptoms? Such a condition is far from unknown to psychotherapists. 'I neither see nor smell anything but wounds,' she wrote in August 1870. 'And the first Anblick [glimpse] which sometimes one does not escape meeting is very shocking.'[12] The anxiety built up as the war progressed and in February 1871 she wrote to Louis: 'I am more out of my mind than in it.'[13] Here she was certainly speaking from that other 'level' of existence that had by that time invaded her life; from that dark tunnel that she had seemed to see ahead of her even during the happy interlude with her sister in Cannes at the end of 1869. At that time she had dreaded her return to the increasingly narrow and 'stifling atmosphere' of Darmstadt after the 'stimulating company' of her sister. But it so happened that there was one person in Darmstadt who was very far from being either narrow or stifling. His name was David Friedrich Strauss.

Strauss was already well known, not to say notorious, in Europe's theological and academic circles. His *Life of Jesus*, published in 1835, was a turning-point in nineteenth-century religious thought; it had questioned the historicity of the Gospel narratives and sought to demythologize the biblical accounts of Christ's earthly existence. Such accounts, he felt, were clouded by the legends superimposed through subsequent human error, enthusiasm or erroneous interpretation; these legendary accretions detracted, in his opinion, from the loftier message that should, in an enlightened scientific age, be the true inspiration to men of genuine faith. Such a theory – not entirely new even then, and paralleled to some extent by the work of Charles Hennell in England – was anathema to Christians of the strictly evangelical and fundamentalist type; it was scarcely less repugnant to the scripturally minded outlook of orthodox Anglicans; and to Roman Catholics it was akin to the 'heresy 'ultimately condemned under the name of

'Modernism'. But it was a theory that offered irresistible attractions to the analytical and inquisitive mind of Princess Alice. 'In 1871 she was 28, a tired woman open to every ill, consumed with a desire to better the lot of the sick and further the emancipation of women, her restless mind probing into the mysteries behind the painted picture of God.'[14] The words are strikingly apposite, since Alice never actually lost her faith; but the unreal picture some 'Victorians' painted of God positively nauseated her. It must be admitted that she was impatient with dull-witted and unimaginative people. And though she had inherited her father's brain in full measure she had also, unfortunately, inherited his lack of humour. To have seen the lighter side of things more readily might well have produced greater tolerance toward narrow-mindedness. But she had never been able to accept facile explanations for religious difficulties and scriptural inconsistencies. It was her father who had urged her to probe deeply into such subjects and this – through omnivorous and liberal reading – she had always done. A sounder religious sense than that possessed by many of her critics was what prompted her pursuit of an intellectual assent for faith.

Two of the foremost thinkers in this field were Strauss and Ernest Renan, whose respective lives of Christ had been similarly inspired and written almost simultaneously, but independently of each other. It was the object of Renan's book, however,

> ... to be as welcome and intelligible to a reader of the female sex and in particular of the French nation as to any reader whomsoever. . . . Strauss, on the other hand, addresses himself to men who indeed do not require to have engaged in learned studies, but who are penetrated sufficiently with the spirit of German science not to shrink from mental labour however serious and continuous; who would wish to be acquainted not only with the results of scientific investigation, but also, more than superficially, with the grounds of those results; to whom beauty of form is no reason for being more easily satisfied with the internal substance, and whom the attractiveness of a combination cannot bribe into acquiescence with defects of proof.[15]

This, in view of the magnetic effect of Strauss's general work upon Alice, gives some indication of the calibre of her mind. As Strauss's work developed – involving a vast amount of research and writing – it paradoxically became more susceptible of analysis and even reduction to relatively simple terms by the intelligent lay person. His *cri de cœur* – and he wrote better when angry – was against what struck him as hypocritical in so much of the contemporary Christian outlook. He pleaded, by contrast, for candid admission that the Bible stories were a compound of fiction and truth and that the dogmas of the Church were in reality no more than significant symbols. Only then, he argued, could men 'remain attached to the moral value of Christianity, and to the character of its founder, so far as the human form is recognisable amid the accumulation of miracles in which its first biographers have enveloped it'.[16]

Alice became for a time not only an apostle of Strauss but also his most intimate friend. This fact springs in part from the personal threads of a rather peripatetic life that eventually brought him to Darmstadt. In 1842 (the year before Alice was born and when he himself was thirty-four) he had married a talented actress called Agnese Schebest. But he soon found that he lacked at home – not unlike Alice at certain periods – 'that harmony of mind for which nothing can compensate, however valuable. The characters, the mode of education, and the past life of Strauss and his wife were too dissimilar, their demands upon each other and upon life were too different and both were too firmly rooted in their peculiarities.'[17] They thus parted within a few years of marriage, though they never divorced. Thereafter Strauss's wandering life – partly conditioned by his unacceptability in certain orthodox academic circles – brought him in 1866 on a visit to Darmstadt. He returned briefly there the following year, when he met Princess Alice for the first time; and he lived in Darmstadt continually from 1869 to 1872. The most notable feature of the first meeting on 31 May 1867 was that it came about entirely on the initiative of Princess Alice. Her secretary came personally to Strauss with an invitation to call on the Princess.

Not believing [as the astonished Strauss put it in a letter to

his friend, Vischer, in Ohringen] that high placed personalities should be interested in us, I resisted the invitation for
45 minutes and would not have agreed to accept the invitation if it had been given by a Prince. However, the persistent
refusal to visit a lady seemed to be a little uncouth and I
could not allow this to be thought of a German scholar. I
therefore went there as arranged in my everyday suit and
was very agreeably surprised. The most natural, open personality, a person with whom one immediately felt at ease.
Her father had himself educated her and the eldest sister
(the German Crown Princess) in religious subjects using a
popular text book of the late Mr. Bretschneider, and had
taught them to reflect and question. For this reason she and
her sister in Berlin had become more free thinking, but their
mother was not allowed to know anything of this.[18]

What Strauss presumed would be no more than a 'pleasant
episode' in fact ripened in the early part of 1870 into a remarkable friendship, the main impetus for its growth and development coming at all stages from Alice. Up until this time
Strauss, in so many ways a disappointed and frustrated man,
had found that the most tender and loving relationship of his
life was that which he enjoyed with his daughter; with her he
often spent long happy periods at Bierbrich and Bonn. Alice,
in so many ways a disappointed and frustrated woman, had
never forgotten the particularly tender and loving relationship
she had had with her father. It may be no more than an
interesting coincidence that when Alice got to know Strauss
she was about his daughter's age and he was about the age the
Prince Consort would have been had he lived. But a surrogate
father and daughter relationship is obviously not impossible
in the purely intellectual but extremely close feelings that
came to exist between them. And one of the reasons for Alice's
being the chief promoter of the friendship may well have been
the vacant spot in one department of her life at this time. Her
letters written to Louis from Cannes at the end of 1869 show
how unusual was one aspect of her relationship with him:
how something – difficult to define – was lacking in it; how
Louis, much as Alice needed and missed him, sometimes
appeared as the lovable 'simpleton' almost more reminiscent

of a son than a husband. If a fairly close psychological *rapport* is essential for the full satisfaction of marital life, then there was something incomplete for Alice about their marriage. During the period when she and Strauss saw most of each other – in the first half of 1870 – she appeared to be unusually relaxed; the summer that year at Kranichstein was particularly happy. She mentioned in her letters to her mother no symptoms of the various ailments that cropped up so frequently in what she wrote before and after that time. A mildly hysterical element in such disabilities, especially as to eyesight, cannot therefore be entirely ruled out; such a condition would tally with her assumption at such times – however unconsciously – of the symptoms of disability (in order to attract love or attention) for reasons connected, however remotely, with sexual repression or frustration. This unprovable theory imputes unworthy motives to no one and is consistent with the wholly blameless, indeed healthy and stimulating friendship between the German scholar and the English Princess; but it does at least explain certain events and tendencies that are otherwise puzzling, for example, her apparent need to identify her religious search with one particular person; her investment of the resulting friendship with a permanent stamp; and the hints in her letters to Louis of a defect in their marriage about which she was to be devastatingly frank later on.

By autumn 1869 Alice and Strauss had got to know each other fairly well. Before going to Munich after their first meeting he presented her with his photograph, after being asked to write in her album. Their acquaintanceship was renewed with enthusiasm on both sides after his return to Darmstadt and she visited him at his home, accompanied by one of her ladies-in-waiting. Louis also got to know and to like Strauss and sometimes took part in the dramatic readings that were arranged. Alice was particularly concerned about Strauss's weak eyes and always made sure that green lampshades were used. She introduced him to the Crown Princess and her brother-in-law, who invited him to Berlin. This byproduct of their friendship particularly gratified Strauss, who shared passionately in the liberal dream for Germany's future. Before going off to Cannes with her sister in October 1869

Alice and Strauss discussed a possible new subject for him to write about. That of Voltaire 'was suggested to him by the whole tendency of his studies at that time' but

> . . . its final form was determined by its special personal purpose. The six lectures on Voltaire are real lectures which were written for the Princess Alice and were listened to by her; and with reference to this circumstance, when they were published, they were dedicated to her; and thus their purpose was at all events not without its influence in leading their author without detracting from their historical profoundness, to surpass himself in the spiritual eloquence and lucid perspicuity of his style and to give us in them the most perfect biographical work of art which our literature possesses, after Goethe's *Truth and Fiction*. As such they have been acknowledged by the reading world.[19]

The intimate circumstances in which Strauss read his lectures to Alice came about by accident. The original plan was that they should be read to a select circle including Louis and Alice, one of her ladies and Robert Morier, the British Minister in Darmstadt, who was a great friend of the Princess's and shared many of her views. The readings were to take place in the early part of 1870, but the arrangement fell through when Louis contracted scarlet fever. Alice thereupon wrote to Strauss asking him to come and read the lectures anyway, if he was not afraid of possible infection (as Alice was nursing Louis herself) and if he could put up with her as the sole audience. He agreed only too willingly; and it was thus that he came privately, every other evening for nearly a fortnight in January, to read for an hour or so on each occasion from his manuscript. Though he had originally hoped to dedicate the published work to the Princess he found himself when the time came lacking the courage to ask her if he might do so. No doubt reading his mind, Alice solved the problem by asking him to dedicate the work to her and telling him how much their friendship meant to her and how greatly it had helped her to clarify her views on a variety of matters. Strauss was naturally delighted, but once again failed to act on his first impulse. The form of dedication he favoured was: 'To Her

Royal Highness Alice, Princess Louis of Hesse, Princess of Great Britain and Ireland for whom they were written who was kind enough to listen to the author who now dedicates the printed lectures respectfully and loyally to her.' He then felt that this form of wording might be too personal for anything but a purely private dedication; that it would seem to make the Princess a sort of 'accomplice' in the writing of the book, possibly with unpleasant consequences for her. Alice, however, insisted on the wording suggested and said that the recollection of the pleasant evenings of the original readings would far outweigh any unpleasantness that might arise from the dedication.[20] And when in June 1870 she received from the author a special copy of the book, she wrote to apologize for not thanking him immediately: 'The book itself is the cause of the delay, as I devoted my spare time to reading over what you had read to me so beautifully last winter. I seemed to hear your voice and all your observations again. I must thank you again for that great enjoyment, and for the kind terms of your dedication. – Alice.'[21]

It was one of the happiest moments of her life. Nothing that Louis could have done would have given her equal pleasure in the same way. This did not in any sense diminish her love and affection for her husband and her gratitude for the quite different things he was able to give her. She was genuinely, almost ingenuously, proud to be the only person to whom the great Strauss had ever dedicated one of his many works. 'But for Strauss also this book was henceforth inseparably linked with the memory of this lady and represented one of the happiest and most humanly beautiful relationships of his life.'[22]

How does all this link up with the earlier suggestions that Alice suffered some sort of suppressed nervous breakdown during these years? One must be careful of exaggeration, but a distinct 'two-level' pattern is definitely discernible in her psychological life between 1869 and 1873; and she was probably at her most vulnerable in autumn 1871. There was no question of madness or mental derangement in any form; merely excessive strain upsetting the normal rhythm of life – at certain moments more than others – but at no time getting

out of control. The years 1870–1 contained the most extreme
of the ups and downs, the earliest period being enlivened by
the Strauss–Voltaire diversions. There followed the war, which
took a particularly heavy toll on Alice, bringing on nervous
exhaustion and reaction in autumn 1871 (when her daughter
Alix was conceived); the winter agony over her brother was
followed by a year of successes for the Alice Societies, even
though the dark night of the inner soul went on. A shattering
dawn came in 1873.

As regards the future Empress Alexandra of Russia no
certain or provable connection is known to medical or psychological science between a human being's future personality and
the temporary condition of the mother's mind at the time of
that human being's conception.[23] But it is interesting to
remember Alice's own fear that high tension affecting her
during the Prince of Wales's illness might be having some
adverse effect on the child then coming to life inside her.
What of course is certain is that the future Empress inherited
much from her mother: her hyper-anxious nature, and possibly
a latent mystical tendency, but not, unfortunately, her (and
her father's) brains. For Alice the sojourn of a part of herself
in a private wilderness meant, above all, a sort of refuge,
thanks to Strauss, from the purely pedestrian and uninspiring;
it also meant a continual struggle within herself – never fully
resolved intellectually – over religious difficulties. But it has
been said that difficulties do not in themselves constitute
doubts; and for Alice the basic conflict was the same as that
which has plagued thousands of other people in every century, that is the conflict not between science and religion, but
between 'religion' and faith.

The former conflict is basically no more than a human one
between two sets of opinions as to allegedly verifiable facts.
But faith totally transcends both these fields and often finds
that 'religion', in its conventional and mundane garb, is a
major obstacle to progress. So it was with Alice, whose tran-
scendent belief was at all times heroic; but her unusually keen
intellect prevented her from accepting at face value some of the
man-made religious formulae that many people mistook for
faith itself. In the heyday of 'conventional' morality and
evangelical fervour her private struggle inevitably brought her

into collision with some of her conformist contemporaries. Nor is it hard to see how an aversion to the impractical and wishy-washy could bring out the tough side of her nature in times of tension or emergency. Hence the alleged 'outburst' against the use of the word 'Providence' during the Prince of Wales's illness. Alice knew that God controlled life and death; she also knew that human agents were expected to act with resource and intelligence. In so highly subjective and emotive a context her God was unfortunately nothing like the one existing in the imagination of Lady Macclesfield. Lutheran training had moreover inevitably made her view the theological value of human 'good works' as insignificant compared to the omnipotent and salvific will of God. But she had no doubt as to the need of good works in order to achieve good effects. Hence the immense success of the Alice Societies and all that they implied. If Alice had stopped short, as many did and do, at mere lip-service to human reflections of God's love in worldly affairs she would have achieved little. By insisting on a practical application of this in terms of human rights, duties and capabilities she achieved much. But regrettably she made enemies on the way; and Queen Victoria never pretended to understand this area of her life.

The more intimate and personal side of all this is distinguishable from the almost abstract nature of her spiritual search, for the friendship with Strauss had an independent significance. It coincided with a period of strained uncertainty and interacted with it at many points. But it had an importance entirely of its own in the overall context of Alice's biographical portrait. For it represented something intensely romantic in the truest sense of the word about Queen Victoria's second daughter. It was the nearest thing that she had to an 'affair', and it clearly had vaguely sexual undertones. But its essential innocence made it a poetic exploration of trust rather than a prosaic exercise in infidelity. It was a union of intellect and imagination to which Louis was a friendly outsider; but it was also a simple Agape to which Eros was not invited. Its quintessence is evoked by a volume bound in red leather and preserved in the Darmstadt Archives.[24]

Princess Alice has written on the title page of this volume (in German), 'Poems by David Strauss. Extracts from his commonplace books – Letters etc.'. There follow about fifty poems, alternating with a few epigrams and a number of brief essays and commentaries on various topics. The first poem declares that all the verses that follow are intended for the author himself and his friends, not for publication. Generally they are poems in a serene, romantic vein, about nature and life and death, with titles like 'Idylle' and 'Linda', though some are full of strong personal emotion, such as an ode on the death of the poet's mother. One poem in particular, copied in Princess Alice's hand, expresses Strauss's bitterness at the vilification that his free-thinking views have brought upon him. It is called 'Misfortune' and affirms his unwavering belief in 'that much-discussed book', for which he is still, after so many years, notorious; and it expresses his resentment that his motives should still be so misunderstood and maligned. Later there is a neat epigram on Hegel and Schleiermacher:

1. Hegel

His system was cleverer than he; that is why his pupils
Expounded the master better than he himself knew how.

2. Schleiermacher

He was cleverer than his system; that is why his pupils
Who lack his genius, cut such a sorry figure.

After the poems come a series of essays, commentaries and so on. First, a table comparing the four Gospel accounts of the baptism of Jesus; then commentaries, in Strauss's hand, on theological subjects – for instance, on *Revelation*, on Buddhism, and one, dated 22 May 1869, on comparative religion. There is also an essay on Schiller's plays; and one on language as being in itself the greatest work of art. There follow fourteen letters from Strauss to Princess Alice, mounted at the end of the volume. The letters extend from June 1870 – at the time of the Voltaire dedication – to the end of 1873. Perhaps their most remarkable feature, apart from their warmth and affection, is that the guard of respect and formality is never dropped – except, in a very limited and very poignant sense,

in a letter written by Strauss in June 1873. This letter refers
to the event that proved to be the shattering dawn bringing
Alice's dark night to an end. For on 29 May 1873 there was a
terrible accident: Alice's little haemophiliac son, Frittie, not
yet three years of age, fell from a first-floor window and died
soon afterwards. It was a moment of unspeakable agony, the
aftermath of which was reminiscent of the worst death-in-life
mental agonies of Queen Victoria. Alice's increasing concern
thereafter with the next world rather than this was dictated
by her heart more than by her head. Of what value now were
the exciting speculations as to the here and hereafter? 'Even
the best-intentioned friend feels himself shamefully empty-
handed before such a blow of fate,' wrote Strauss to her on
6 June 1873.

> In the end all he has to offer is his own poor sympathy, and
> all he can do is to guide the bereaved towards thoughts
> with which the latter is already familiar, because they lie in
> the essence of human things. And how completely helpless
> he is when all this must be done in writing! Yes, if I were
> still living in the same place as Your Royal Highness, and
> if I were given the opportunity to hear you speak of your
> feelings, face to face, the living communication with you
> would put living words in my mouth, and perhaps, when we
> parted, as so often before in happier days, we should both
> feel our spirits raised.
>   Before me, as I write this, lie two photographs, gifts from
> you, which show the dear child at different ages; his
> thoughtful eyes, especially in the later one, look right into
> the heart of the beholder, and give him a sense of the distress
> which the mother must feel at his loss in such heartbreaking
> circumstances. But of these circumstances, it seems to me
> that some reassurance can be drawn from the one that the
> child had the accident in the presence of his mother. For
> that removes the sting of suspicion that he was not being
> looked after as he should have been. For there is no doubt
> that you, dear Princess, were watching over him as far as is
> humanly possible. But complete supervision every single
> second is not humanly possible, and of course one may trust
> a child who has been well brought up and taught to be

careful to take care of himself for a moment. In a thousand cases to one he will do this, and if the one case in a thousand when he does not do this should arise, could anyone have foreseen it? It is enough, in circumstances which we cannot foresee, for the mother to turn towards the opening door, for the child at the same moment to see a brother or sister playing, or a bird hopping, beneath the window, and the accident has happened. Therefore, dearest Princess, do not torment yourself with fruitless and, I am sure, unfounded reproaches in this respect. You watched over the dear child – I am as sure of this as of my life – as only the most careful mother can; that your care was not sufficient is the result of circumstances which lie beyond human control and human foresight.

I can imagine that this son, who has been so cruelly torn from you, may have united in a particularly pleasing way the good qualities which you love in his brother and sisters, and may thus have become your favourite. But now you will seek out these qualities, in the different combinations in which the children remaining to you possess them, with a love that is twice as strong, and in so doing you will discover how, thanks to the mystery of individuality, each such combination has its own peculiar advantages, and each only needs the right care for it to develop satisfactorily in its own way. In such a rich garden of young saplings, full of shoots and buds, of course you will always sorely miss the one which was so suddenly uprooted by a violent gust of wind, but you will also find ever increasing comfort in the healthy growth and ever more beautiful flowering of the others.

It was these 'others' who now became the firm centre of Alice's life. The 'great exhaustion' had set in; the world of Alice, the woman, was for all intents and purposes over for ever. Pride of place now belonged to that aspect of life that concerns itself with Alice as a mother. It has hitherto been neglected in these pages; but it was an aspect never neglected by the bereaved Princess herself.

Part Four

MOTHER

Grand Duke Louis IV and the Grand Duchess with their family at Kranichstein, summer 1878. Prince Ernest Louis is seated opposite to his mother. The Princesses are (left to right) Victoria, Irene, Alix, Elizabeth and Marie (on pony)

Family Group, c. 1878. (Standing, from the left) *Prince Ernest Louis, Princess Alice, Grand Duchess of Hesse, the Grand Duke of Hesse, Princess Elizabeth.* (Seated, from the left) *Princess Irene, Princess Victoria*

Chapter Twelve

THE THREE GRACES AND A SON

Only ten years had elapsed between the birth of Alice's first child and the death of the three-year-old Frittie in 1873. Yet the worn-out woman was already approaching the end of her life. At the time of Frittie's death she had five other children. The eldest three had been girls, Victoria, Elizabeth and Irene, 'the three graces' a friend had called them, prophesying that a son would come next. The prophecy came true in the person of Ernest Louis, while Frittie's birth had been followed quite quickly by that of Alix. One more daughter, May, was born in 1874.

Alice, as a mother, left an unusually strong mark on all of the children who survived their earliest years; and a graphic impression of her has been written down by her surviving son, Ernest Louis, usually known as 'Ernie'. And yet it is as a mother, as much as in any other way, that Alice has often been forgotten – or remembered only as a rather shadowy figure – when the exploits of her famous descendants are recounted. Having died so young she tends to be a 'missing link' in people's minds when a mental picture is conjured up of the nineteenth-century British royal family. Yet of course the present heir to the throne is directly descended from Alice as well as from King Edward vii. She was the mother of Russia's last Czarina and the grandmother of the man who, for many, is the greatest living Englishman of modern times, Earl Mountbatten of Burma. She was the sister whose shrewd care may well have saved her favourite brother's life; the daughter who stood between a widowed Queen and a monarchy in peril; the woman who preserved life for men and gave hope to women; and finally a mother who died after only half the allotted three score and ten years, but lived on with such tremendous vividness in the memories of her children and her children's children. It is the pen of Lord Mountbatten's mother,

Victoria, Marchioness of Milford Haven, that yields the most detailed account of her first years as a mother.[1]

Victoria was born during that first long stay back in England soon after Alice and Louis were married. The Easter bells were in full chime at Windsor and in Darmstadt a twenty-one-gun salute was fired. The day, 'supposed to be a very lucky one', was 5 April 1863, though the Tapestry Room in Windsor Castle in which she was born was one that Queen Victoria detested. In it she had been scolded by her mother for 'making up to William IV' at the dinner he had given for her birthday and at which he had insulted the Duchess of Kent. But it was also the room in which another Alice was to be born in 1885: Victoria Milford Haven's own daughter, the future Princess Andrew of Greece and mother of Prince Philip, Duke of Edinburgh. It is by this route that the children of the present Queen are directly descended from Princess Alice.

The Queen's account of little Victoria's birth and the circumstances surrounding it – in a letter to her eldest daughter – show how much was still happening in a Windsor darkened by the shadow of the Prince Consort's death; but it also shows how greatly the Queen's views on childbirth and children differed from Alice's.

> Thank God [the Queen began her letter] all goes on most prosperously. . . . I shall take great interest in our dear little grand-daughter, born at poor, sad, old Windsor in the very bed in which you all were born, and poor, dear Alice had the same nightshift on which I had on when you all were born! I wish you could have worn it too. But I don't admire babies a bit the more or think them more attractive. She is very like Alice, has a long nose and beautiful, long fingers like Alice. Alice . . . is very calm and quiet, but not as strong as I was. She reminded me so much during the labour and even now lying in bed, of dearest Papa when he was ill. I was dreadfully shaken and agitated by it all. . . .[2]

Louis was a touchingly proud father and after the christening of the future Princess Louis of Battenberg he seemed twice the man he had been before. (Little Victoria's future husband was the young Prince whom Alice was to help on the way towards his spectacular career in the British navy.) A few days later Louis made his 'maiden speech' at the Royal Academy Dinner, which was – according to the Duke of Cambridge – done 'exceedingly well'.[3]

Alice always took a more active day-to-day interest in her children than her mother ever had. And far from sharing the latter's revulsion against breast-feeding she particularly favoured this natural and intimate function of maternity. It corresponded to one of her two overriding lifelong interests: the workings of the human body in terms of nursing and love, and the workings of the human mind in terms of religion and faith. Just over a month after the baby's birth she went with her mother to the Military Hospital at Netley, whose foundation-stone the Queen had laid seven years before.[4] It was the Queen's first 'public' appearance since her husband's death; and with the wards full of wounded men recently back from India it was a moving experience. But for the Queen it was chiefly a rather painful exercise demanded by the call of duty; for Alice it was the foretaste of a vocation that would also one day attract her recently born daughter.

The first three years of little Princess Victoria's life were spent in her parents' first Darmstadt home, that tiny house in the Upper Wilhelminestrasse annexed to her grandparents' house. Its most cheerful feature was the vast garden in front reaching down to the Heidelberger-strasse. But compared to the kind of houses Alice had lived in this one was poky and depressing in the extreme. It seems to have had a rather eerie effect on baby Victoria because of the 'tiny hidden staircase leading from my father's room to my mother's room upstairs'. She dreamt of little staircases for years afterwards. She was in fact highly impressionable in her earliest years; she could talk quite clearly when she was nine months old, saying not only 'Papa' and 'Mama' but also 'Louis'. She already adored her father, and even before her first birthday Alice found that she was more like a child of two.[5] Before she actually was two, another daughter had been born in the little house at Darmstadt, on 1 November 1864; away from the somewhat inhibiting atmosphere of Windsor, Alice could freely nurse the child herself, to her infinite satisfaction. The parents' disappointment that the new arrival was another girl was only 'momentary'.[6] It was customary in Hesse that the name of one of the sponsors should correspond with that of the child. It was thus that Louis's mother, Princess Charles, whose name was Elizabeth, was godmother to the girl called after the saintly ancestress of the Hessian and Saxon houses. Her full names were Elizabeth Alexandra (after the Princess of Wales) Louise Alice. The association with St Elizabeth was to prove only too grimly real: the fortitude based on faith displayed by Alice's second daughter was one of the most tangible tributes to her inheritance and upbringing. Her adult life story was that of a Cinderella in reverse. Having married, at twenty, the Russian Grand Duke Serge she entered St Petersburg in a glass coach; she ended her life in a mine shaft, hurled to her death by revolutionaries. A more ironic martyrdom is difficult to imagine for a woman in whom Alice's liberalism and liberality had lived on so strongly. The account given by her brother, Ernest Louis, loses none of the drama by its succinctness:

This childless, beautiful woman, after her husband was murdered by the Anarchists in 1905, devoted herself totally to the work of helping the suffering poor and especially the sick. She founded a new and active order of nuns, because in the Russian Orthodox Church nearly all such orders were purely contemplatative. This new order was largely influenced by the example of some of the German Protestant Nursing Sisters. In the aftermath of the terrible Russian Revolution she suffered the death of a martyr like her sister the Czarina Alix. A faithful priest brought her undecomposed body, via Peking, from the Siberian mine into which she had been pushed, to the Orthodox Church in Jerusalem, which during happier times she had dedicated with her husband.* Amongst the Russian immigrants who still know something about the old Christian Russia, her memory is venerated like that of a saint. In her work she proved to be

* It was Elizabeth's sister Victoria and brother-in-law Louis who arranged for her body to be brought home from China. They personally received it in Jerusalem, where they attended the committal.

the true daughter of the Grand Duchess Alice.[7]

'Ella' – as she was called in the nursery – mirrored her mother's outlook in important directions. She favoured the spread of liberal ideas as the best antidote to violence, as well as for their own intrinsic value. But her husband, though conscientious, proved himself to be an authoritarian absolutist as Governor of Moscow. Among the many enemies he made was the young and fanatical anarchist Kalajew, whose bomb killed him in a Kremlin square a few yards from Elizabeth's room. At the sound of the explosion she rushed out of the Palace to find the gruesomely scattered remains of her husband's body at her feet. What she did subsequently one can imagine being done by Alice. She went to visit the assassin in prison, imploring him to repent before undergoing his final judgement. She was unsuccessful.[8]

These two eldest daughters of Alice, though very different from each other in character, were very like their mother in their own respective ways. Victoria, Princess Louis of Battenberg, was less demonstrative than Ella, despite a warmth of heart with which was combined wide culture and no little scepticism.[9] She thus resembled Alice more closely on the intellectual side than did the Grand Duchess Serge.

Alice was at the peak of well-being, physically and mentally, in the summer following Elizabeth's birth.

I have weaned Ella last Saturday [she wrote her mother in June 1865] and can only say that my health has never been so good, nor have I been so strong or looked so fresh and healthy as I do now. When Uncle Ernest* saw me he said I looked again as I did as a girl, only rather fatter. Ella crawls now and is very strong; she has her first two teeth. Victoria is very wild and speaks more German than English. I think her rather small, but other people say she is not. She goes out walking with her Papa before breakfast quite alone, with her hands in her pockets, and amuses him very much.[10]

This makes it all the more sad to see how symptoms of

* Ernest II, Duke of Saxe-Coburg-Gotha, brother of the Prince Consort.

Alice's later physical weaknesses were already showing themselves at the time when the third of the 'three graces' was
born. Her letters are full of her concern over the Austro-
Prussian War and contain references to insomnia and lack of
appetite. The rheumatism and neuralgia were also now beginning, but the happiest circumstance was that the third
daughter – born on 11 July 1876 – could be given a name
commemorating the peace that soon came about; and Irene
Louise Marie Anna was duly christened on 12 September.*
The christening took place in the New Palace, in which the
family was now happily installed. The financial worries had
not yet begun in earnest, though the upkeep of this very palace
was one of their prime causes as time went by. But Alice
already knew how to be thrifty; and in the young days of the
'three graces' her needle was plied with skill and energy. 'I
have made all the summer out-walking dresses . . .,' she told
her mother. 'Likewise the new necessary flannel shawls for
the expected. I manage all the nursery accounts, and everything myself, which gives me plenty to do, as everything
increases, and on account of the house, we must live very
economically for the next years.'[11] By the time of Irene's birth
the energy was flagging somewhat, and she would fall asleep
in the evening while sewing her daughter's dresses.

Ever-anxious over her children's physical health, she also
expressed concern for what she called 'those little lent souls'.
She saw to it that during the happy Christmas of 1866 the two
older ones should give some of their presents to poorer
children. 'The young mother had wisely determined that they
should learn to be generous and kind to the poor. And she
wrote gladly that they even wished to give their own things
and such as were *not* broken.'[12] More important lessons regarding charity and the things of the spirit were to bear fruit in
the coming years. Alice's daughters were apt pupils, Victoria
being particularly quick to learn. She had a real chance to
enjoy their company during the respite from childbearing in
1867. The flagging energy was replaced somewhat and given a
stimulating outlet in the first fruits of her societies' work. Less
stimulating was Darmstadt's social life, which held few real

* Irene married Prince Henry of Prussia and was the last survivor of
Alice's seven children, dying in 1953.

charms for her. One particular ritual is mentioned by Princess Victoria among her earliest memories. The Grand Duke liked visiting his various residences, where family 'dinners' were held at 4.30 on Sundays. These 'greatly bored' Alice, who felt they 'spoilt the Sunday', especially when Louis was free of military duties. Such duties involved Louis, in autumn 1868, in the manoeuvres of the Hessian division in the neighbourhood of Kranichstein. Here Alice, dividing her time between her three daughters and occasionally watching the manoeuvres, awaited the birth of her fourth child.

The prediction that her next child would be a son came true on 25 November. Little Victoria wondered why more guns were fired than when she had been born; a nurserymaid explained: 'It is for a brother.' On 28 December the Hessian son and heir was christened Ernest Louis Charles Albert William. This son was to be the most important link between his parents and the future, at least as far as Hesse was concerned. Inheriting a balanced mixture of their characteristics and qualities, his liberal-mindedness was later to earn him the nickname of the 'Red Grand-Duke'. As an enlightened ruler he took his father as a model. But he imbibed his most formative impressions between the tender ages of five and ten, when it is probably true to say that no one was closer to Alice than he was. For it was when he was five that little Frittie died and, as Ernie put it,

Now I was the only son and my mother and I clung to each other. Probably that is why she spoilt me because my elder sisters were jealous of me. Later on I often felt lonely as I was the only boy; my sisters took precedence over me and three of them were older than I. When we went out driving I always sat at the back with the coachman or if we had lots of relatives staying with us and several carriages were required, I always had to drive with the entourage.[13]

But even if she spoilt him, Alice was still 'the careful teacher who gave him his first lessons, who taught him that man should be noble, helpful and good. . . . An especially active mind, a thorough knowledge in the most varied fields, a muscular, supple, truly manly appearance were the result

of . . . the foundations [which] were laid by his mother.'[14]
Ernie amplified this in writing:

> My mother was one of the very great souls who, although
> she died young, accomplished a great deal and all ladies
> with whom I talked told me that they had been changed by
> her personality. They had become more serious and had
> learnt to take an interest in suffering humanity. One can
> imagine what kind of a person she was, I was only a little
> boy when she died, but nevertheless she had left her mark
> on me to such an extent and we had become so much at one
> with each other that even now as an old man, if I have any
> problem I only have to think what she would say to what-
> ever it is and I know I have made the right decision.[14]

It is to Ernest Louis that we owe a detailed account of many
lesser-known aspects of the life and character of both his
mother and father. Some valuable observations occur on the
kind of situations that could soften Alice's habitual seriousness, which Ernie attributed to the intense sufferings she
experienced early in her life. He claimed that she nevertheless
had a 'great sense of humour' and enjoyed comic occasions to
the full.

> So, for instance, when she and I stopped before the house of
> our eye specialist Dr. Weber. She drove her small low car-
> riage herself. She only wanted to ask him a short question
> concerning myself and therefore, Dr. Weber came out to the
> carriage. When talking absent-mindedly he picked up her
> handkerchief from her lap and started to clean the wheel of
> the carriage standing before him. When they had finished
> talking she only said to him: 'Oh Dr. Weber please give me
> back my handkerchief,' and drove off. How we laughed,
> because one can imagine the expression on Dr. Weber's face.
> Another time my parents gave a dinner for the Lower
> House and I was allowed to be present before they went in
> to dinner. I can still hear the conversation which my mother
> had with Mr. Wernher from Nierstein (the father of our
> Adjutant General who was with us for such a long time.)
> He was an old gentleman with white hair and wore a blue

dress coat with gold buttons, as was fashionable at that time. He loved arguing. During conversation, in his excitement, he kept on calling my mother 'Sir' and finally took hold of the pearl brooch which she was wearing on her dress and was twisting it talking all the time. My mother allowed him to do this without any murmur in order not to disturb him. The conversation ended when other gentlemen joined them. Therefore, he never knew what he had done, but I shall never forget the teasing, laughing eyes of my mother.

Ernie could not praise his father's straightforwardness and generosity too highly, and remarks that he never scolded the children. He shows Louis to have been almost childlike himself, with a liking for simple and routine amusements and an extraordinary capacity for taking things as they came. But he was adored by all the children, who spent hours in his room playing, painting, working and talking while he tried to do some writing at his desk. His influence on the children was considerable but chiefly in a passive sense; they never forgot his exemplary good nature. Much more active and forceful was the influence exerted by Alice, from whom Ernest Louis inherited his musical taste and talent. 'My mother not only played the piano but had a beautiful touch,' he recalled.

If it was possible I joined her. Very often she also played duets and eight hands. Many artists came to her and once I sat in a corner of the music room on the sofa to listen to a man with a big red beard playing to my mother and at the same time she discussed a lot with him. He ruled off the notes and asked her to accompany him. She said it was impossible because they were handwritten and only just roughly sketched. He insisted and said she should only improvise if it was too difficult. Then they played. At the end he turned round, his hands on his knees, and said to her: 'Are you I or am I you?' She was able to sense him completely. It was Brahms and I was therefore the first person to hear the Hungarian Dances.[15]

Ernie remarked especially on the 'idea of true art' which he and, in particular, Ella got from their mother. He attributed

her rather indefinable legacy in this connection to her love of
beauty in general and of the marvels of nature; even if all the
children had not learnt to play musical instruments, they all
learned to listen appreciatively.

Also in another way she influenced us children [Ernie said].
Every Saturday morning we had to take lots of flowers to
her hospital in the Mauerstrasse and, having first put the
flowers into vases, take them to the various patients. In this
way we lost all timidness which children so often have when
meeting sick people and we became friends with many
patients and unconsciously learnt to have sympathy for
others. There was no age limit; even the youngest amongst
us, had to come along.[16]

If Alice made a mistake with her children, it was perhaps
in too intense or highbrow an approach to their cultural formation when they were too young for it. 'She always had new
ideas how to educate us. Once she had asked the well-known
actress, Mrs. Sonntag, to read to us children during the afternoon. Amongst other things she read the Elf King to us with
great solemnity. When she had finished she looked at all of us
expecting us to be moved.' Unfortunately they were not; they
obviously preferred Louis's technique of letting them do what
they liked! On the credit side, however, as Ernie added,
'There was no end to the people my mother had around her.
Musicians, artists, professors, doctors and women of all kinds
and physicians because, for her, there were no barriers, and I
was often allowed to be present.'
    In pursuance of her ambitious aims for the education of her
children Alice adopted measures reminiscent of her own young
days. She asked her friend Dr Hinzpeter to draw up a memorandum on the duties of her daughters' governesses, setting
out at some length her own ideas on the subject.[17]

Ideally [the memo stated] the mother should have firm,
clear ideas about what she wants her daughters to be, and
should find a governess whose pedagogical gifts and practical experience will enable her to devise and apply the
means and methods through which the mother's ideas can

be realised. Mutual confidence must therefore be based on the governess's accepting the mother's ideas as right, and on the mother recognizing the measures and arrangements adopted by the governess as appropriate.

As for the correspondingly ideal governess, no less was required of her than that her mental and physical powers should be considerable,

. . . for only the feeling that a certain energy in both these respects is in good supply will give the children the firm, suitable confidence that they should have in their governess; untiring activity on her part is the easiest way of giving the children the feeling that they have a firm support, on which they will willingly lean; and that alone justifies in the child's eyes the consistent strictness which must pervade their entire upbringing. This last is absolutely necessary for the achievement of satisfactory results in both her own personal efforts and to give herself up entirely to the life of the children. Only with perfect concentration of all her powers and all her interests will she be able to fulfil the demands that must be made of her.

It is not hard to detect what one might almost literally call the 'ghost-writing' hand of the Prince Consort in this document. But it would be a mistake to imagine that Alice's somewhat austere views of a mother's vocation cast gloom among the children. Quite a different picture emerges from Princess Victoria's account of her everyday girlhood life. It is true that in the family photographs of this period (about 1870) everyone tends to look very stern and strained. But an interesting explanation for this is given by Princess Victoria in her memoirs. In describing the 'ordeal of being photographed' she says: 'an iron support was put behind your head and one behind your waist to keep you quiet while the photographer counted up to ten very slowly for the exposure of the plate . . . the whole afternoon was spent in the operation.'

Princess Victoria took an active interest in the wartime transformation of the New Palace in 1870. The ballroom – later split up to house the nurseries when they were moved down from the top floor – became a hospital supply depot. 'All the ladies of Darmstadt came to make what was called "charpie". Old linen was cut up and threads pulled out to produce the substitute for cotton wool which was apparently non-existent at the time.' The summers at Kranichstein were remembered with special joy; apart from anything else they were associated with comforting warmth in contrast to the freezing winters. Little Victoria got her first chilblains in 1870–1, a particularly cold winter during which soup kitchens were set up for the poorer members of the population. Alice visited most of these herself, accompanied by her eldest daughter, then aged eight. The children followed the same sort of fixed daily timetable that Alice herself had done up to the age of six or seven: lessons began at 7 am, followed by breakfast with parents at 9. Then came exercise out of doors before and after a sort of 'elevenses' snack that they used to call 'little lunch'. Proper lunch was taken, *en famille*, at 2. The simple diet was favourably compared by young Victoria to the meals they had when staying with her namesake and maternal grandmother, which she remembered 'with a shudder of disgust'. After lunch the children went out, rain or shine, hot or cold, for an hour and a half, before schoolroom tea, playtime and bed by 7. Alice encouraged them to go for long walks, rambles and pony rides. In town their favourite place was the Akaziengarten (opposite which stood Alice's temporary English hospital during the Franco-Prussian War). Kranichstein, however, offered the best scope, with long treks in the woods. They led their Shetland ponies and were followed by Alice's fierce little bull-terrier, Boxer, who chased the wild boar and once got badly attacked. Alice and Louis loved it all as much as the children, whether it was rowing on the lake, in the boat given to them by their cousin Mary of Cambridge, or the long rides. Alice was a skilful horsewoman and according to Ernie it was she who introduced her husband to the thrills of hunting. Louis himself was the best kind of sportsman, unusually magnanimous to fellow-guns or stalkers; and like all true sportsmen he was inordinately, if paradoxically, fond of animals. (Another example perhaps of a somewhat illogical sentimentality.) He kept a number of extraordinary pets, such as wild boar and dwarf sheep or goats at Kranichstein; and at the New Palace a rather smelly fox, a lamb, white rabbits, guinea pigs and some Turkish ducks. It was all grist to the carefree mill of tomboyish young Victoria, who preferred gym and drill to dancing until her late teens. She ruled the younger ones with great success, with only Ella occasionally rebelling. The governesses, despite the formidable criteria for their qualifications, invariably found that Alice's eldest daughter wielded more power than they did. The three girls and a governess would walk in pairs, Victoria and Ella taking it in turns to walk with Irene. They had very different tastes in the stories they liked to tell and hear; Ella's were 'nice little girl stories', while Victoria's were about Homeric heroes and Knights of the Round Table.

It is remarkable how much time Alice and Louis managed to spend with their children, despite pressure of duties and other commitments. Seaside expeditions, about every other year, were greatly looked forward to. Financial stringency naturally went unnoticed by the children, and Alice put as brave a face as possible on the 'economy' excursions to such places as Blankenberghe and Houlgate. At Ostend one winter they met 'Cousin Leopold',* as Alice called the King of the Belgians. Princess Victoria remembered him as 'a tall, thin man, with a nose nearly as long as Cyrano de Bergerac's and his slow drawling voice seemed to proceed from it'. He was the creator of Ostend but, wanting to flatter the town's mayor, presented him to Alice, speaking French, as 'my friend and collaborator'. The mayor was delighted even when Leopold continued in German with equal apparent politeness, 'but he's also very boring'. The mayor merely thought this was a 'continuation of the compliment' and went on beaming.

Returning to Darmstadt after this particular visit entailed the kind of rail journey that was not untypical in those days but was obviously tedious and excessively uncomfortable. There were no sleepers and the chief antidote to the intense cold was footwarmers containing tepid water that were occasionally 'shoved into the carriages as they went along'. The young Victoria was only ten when she began to notice how ill-equipped physically her mother seemed to be against such

---

* King Leopold II, son of Queen Victoria's uncle, King Leopold I.

hardships. She also noticed how she came more and more to take refuge in her favourite pastimes of painting and music. She also drifted increasingly into the company of the growing English colony at Darmstadt, whose numbers were greatly swelled in the middle 1870s by the arrival of Colonel Williamson's Army Cramming School. The stodgy locals were horrified by the pranks of the would-be young officers who were being crammed, and were totally amazed at the spectacle, hitherto never witnessed by them, of football being played. Alice was careful not to make her friendship with the English in Darmstadt in any way ostentatious. She was not in any event addicted to pomposity or superfluous formality. One particular story was often told about her. It even appeared in the *Annual Register* for 1878:

> An English lady of high position residing at Darmstadt received a note from the Princess, saying that she would call and take tea with her the following afternoon. Scarlet cloth as etiquette seemed to demand, was laid down, and a man was sent to the top of the house to watch for the Royal Carriage and give due notice of its approach, so that the Princess might be received at the entrance with all due honour. But up to the time named by the Princess, no carriage of any kind had come in sight. Suddenly a ring at the street door was heard, and a Lady attired in a waterproof and wearing goloshes made her appearance. 'I have made a point', she said, 'of not treading on your beautiful scarlet cloth;' and she intimated that in future she should be glad to be received, not as a Royal Princess making a State visit, but as a private lady 'dropping in' upon a friend.

Unfortunately, however, Alice's closeness to the English colony was yet another cause of resentment on the part of native Darmstadters; but Louis's friendship with the former was just as firm and went on uninterruptedly after Alice's death. To Princess Victoria and her sisters Alice was 'the mistress of the house, a wise and loving wife and mother whom we respected as much as we loved'.

If there is a hint of reservation in this assessment it is perhaps attributable to the tinge of remoteness that sometimes characterized Alice the mother. It did not seem to arise in the case of Ernie, and certainly not with her other adored son Frittie. He was the first to be born of Alice's three youngest children; and their lives, two of them pathetically short, mark out a rather different side of Alice's family life.

Chapter Thirteen

THE 'CURSE OF ENGLAND'

'It is difficult either to find a disease which is more dramatic and tragic than haemophilia, or to name a clinical entity (if one excepts tuberculosis, syphilis and insanity) which has influenced modern history more than this hereditary defect. There can be no doubt that the presence of this disease in the royal families of Russia and Spain played a part in shaping the destiny of present day Europe.'[1]

Of Alice's seven children at least three of them were definitely affected in different ways by this disease. But she herself lived to see its effect only on the life of one of them, Frittie. Its effect on another, Alix, was indirect but no less tragic, and of immense relevance to world history.

Alice doted on Frittie, as she mostly called her second son, though other members of the family sometimes called him 'Fritz'. His birth during the Franco-Prussian War (on 7 October 1870) gave his mother 'a difficult time, but it went quickly'.[2] In writing to Louis she tried to make light of her poor state of health at the time. That this second son and 'new proof' of their love was 'fat and healthy' was all that mattered to her. It was not for over two years that she had any cause to suspect bleeding problems. And in the meantime the delightful little Frittie was a principal distraction from war-weariness and spiritual doubts. There was also, after the relief over the Prince of Wales's recovery at the end of 1871, the reward for Alice, during the following year, of seeing the first fruits of her pioneering social and medical work firmly consolidated. It was, as already mentioned, in the course of this year, on 6 June, that her fourth daughter was born. She was to have been called after her mother, but it was a name 'they pronounce too dreadfully in German', Alice wrote to Queen Victoria.[3] So she was called Alix, her full names being Victoria Alix Helena Louise Beatrice. She was 'a sweet, merry little person always laughing, with a deep dimple in one cheek just like Ernie'.[4]

She came to be called 'Alicky', 'Sunny' or 'Princess Sunshine'.

At this stage life for Alice, still in her twenties, should have been entering the golden years as far as motherhood and family contentment were concerned. The four eldest children were happily and promisingly growing up. The latest addition seemed robust and of an unusually cheerful disposition. And above all at this particular juncture Frittie, at the interesting age of nearly two, was a playful, extremely bright and highly engaging little boy. 'A very pretty winsome child,' Princess Victoria described him as being,[5] and he was the apple of his mother's eye. But his health gave cause for concern for reasons that were not at first wholly apparent. Then in February 1873 there was a three-day flow of blood after a cut on the ear. Alice's fears of haemophilia were confirmed. There seemed, however, no call for exaggerated alarm, despite an obvious need for caution and constant vigilance. In general, in fact, despite the cut ear incident, Frittie seemed stronger and better in spring 1873, and Alice set off in March on a long-planned visit to Italy. She was escorted round the Vatican by Cardinal Howard and received in audience by Pope Pius ix. She was fascinated by early Christian and medieval Rome but was not greatly impressed by the Holy Week ceremonies favoured by Roman Catholics, of whose religion she was not enamoured at the best of times. She also visited Florence, Sorrento and Naples, and arrived back in Darmstadt refreshed in mind and body on 2 May. The family reunion that followed was particularly happy as even Alix was old enough to join in most of the fun. Louis had to go off early on 29 May, so on the day before the whole family spent the afternoon on the Glasberg. Ernie was only four at the time but afterwards remembered vividly the events of that afternoon:

> We gathered lilies-of-the-valley and Fritz, who had a special love for me had some in his little hand which he wanted to give me. I ran further and further away and he with his short little legs trotted behind me and I can still hear how he called out: 'Ernie I wants ou, Ernie I wants ou so much!'; he wanted to give the lilies-of-the-valley to me. This cry was with me for many months, yes, even years. I could not get it out of my head and at first I felt quite desperate. . . .[6]

Ernie's desperation was caused by the nightmare events of the following day, 29 May. Louis left early as planned to review the troops in Upper Hesse. There are various accounts of what followed while Alice was still in her bedroom. It was a room from whose window you could look, at right angles, through the window of the sitting-room next door. As Ernest recalls the scene: 'My mother was still in bed in the morning and my brother and I were playing near her. (The house goes round a corner there). I ran into the sitting room in order to look across at my brother. My mother jumped out of bed to pull me back from the window. During this time my little brother got up on a chair to enable him to look out and before my mother could return the chair tipped forward and he fell down on the steps.'[7] He did not fall very far but the hours that followed were ones of despondency and dread. Queen Victoria received an alarming telegram and then a long letter from one of Alice's ladies, Fräulein Bauer. The Queen appended a translation of this letter to her *Journal* since it gave (and gives) the most detailed account of what happened that day. Reporting as of 'Thursday forenoon' from Darmstadt on 29 May, Fräulein Bauer wrote:

Through the telegram which I despatched to Your Majesty by the Princess's own desire, you have already received the terrible news, which since this morning, agitates the town. Prince Frederick fell out of the window from his Mama's bedroom upon a balcony below. He, as well as Prince Ernest, was with his Mama, no nurse being present at the time; and whilst the Princess went for a moment towards the door to call for the nurse to take the two Princes away, the melancholy event happened. The poor boy was lying on his arm, when they came to pick him up, and was senseless, though no external injury was visible. Doctors were speedily at hand and found that the skull was not fractured nor any limb broken; but they fear that an extraversation of blood on the brain may take place. It is now some time since we have observed a considerable swelling on the side of the forehead; but the breathing is pretty quiet, the feet are warm and at one time the Prince moved his little arm! Sensation is complete but otherwise he rests without uttering a sound. The doctors are not without hope but at the same time do not conceal from the Princess the extent of the danger. . . . The Princess is dreadfully alarmed but now calm and composed after having been almost stupefied by the terror at first. She does not for a moment leave the bedside, but watches constantly by the darling child whose life, short as it has been, was already such a source of anxiety to her. . . .[8]

Prince Louis having been sent for to return as quickly as possible Fräulein Bauer continued her letters with a section headed 'Thursday afternoon':

Thus far I had written when things got worse, and after an hour of dreadful suspense all hope was gone. The doctors were right when they feared that there might be an effusion of blood on the brain, and we had hardly realised the idea of the case being hopeless when the terrible news was announced that *all was over!* Breathing had gradually become more irregular and heavy; all the feeling of the nerves had ceased and without pain and struggle the young soul had departed. . . . [The Princess] was able to give vent to her grief by tears, and God may give her strength in this hard trial of a mother. . . . I have just seen the Princess at the bedside of the poor little Prince, who represents death in its loveliest form. [The Princess] wishes me to tell Your Majesty that she trusts this trial will not be more than she will be able to bear!

Alice never completely recovered from the blow of this loss. Apart from anything else, she knew that Frittie might not have died but for the internal bleeding brought on by the fall. It is true, as his sister Victoria later put it, that Prince Frederick's 'early death might have saved him from a semi-invalid life'.[9] But this is a grim sort of consolation voiced at its most hollow by Alice's younger brother Leopold, who had been Frittie's godfather. He too was a haemophiliac. He was very close to his sister, to whom he confided his frustration at all the restrictions the Queen imposed on him, and his preference for being

away from home. His letters were often very bitter, but on 11
May 1873 he had written to Alice from Oxford: 'I hope my
godson is keeping quite well, and not having any more bruises,
and in every way unlike his godfather except in being very
fond of you and Louis. . . .'[10] But all the horror of 29 May
returned when he wrote to Alice from Osborne just after
Christmas to thank her for a bust of Frittie she had sent him:

> It is such a dear, sweet and innocent little countenance, that
> I cannot help saying to myself that it is perhaps well that
> the dear child has been spared all the trials and possibly
> miseries of a life of ill health like mine for instance. Oh dear
> Alice, I know too well what it is to suffer as he would have
> suffered, and the great trial of not being able to enjoy life
> or to know what happiness is, like others. That old saying
> (I don't know whether I quoted all right); 'Everything
> works for good', seems always to me such a truly comforting
> and good one. When first darling Frittie was taken away
> from among us, I remember so well people saying: 'It is all
> for the best, he would never have been well etc.' And I said
> to myself: 'If anything happens to me, that is what every-
> body will say', and it made me feel so bitter for a time, but I
> think that I have now come round to see the justness of the
> saying which I quoted above. . . .[11]

The effect was very terrible on Ernie, who suffered intensely
and in secret as only very sensitive children can sometimes
suffer. The fact that on the previous day he had run away
from his little brother and upset him by not accepting the
flowers preyed on his mind. 'I cried through many nights,' he
wrote, 'and everyone thought I was grieving at his loss; it was
only partly that, but it was also my conscience. I had told
nobody about it and as he was laid amongst all the spring
flowers my mother held me up and I placed the lilies-of-the-
valley into his cold small hands. Can grown-ups ever realise
what a child can suffer?'[12] The various members of the family
reacted in their different ways to this whole pathetic event.
Princess Victoria came to her mother one day and handed her
a poem she had written in English:

> Oh weep not mother I beseech thee
> For Fritzie is in heaven
> In heaven where angels sing with glee
> And sins are all forgiven.[13]

The stricken and sentimental but less vocal Prince Louis made no written entry in his diary; but he inserted on 2 June a photograph of the little boy's dead body surrounded by flowers and a press account of the funeral.

Flowers – and music – were the two things that most quickly made memories flood back to Alice of a life that she couldn't believe had gone. She couldn't see a flower along the roadside without having the urge to pick it for her dead son. And the piano that she loved remained silent for many many days. She could not face the keyboard from which Frittie's tiny hands had so often pulled away her own when he wanted her to come and play with him. The last piece she had played before his death happened to be Chopin's 'Funeral March'. 'The wish that *all* have who love their own' – as Alice put it – was expressed by Ernie to his mother a whole year later: 'When I die, you must die too, and all the others; why can't we all die together? I don't like to die alone like Frittie.'*[14] Ernie, who sometimes dreamed of his dead brother, often returned to his theme of wishing that they should 'die all together'.

As for the 'heaven' depicted by Princess Victoria in her poem, Alice certainly believed that Frittie was there.

'She could not for long,' we are told, 'believe that a life so sweet and promising as Frittie's, or one so energetic and influential as her father's had belied her instincts and ceased to be, through the violent contact of its physical framework with a stone pavement or by the introduction of a few germs of deleterious matter into the blood.' She said, 'The whole edifice of philosophical conclusions which I had built for myself, I find to have no foundation whatever; nothing

---

* Prince Ernest Louis died on 9 October 1937. Just over a month later most of his family perished together in an air crash at Ostend. They were flying from Munich to Croydon for the marriage of Ernest Louis's younger son Louis to the Hon. Margaret Geddes, now Princess Margaret of Hesse and the Rhine.

of it is left, it has crumbled away like dust. What should we be? What would become of us if we did not believe that there is a God who rules the world and each of us?'[15]

The dark night of intellectual doubt had passed. It was followed by a long grey day in which a broken heart dictated acceptance of the data of faith whose denial would have created an even greater mystery. Such a denial would also have presupposed a now unthinkable alternative: that of total oblivion after death. If the explanation of the Rev. Charles Bullock is somewhat sickly and simplistic, it is characteristic nevertheless of orthodox logic in certain quarters at that time:

The tender heart of the Princess was sorely smitten by this agonising trial. Yet the 'angel' sent in 'dark attire' bore no uncertain 'embassy of grace'. It is said that in Alpine lands when the shepherd finds his flock unwilling to leave the rich grass of the valley for the mountain pasture to which he would lead them, he takes up a lamb in his arms, and going on whither he would bring them, the mother presses close behind him and the flock are drawn to follow. Thus the good shepherd carried into the heavenly fold the little Frederick, and drew the tender mother's heart to follow after. Not at once, however was the Princess enabled to rally from this terrible stroke. There is reason to know that through the adverse influences of Rationalism to which she was exposed in Germany, she failed to realise the confiding trust of simple faith. But she was not left alone in her conflict. For a season the dark cloud remained, hiding the bow of Divine promise; but at length, instrumentally through some words addressed to her by a humble Scotchman,* she was enabled to look beyond the cloud. She saw the Divine purpose of grace in the dark mystery of trial, and could henceforth speak of

* The only clue as to this 'Scotchman's' identity occurs in Edith Kenyon's *Scenes from the Life of Princess Alice*, a work that relied entirely on oral evidence. The author says: 'In reference to the Scotchman whose words of advice, Mr. Bullock said, were instrumental in enabling her to look beyond the dark cloud which had hidden the bow of divine promise, we learn that he was a Scotch gentleman, a friend of the Grand Duke and Grand Duchess, who was residing with his family at Darmstadt' (p. 190).

'much tribulation' as leading her nearer to the Redeemer whose Atoning merit and Divine Sympathy can alone meet the need of sinners and sorrowers.[16]

Such well-meant and high-flown sentiment barely scratches the surface of what Alice actually went through during the rest of 1873 and the years that followed. She could scarcely get Frittie's death out of her mind, even though outwardly life had to return to its normal routine. Queen Victoria did not refrain from speaking her mind in opposition to Alice a few months after Frittie died. For 'to Queen Victoria by far the most overwhelming event of 1873 was the engagement of Prince Alfred Duke of Edinburgh* to the Czar of Russia's only daughter Marie. She displayed unusual tetchiness.'[17] Much of the Queen's tetchiness was directed at Alice, whose views over Princess Helena's wedding had evidently been neither forgiven nor forgotten. She had even as early as April 1873 written to Lord Granville laying it down that 'the Queen wished Princess Alice (who is at home)† to be in *no* way consulted or taken into confidence about this affair of Prince Alfred'.[18] The Czar unfortunately refused to present his daughter for premarriage inspection at Balmoral, and the Queen was instead invited to meet the Russian royal family in Germany. When Alice supported this suggestion 'Queen Victoria's indignation with her second daughter knew no bounds'.[19] 'You have entirely taken the Russian side,' she wrote indignantly to Alice, 'and I *do not* think, dear child, that *you* should tell *me* . . . *what I ought to do.*'[20]

This remonstrance was directed at Alice just two months after the death of Frittie. The very day it was sent off, as it happens, Alice was writing to her mother from Seeheim, and saying:

I am glad that you have a little coloured picture of my darling. I feel lower and sadder than ever and miss him so much, so continually. There is such a gap between Ernie and Sunny, and the two boys were such a pretty pair, and were to become such companions. Having so many girls I

* Alice's younger brother.
† Princess Alice was in fact in Italy at the time.

was so proud of our two boys! The pleasure did not last long, but he is *mine* more than ever now. He seems near me always, and I carry his precious image in my heart everywhere. That can never fade or die![21]

And indeed the shadow thus cast remained for the rest of her life. If its enveloping quality rekindled the strong basic faith of a soul paralyzed by intellectual doubt it was something like restoring life to a frozen limb by casting it in a flame. But a much more philosophical and more tender strain was introduced into her letters to her mother from now on; her thoughts kept going back to the past and to her father; her present attentions and affections were increasingly wrapped up in her children, especially Ernie; and her whole outlook was now summed up in 'the feeling that all is in God's hands, not in ours'.[22]

Thus did haemophilia lay its hand for the first time on one of Alice's children. A generation later another beloved son was to be the object of the same anguished parental worry. This was Alexis, the only son of Czar Nicholas II of Russia and Alice's daughter 'Alicky', known to history as the tragic Empress Alexandra Feodorovna. The desperate efforts of this pathetic Empress – including, above all, the enlisting of help from the sinister Rasputin – are part of one of the best-known tragedies of modern times. So irresistible has the colourful, grotesque and fantastic Rasputin proved to novelists, biographers and film-makers that his place in real history has probably been distorted. But the story could well have been different had Alix inherited more of her mother's blend of firm belief and sharp intellect. She relied instead more on that aspect of 'religion' that is readily distinguishable from an intelligently directed faith. She also possessed the kind of sentimentality – perhaps inherited from Louis – that lent itself at times to credulity. She was thus vulnerable to the almost hypnotic persuasiveness of Rasputin. And the belief that he might save their son by a form of faith-healing, necessitating his acceptance as a close friend, outweighed the political implications of his being so widely hated in Russia. But any generalization about this period is dangerous. The importance of what she did or did not inherit emotionally and intellectually from

Alice is to some extent academic, but cannot be omitted in any account of Alice's life, because of the hitherto neglected historical links involved. What is undeniable is that Alix's whole personality underwent a radical change when Alice died.

The death of her mother, at 35, had a shattering effect on six year old Alix. She sat quiet and withdrawn in her playroom while her nurse stood in the corner, weeping. Even the toys she handled were new; the old familiar toys had been burnt as a precaution against the disease [of diphtheria]. Alix had been a merry, generous, warm little girl, obstinate but sensitive with a hot temper. After this tragedy she began to seal herself off from other people. A hard shell of aloofness formed over her emotions, and her radiant smile appeared infrequently. Craving intimacy and affection, she held herself back. She grew to dislike unfamiliar places and to avoid unfamiliar people. Only in cosy family gatherings where she could count on warmth and understanding did Alix unwind. There, the shy, serious, cool Princess Alix became once again the merry, dimpled, loving 'Sunny' of her early childhood.[23]

The other decisive factor, without which subsequent history must in some way have been different, was that of the haemophilia. And the description of Alix as she dealt with the consequences of this might almost have been a description of her mother Alice nearly half a century before: 'As one precarious year followed another, emotional stress took a terrible toll. . . . Dr. Bodkin . . . mentioned years later to an officer in Siberia that the Empress has "inherited a family weakness of the blood vessels", which often led to "progressive hysteria". In modern medical terminology, the Empress Alexandra undoubtedly was suffering from psychosomatic anxieties symptoms brought on by worry over the health of her son.'[24]

There was for a long time, and to some extent still is, much mystery and controversy about this disease, especially as it affected the British royal family in the nineteenth century. Some of the mystery persists, though new light has been shed on it by recent research, particularly that of G. H. Green, whose findings I have relied on.[25] The fact is that Queen

Victoria's outwardly robust health concealed a grave defect, destined to appear – because of her – in the most important royal families of Europe and to prove fatal to many of her descendants. The deadly disease is thought to be older than recorded history but was never mentioned by Latin or Greek writers. But the existence of haemophilia is implied by passages in the Talmud relating to the dangers of death from haemorrhage after circumcision. And 'Albacusis, the great Moorish surgeon of the eleventh century, related that in a certain village were men who when wounded suffered an uncontrollable haemorrhage which caused death, and boys who bled often fatally when their gums were rubbed harshly'.[26] Strangely, however, the disease received no medical recognition until the nineteenth century and the name haemophilia did not come into use until shortly before the birth of Princess Alice. It can perhaps be argued that apart from Queen Victoria herself she was the most important of all the carriers of the disease as far as subsequent dynastic history was concerned; for through her it affected the royal houses of both Russia and Germany, the former with devastating results. The supreme irony consists in the uniquely heritable quality of haemophilia, which is generally transmitted through apparently normal females but appears predominantly in the male.

The question is, how did it appear in Queen Victoria, when it cannot be traced in either the Hanoverian or Saxe-Coburg-Gotha royal families? The answer is that when these two families were united in the persons of Edward, Duke of Kent and Victoria of Saxe-Coburg the disease made its appearance in the only child of this marriage, the future Queen Victoria, through a spontaneous mutation in the x-chromosome handed on by one of her parents. Which parent? Mutations are known to occur much more often in the germ cells of older fathers and the Duke of Kent was fifty-one (Victoria of Saxe-Coburg was thirty-one) when the future Queen Victoria was born. Later the Queen often spoke of the disease, but was convinced that it was 'not in our family' – meaning the House of Hanover. 'This was strictly correct but the mutation almost certainly occurred in a Hanoverian gene and not [as has generally been thought] in the Saxe-Coburg genes Queen Victoria inherited from her mother.'[27] The disease can be inherited through males or females, though it normally exists only in the carrier state in the female, with the bleeding characteristics not manifested. And while an affected male has normal sons, all his daughters are carriers. It is thus not difficult to see why the disease spread so rapidly in nineteenth-century royal circles, with arranged marriages between close relations being an added complication and danger. 'Because cousins have one-eighth of their genes in common, the wonder becomes not so much that so many of Victoria's descendants (at least sixteen in three generations) were affected but that an affected male did not marry a carrier female cousin and produce that rarity of rarities, a true female haemophilic.'[28]

Prince Leopold was the only haemophiliac among Queen Victoria's four sons. He himself had a normal son and a carrier daughter. Of the five daughters, Alice and Beatrice were definite carriers. The Crown Princess probably was as well. (Two of her sons died in infancy, possibly but not certainly from haemophilia.) Well might the Queen have exclaimed in despair: 'Our poor family seems persecuted by this awful disease, the worst I know.' Alexis, Alix's son, had four sisters, but the whole family perished at the hands of the Bolshevists. Whether any of the daughters were carriers will never be known.

Irene was another of Alice's carrier daughters. Her marriage was a good (and potentially dangerous) example of matchmaking between relations, her husband being the Crown Princess's younger son, Prince Henry of Prussia. But even with the death in infancy of one haemophiliac son of this marriage and the murder of the Russian royal family the diseased gene had not yet died out in those branches of Queen Victoria's family with which Alice was the link. It persisted until 1945, with the death of Prince Henry's other haemophiliac son, Waldemar.

Alice was thus both a victim and an agent of this blight that ravaged dynastic Europe. The dreaded 'bleeding disease' has been called at different times the 'Curse of the Romanovs' or the 'Curse of the Bourbons'. It is ironical to reflect that in origin it was the 'Curse of England'.

Chapter Fourteen

MOMENT OF TRUTH

Alice's seventh and last child was born almost exactly a year
after the death of Frittie, on 24 May 1874. On 11 July she was
christened Marie Victoria Feodora Leopoldine. Her short life
corresponded almost exactly to Alice's last years. They were
years during which her maternal instincts, as a reaction to
Frittie's death, directed themselves with increased intensity
toward her three youngest children. She made no bones, in
writing to her mother, of the desirability of herself feeding
baby May, as they called their last child. She was adored by
little Alix and was especially close to Ernie, who wrote, as will
be remembered, 'Now I was the only son and my mother and
I clung to each other.'[1] One might have thought that Alice
would have clung first and foremost to her husband; that the
loss of Frittie would have made her less conscious of those
barriers between them at which some of her letters had
hinted in days gone by. Instead of this the astonishing truth
finally became apparent, though not all at once. It emerged
in stages in the letters she wrote to Louis between 1874 and
1877. And it was not a question of her having become hard or
bitter about life; her letters to her mother show an exactly
opposite tendency. Strauss's death (in February 1874) naturally saddened her, but it was through sadness that her whole
outlook on life had already become considerably softened. And
she was one of the many former devotees of Strauss who
found that they could not follow him in the extremes to which
he went towards the end of his life, particularly in his work
The Old and New Faith.

If she was hard on anyone at this time her views took the
form of frank self-criticism; and it is not difficult to guess that
she was thinking of Louis and herself when contrasting people
with equable dispositions with those of violent emotions:
'People with strong feelings and of nervous temperament, for
which one is no more responsible than for the colour of one's

eyes, have things to fight against and to put up with,unknown to those of quiet equable dispositions, who are free from violent emotions, and have consequently no feeling of nerves – still less, of irritable nerves. If I did not control mine they would be dreadful. . . . One can overcome a great deal – but *alter* one's self one cannot. . . .'[2] But in the last few years of her life she was not always as successful as formerly at keeping a taut rein on her nerves. It was partly because 'being strong and healthy by nature' she resented 'not being well, and feeling so weak'.[3] And to Louis she wrote, towards the end of 1874: 'Every little emotional upset, for instance over . . . your being cross – or any disturbance of my usual life, is a strain on my nerves.'[4] What was really in the back of her mind was revealed in her letter of ten days later, when she wrote: 'The wound that his [Frittie's] death inflicted on me is not yet healed – and so painful – I sometimes need to talk about it, when my feelings become too much for me to bear – then I feel stronger again. But I don't do it with you – I know it hurts you – and men react differently to sorrow from women.' (In this letter she also laments the extent to which the former Liberal Minister Lord Ripon had lost his intelligence and common sense in becoming a Roman Catholic!)

A whole year later – five years after Frittie's birth – found Alice, on his birthday, less able than ever to keep her eyes dry. But 1876 saw her fighting back on a new front. She had begun to pick up the loose threads of the medical and social work that had never ceased to interest her. Though her main labours were over and the firm foundations for lasting progress solidly laid, 1875 saw her once more involved in fund-raising and similar activities. And in 1866 she widened her personal horizons by visits to some of the worst parts of London's slums with her friend and collaborator, the celebrated social reformer, Octavia Hill. She described one of these visits in a letter to her daughter Victoria:

With a charming excellent lady Miss Octavia Hill . . . I have been this morning in some of the very poor courts in London, garrets and streets . . . such quantities of little children and so many living in one dirty room. It was sad to see them – in one way, but beautiful to see how these ladies

worked amongst them, knew them, did business with them.
I have been trying to see as much and learn as much as
possible of what is done for the poor in every way and have
heard of such good and unselfish noble people. . . .[5]

She subsequently exchanged numerous letters with Octavia
Hill[6] and was as much of a help and encouragement to Miss
Hill as the latter was a source of instruction and inspiration to
her. But she was also beginning to be concerned with her and
Louis's political future. Her prompting looked distinctly more
'maternal' than uxorious when she wrote to him, in June 1876:

I am very pleased when you mix with other people a *little*
more – it is not manly, – it is too easy-going to spend all
one's time in the company of governesses and children;
when I hear you talking about Uncle Louis I think how
soon your position could change, and then you will have to
set yourself standards – as St. Paul says – 'But when I
became a man I put away childish things' – in these words
lies the whole secret of your future – with this resolve you
could *really* be to me and the children and your subjects
what you outwardly seem to be now. This is your stumbling
block dear boy – forgive my saying it – it is but for your
sake, for your good, that you may be thus enabled to use
your good qualities and to put some serious purpose into
your life. My faults are so many – I have no right to preach,
tell me of mine as I tell you of yours. . . .[7]

But Louis did not respond to the invitation to be critical. He
ever preferred to avoid the troublesome issue and Alice now
distinctly felt that, for her at least, time was running out. It
was a fight, almost, against his excessively 'easy-going' attitude and her own growing physical lassitude, which she began
despairingly to think she would never now throw off, despite
her strength of will.[8] But Louis must have smiled at her female
inconsistency when she sent him warm greetings on his birthday, 11 September, but begrudged his having to spend it 'in
military style and not with your family'.[9]

Things were not made easier for her towards the end of 1876
when she had to undergo some extremely painful treatment in

England for a long-standing internal complaint due to a back-
ward curvature of the womb. But her own familiarity with
medical matters fortunately enabled her to brush this off in a
more or less matter-of-fact fashion. She was much more concerned (writing from Balmoral while convalescing) with
Louis's apparently chronic immaturity:

> It is kind of you to write so often and it gives me such
> pleasure, but, darling Louis, if my children wrote me such
> childish letters – only short accounts – of where and what
> they had eaten or where they had been etc., and nothing
> else, no opinions, observations and remarks, I should be
> surprised – and how much more so when *you* write like that!
> . . . Mama is *so* considerate and kind to me – it is all going
> on smoothly and well, but I am still so tired and lethargic.
> . . . Bertie wants you to go to Sandringham for his birthday,
> and Alix too – I have accepted for you. You ought to shoot
> with him at Windsor. . . . I benefit too when I know that
> you are enjoying yourself. After all, it is nicer than man-
> oeuvres, and it is better for you intellectually than always
> 'doing one's humble duty.' It is unjust of me, but I feel
> more and more how *little* I like Germany and the Germans.
> Especially the kind of relationship and the tone adopted
> between members of Princely families and other mortals.[10]

It was on 3 October 1876 that Louis received his first real
bombshell from Alice, who was still at Balmoral; it was as if a
catapult containing the pent-up emotions of a married lifetime
had suddenly been released; as if the perennial forbearance
and affection that had cushioned a basic incompatibility had
been brusquely cast aside:

> You write so sweetly about the old days when we first got
> to know each other. But you must not deceive yourself and
> think that the other little affairs were chiefly to blame for a
> rather disappointing life – the real reason was that I on my
> side expected too much – or just expected something differ-
> ent – from my husband. There has never been any lack of
> love – only with time, the disillusion became hard to bear.

I longed for a real companion, for apart from that life had nothing to offer *me* in Darmstadt. I could have been quite happy and contented living in a cottage, if I had been able to share my intellectual interests, and intellectual aspirations with a husband whose strong, protective love would have guided me round the rocks strewn in my way by my own nature, outward circumstances, and the excesses of my own opinions.

So naturally I am bitterly disappointed with myself when I look back, and see that in spite of great ambitions, good intentions, and real effort, my hopes have nevertheless been completely ship-wrecked – and this realisation, my darling, often makes me unjust towards you – for one carries the blame for everything in one's self – I know that *now*. It always grieves me, too, to see how you have been disappointed – for the fault is *mine*. But let us go on helping each other honestly – we cannot let ourselves be paralysed by the past – and there is nothing I want but to make your life happy and to be useful to you.

You say, darling, that you would never have caused me hardship *intentionally* – indeed it would have been terrible if you could have done such a thing, or if I could have believed it of you. I only regret the lack of any intention or desire – or rather insight – to be more to me, and that does not mean spending all your time with me, without wishing to share anything with me at the same time. But I am wrong to talk of these things. Your letters are dear and kind – but so empty and bare – I feel myself through them that I have less to say to you than to any other person. Rain – fine weather – things that have happened – that is all I ever have to tell you about – so utterly cut off is my *real self*, my innermost life, from yours.

I have tried again and again to talk to you about more serious things, when I felt the need to do so – but we never meet each other – we have developed separately – away from each other; and that is why I feel that true companionship is an impossibility for us – because our thoughts will never meet. There are so many things that are necessary to me, of which you know nothing, but which, at my age, form a part of my own personality, and make up my life. You would laugh, you would not understand, if I expressed what I think and feel. I shall never forget your *great* goodness, nor that you are still so fond of me – and I love you too so very much, my darling husband, that is why it is so sad to feel that our life is nevertheless so incomplete – and sometimes so difficult. But you are never intentionally to blame for this – I *never* think that, *never*. . . .[11]

This was one of the longest and one of the most important letters that she ever wrote to Louis. She followed it up the next day with a very short one based, it would seem, on the rather surprising assumption that a few lines would suffice to put everything right again: 'Dear good Louis, I hope you are well and enjoying yourself. I am so much looking forward to our meeting. I hope my letter to you yesterday did not distress you – but it is always better to be quite honest about all one's feelings.'[12] Perhaps this letter, more than the previous one, puts the marriage relationship into its proper perspective, with Louis once more the lovable 'boy' figure and Alice the affectionate maternal friend.

The question naturally now arose as to how this married relationship – as well as Alice and Louis individually – would stand up to the rigours of granducal status if this should suddenly be thrust upon them. The matter was not long in being put to the test, for Louis's father, Prince Charles, died of erysipelas in March 1877. This put Louis next in line for the throne; in the same year his uncle was taken ill at his summer residence at Seeheim and died on 13 June.

More suddenly than either of them could have thought possible Louis and Alice found themselves Grand Duke and Grand Duchess of Hesse. Alice became a new kind of mother, the *Landesmutter*, or 'mother of her country'. The actual accession to sovereign office occurred during a period of overpowering heat. This increased the exhaustion brought on by the receptions and official duties that had followed so swiftly after the ordeal of the two deaths coming so close together. All too justified were Alice's grim forebodings as expressed to her mother just before the Grand Duke had died: 'The questions long discussed between Louis and some people, as to complications and difficulty of every kind that will at once fall upon us are really dreadful, and I am so unfit just now! The confusion will be dreadful. . . . I am so dreading everything, and above all the responsibility of being the first in everything, and people are not *bienveillant*.'[13] The lack of goodwill towards Alice in some circles, after all that had gone before, was indeed a bitter pill to swallow. The immediate burden of events did indeed prove too much for her and she was forced to seek refuge from the blistering heat of Darmstadt. She and the children spent July and August in the cool watering-place of Houlgate in Normandy, where Louis visited them whenever possible. As he struggled meanwhile to initiate himself into his grandducal responsibilities Alice sent him frequent, loving and encouraging letters. And just as, the year before, the moment had seemed to arrive for the truth to be faced, it now appeared as if the depth and extent of such truth called for yet further analysis.

Far from being angry with Louis or contemptuous in any way of him, Alice felt indignant at the thought of his abilities not getting their rightful deserts. She was touched by his recognition of her help but desperately keen for *him* to have as much confidence as she had in his own judgement.[14] And she was furious when a Roman Catholic bishop was appointed from Rome without the consent of Louis's government.[15] No 'ultramontanist' pretensions were likely to endear themselves to Alice, the fierce champion of Protestantism! The next thing that happened showed how quickly and completely she could snap out of her doldrums when anyone lively and intelligent was in Darmstadt. It has been made clear above that Louis seldom if ever had this revivifying effect on her. She was joined by Lina Hocede, who had once been her French governess. This prompted her to weave plans for injecting more urbanity, culture and cosmopolitanism into their family life in Darmstadt: 'Besides good Wilhelm,* there ought to be other influences from time to time, bringing fresh culture and new interests – and one gets bogged down with the ladies of Darmstadt – *I* certainly do, completely – such a contrast when Lina is here again – so stimulating – so much to hear about and discuss together – books, people – ideas.'[16]

* Family tutor.

Her letters to her mother meanwhile displayed only apparent harmony. In reality she was deeply hurt by the Queen's
obviously not wanting her in England. She would have welcomed a chance to go 'home' at this particular time, as the
prospects of returning to the 'narrow-minded, malicious criticism of intolerant interfering people' in Darmstadt positively
appalled her.[17] She was convinced, moreover, that the physical
strength she craved for the fulfilment of her many plans would
never return.[18] Louis meanwhile hoped: 'As you go on with
your sea-bathing the bitterness of the salt water will drive
away the bitterness that you still feel against Darmstadt.
Please my darling, don't speak so harshly of it when I come to
join you – it would quite spoil my happiness at seeing you
again – I was so happy to think that you are contented, and
I secretly hoped that you have recovered your old carefree
self.'[19]
Alice's reply is the last letter of her life that needs to be
quoted at any length, expressing as it does – far better than
any extraneous comment could do – the final judgement on
her marriage once the moment of truth, the point of no return,
had finally been reached:

When I came home I found your letter of the day before
yesterday, for which I thank you. I shall certainly say
nothing to you about Darmstadt when you come. What is
difficult and unpleasant for me there naturally does not
affect you so much – and so in your eyes it is only something
which emanates from me myself. However wrongly you see
these things and however much you misinterpret my feelings, I should not say such things to you. Forgive me – I do
not want to hurt you. You were made for a smooth, cheerful, happy life – and so your wife must want that too. She
can share your joys with you, and your worries too, but she
may not, or rather cannot, expect you to enter into hers; my
mistake is to forget this sometimes. I can share with you –
but not you with me. But do not let us talk about these
things any more – I have no intention of saying anything
unpleasant, least of *all* to you. You shake off anything
serious or unpleasant like a poodle shaking off the water
when it comes out of the sea – natures like yours are the

happiest in *themselves*, but they are not made to help, comfort and advise others, nor to share *with* others the heat of life's noon-day or the cool of the evening, with insight, understanding and sympathy. . . .

Do not write any more about what I have said – I am really looking forward to your arrival so much, and I have overcome the old feeling of disappointment which has often made me unhappy in the past few years – and I shall not torment you any more. It takes a few years for a nature which thirsts for strong mutual love and intellectual communion to reach the point of cheerfully and contentedly renouncing what it seeks. I must reach that point, and if God wills, I shall reach it. The more one's own self dies, the more one can be to others, and, renouncing one's own personal desires, live in search of something higher and better.

Goodbye, and come soon. . . .[20]

Pour Louis replied, pouring his heart out to the wife he loved so much. He did so in English, which seemed to free him of his inhibitions, and his letter touched its recipient's heart; it represented his delayed reaction to recent bombshells. Alice was moved to answer without delay, saying: 'Your nice dear letter really made me cry – you have a heart of gold – if only you will let me have a glimpse of it sometime.'[21] The gloomy spell was broken, even though Louis was not able to come right away to Houlgate as planned. In her letters from now on Alice concentrated more on encouraging her husband in his work, urging him to make decisions for himself, and assuring him that he could have the fullest confidence in his own decisions. He was finally able to get to Houlgate at the end of August, and together they journeyed back to Darmstadt.

Chapter Fifteen

14 DECEMBER 1878

It was perhaps a pity that Alice had not returned sooner. Too much time had been available for rumination, for introspection, for self-analysis. But the truth was now more apparent than ever that her dispirited outlook was not due to any basic defect in her health nor to an exceptionally hard life since getting married. The key to her unusual vulnerability to trials and strains, to mental fears and spiritual doubts, must surely be sought in the period immediately preceding her marriage. No other member of her generation in the royal family had to go through an experience in any way comparable to this. In this year of 1877 she wrote to her mother on the eve of 14 December: 'For tomorrow, as ever, my tenderest sympathy! Time shows but more and more what we all lost in beloved Papa; and the older I grow, the more people I know, the more the remembrance of him shines bright as a star of pure lustre than any I have ever known.'[1] And though the events happening immediately after 'the dreadful 14th' had evidently been 'defaced' from Queen Victoria's memory,[2] they had on the contrary burned themselves deeply into the conscious and subconscious life of Princess Alice.

Her return to Darmstadt as its Grand Duchess was much more auspicious than anything she had expected: flags out, bells ringing, people bombarding her and Louis with nosegays; all the schools on special holiday, Louis's old soldiers out in force and singing their welcome; serenades under the palace windows. It was like 1862 all over again, except that Alice was now Grand Duchess and 'mother of her country'. 'We are all very glad to be at home again,' she wrote to her mother, 'and, please God, with earnest will and thought for others, we together shall in our different ways be able to live for the good of the people entrusted to our care!'[3] Old hopes flickered of being able to carry her already well-established work on into a new dimension. Her recent slum visits in London with

Octavia Hill had been both instructive and thought-provoking. She had been determined at the time to adapt to Darmstadt and elsewhere the methods of Miss Hill, many of whose pamphlets she arranged to be translated into German. The first practical steps had been an incognito visit to the poorest parts of Metz at the beginning of 1877. But the attempt at the end of this year to make a new beginning had its own special perils.

A flurry of activity in September and October meant that more and more demands were made on the new Grand Duchess. The very fact that she herself had initiated so much new activity, and erected in the past so fruitful a platform for further development, came home to roost. Naturally it was *she* above all others who was constantly being sought out. And the effect on her was uncannily and tragically similar to what had happened to her father. It all became too much for her. Her spirit all but broke. 'Too much is demanded of one,' she wrote to Queen Victoria, 'and I have to do with so many things. It is more than my strength can stand in the long run.'[4] To add to her troubles she seemed to sense no gratitude among the so-called 'right people' in Darmstadt. Little did they know how much her efforts were costing her; that they were producing something akin to a slow death. Alice wrote to Louis during one of his absences from Darmstadt:

> I feel only moderately well and certainly not cheerful – I am 'sore' about all the many little unkindnesses which the endless gossip and stories about me cause. [There had been malicious stories about her supposed unkindness toward the former Grand Duke's wife at the time of his death.] Lies, envy – I am no match for such baseness, and it leaves a sting – because it is the 'foreigner' that they are always carping at. I am so tired of it, so sick of it – why can they not leave me in peace?[5]

The petty-mindedness that in certain quarters had never really abated became an increasingly heavy cross; and the death at the end of November of long-time friend and collaborator, Louise Büchner, was a heavy blow. The whole unhappy situation was made all the more irksome when it was contrasted to the stimulation she invariably received from some of her more notable friendships when she was in England: with Ruskin, for instance, who admired her painting; with Carlyle, who agreed with her philosophy; with Dean Stanley, who understood her compassion. And the stupidity of ministers in Darmstadt as well as of members of the grandducal household – of which she had been all too conscious – now seemed to irritate her more than ever.[6] But Christmas 1877 produced a sweet respite, chiefly because of united family happiness. She revelled in the company of her precious children, particularly the youngest of them all. Though no one, however adored, could quite replace the lost Frittie, little May, now three, had a very special place in her mother's heart. One incident was particularly calculated to please a mother so desirous that her children's love and interests should have wide horizons. Ella, now thirteen, reported it to her grandmother, Queen Victoria. Talking of Christmas presents, she described how 'for Mama each of us made a frock, pinafore, petticoat and two shifts for a poor child, we put a pocket handkerchief into the pocket of the frock because we thought the child who got it would like to find it their [*sic*]. It took a long time to make them. . . .'[7]

Did Alice have a presentiment that this would be her last Christmas? The question is prompted by her own words in a particularly bitter, undated, black-bordered letter that she wrote to Louis: 'I have had a letter from Mama – so unfair that it makes me cry with anger. I am so cross that I shall not write about it until I am back in D. I wish I were dead – and it probably will not be too long before I give Mama that pleasure.'[8] But she does not give any information as to what occasioned the hurtful letter from her mother.

Few were surprised that Alice was not up to making the trip to Berlin in January 1878 for the wedding of the Crown Princess's eldest daughter Charlotte to the hereditary Prince of Saxe-Meiningen. On this occasion, 'Vicky, marvelling at her daughter's cool and almost calculating attitude to marriage, realised that times had changed and that girls were no longer reluctant to leave their mothers.'[9] Alice had long since anticipated this problem by trying to give her daughters the widest possible interests and to discourage them from regarding a 'suitable' marriage as the be-all and end-all of their lives. Indeed she was getting less 'society-minded' with the passing of every month as winter turned to spring in 1878. She immersed herself more than ever in science and the arts, and in the people connected with them.

A highlight was the visit to Darmstadt in April of the celebrated portrait-painter Joachim von Angeli. His picture of Princess Alice was the last ever painted of her. The visit had been arranged by Queen Victoria, between whom and the Princess better relations must by now have developed once again. Alice had written to her mother in February in terms that could hardly have failed to please the Queen, for she had some very rude things to say about the monarch's *bête noire*, Mr Gladstone. The 'Bulgarian atrocities' in Serbia had outraged civilized opinion, and Russia appeared to be on the verge of war with Turkey to avenge these atrocities. But Alice felt that the fundamental long-term issue was whether Britain or Russia was going to gain the ascendancy in Asia. In fierce indignation Alice wrote to her mother:

'As Mr. Gladstone is so fond of Russia and so partial to them, I wonder what he would think of the mode in Russia of distancing far less dangerous and less mad people than himself, by placing them in lunatic asylums until they are harmless! He is too deluded, mad, unpatriotic and dangerous! All Bismarck has said is very reserved. The Austrian declaration is more decided. But they both evidently discountenance the Russian demands. It is not a question of Bulgaria or Turkey, but of Russia or England in Asia in future; of *this* all are convinced who are reasonable.[10]

Such a vehement show of spirit could not easily disguise her need for some sort of temporary refuge from the escalating burdens of Darmstadt. It was Queen Victoria who provided this by paying for Alice and her children to spend the latter part of the summer in Eastbourne. Louis went with her, but had to return fairly quickly to Darmstadt. He was enjoying life as Grand Duke and Alice, not long before, had written to

his mother, Princess Charles, to report: 'Louis is well, in spite
of everything, and very happy – I am always so glad to see
how he is so perfectly contented with his life – he has such a
fine, childlike, happy nature. . . .'[11] The bathing and sea air of
Eastbourne did Alice some good. But she found it hard, if not
impossible, to rest and relax. Her brain was in a whirl through
her almost constant preoccupation with what she could do for
the forgotten victims of various kinds of social misfortune. She
took a fine toothcomb to the sociological fabric of Eastbourne,
asking searching questions, visiting numerous humble dwell-
ings and wandering through the areas inhabited by the
fishermen and their families. The main interest of her visit
completely escaped the attention of a certain respectable
Victorian worthy. His portentous legacy to posterity consisted
of his 'Eastbourne memories', which recorded:

> In the autumn of 1878 the Grand Duke and Duchess of
> Hesse with their children made a long stay at a house on the
> Grand Parade. The Grand Duchess, it will be remembered,
> was our Princess Alice. They went about freely in the town
> and attended various festivities. On August 21 Her Royal
> Highness went to the Devonshire Park for the opening of a
> Bazaar for the Building Fund of All Saints' Church. My
> wife and I were introduced to her by Lady Fanny Howard.
> The thing which specially struck me in conversation with
> her was how completely she had lost her English pronuncia-
> tion of English. This visit was a great 'lift' for the Bazaar,
> which yielded £720. She also gave away the prizes at the
> College, and inspected the Christ Church Schools. Their
> sojourn in Eastbourne was productive of such good results
> from a health point of view that in the following year (1879)
> the children came again for several weeks.[12]

The author neglected to mention the reason why Alice herself
wasn't able to return the following year.

But the townspeople of Eastbourne remembered the Princess in a rather different way. Soon after her death in 1878
they started a fund for the raising of a memorial to her, but
soon found they had enough to build a small hospital. This

became fittingly known as the Princess Alice Memorial Hospital and it was officially opened by the Prince and Princess of Wales in June 1883.*

One particular activity to which Alice had long given much thought and attention was the question of helping and rehabilitating prostitutes. The term was not then used in polite society, and the homes catering for their needs were often referred to as refuges or penitentiaries. One of the best known was Albion House in Brighton, founded and run by a Mrs Murray Vicars. Princess Alice invited her over to Eastbourne to learn more about the work and subsequently returned the call, 'as one woman to visit another'. She told Louis:

My visit yesterday made a *deep* impression on me. Many young girls and *many* of them beautiful. They are treated with such touching love. They give up their bad life of their own free will, and let themselves be locked in here for two years. It really shows strength of character. I went quite incognito – the girls knew who I was – but the ladies of the world think it is contamination to go near such girls. I opened a new dining hall for them – 85 of them sitting together, opposite me, Mrs. Vicars, and her sister, whose husband, a clergyman made a speech, which was very moving. He finished by saying 'out of sympathy for your endeavours for good a woman is today come to you and she is the daughter of our Queen. She has come to encourage you and God has brought us all together . . .' Many tears were

---

* It was while Alice was staying in Eastbourne in this year of 1878 that the 'butterfly' boat bearing her name was, as mentioned at the beginning of this book, churning up the waters of the Thames. The date was 3 September and about an hour after dusk the *Princess Alice* with eight hundred souls on board was passing Galleon's Reach. The collier *Bywell Castle* was coming downstream at the same time. For reasons no one has ever discovered there was a head-on collision between the two craft. The *Princess Alice* sank and more than six hundred people drowned in less than five minutes. Many of the others died from pneumonia or poisoning from swallowing the noxious and filthy river water. In the whole history of the Thames there had never been – and never has been since – a more terrible disaster. The *Princess Alice* was the last boat of her kind ever to ply London's river, in whose history this catastrophe marked the end of an era.

shed – and mine too – as we knelt in prayer together, a strange gathering filled with the sense of deep solemnity – what were not *my* feelings! Hard to describe – but there is One who has read the thoughts of my heart, and His comfort and His help and His forgiveness will not forsake me. ... It makes me cry too much to write about these things. God bless and keep you. ...[13]

While they were in England the whole family also paid a visit to Osborne. It was Alice's last pilgrimage to the scene of her earliest childhood memories, thirty-three years before. She was followed back to Darmstadt by her brother, Prince Leopold, whose haemophilia always produced such over-protective concern on Queen Victoria's part. She irately telegraphed Alice on hearing that Leopold had gone out shooting during his visit. The telegram successfully upset all concerned.[14]

Shortly afterwards, at the end of October, Louis had to go away for a few days and Alice kept him posted on family and political affairs. She was very shocked about the reported prohibition against certain seemingly quite harmless trade-union associations in Darmstadt: 'We are getting back to a real police state, don't you think?' she pointedly asked Louis.[15] Of herself she wrote very pessimistically, despite feeling able to say: 'I am perfectly healthy.'[16] What was defeating her was her lack of strength, and perhaps by now lack of hope. As with her father seventeen years before, and because of a slow but insidious process – starting in her own case from those very days – something seemed to have gone dead inside her. 'I am but very middling,' she wrote to her mother, 'and leading a very quiet life, which is an absolute necessity. It is so depressing to be like this. But our home life is always pleasant – never dull however quiet. Only a feeling of weariness and incapacity is itself a trial.'[17] This letter was sent off on 6 November 1878. If somewhat gloomy, it portended nothing strikingly out of the ordinary.

Indeed life seemed to be going through one of those periods that was particularly 'ordinary' in the sense of being relaxed and unworthy of any special note. But there is a record, a very full one, of what was happening at just this time, for a great

friend of Alice's, one Katherine Macbean, who lived in Darmstadt, was at this time standing in for one of the ladies-in-
waiting. She was having tea with Alice in the New Palace on
5 November and subsequently compiled a detailed account of
all that happened on that day and those that followed.[18]
Princess Victoria complained of a stiff neck and Alice thought
it might be mumps. She remarked how comical it would be if
it were infectious and the whole household caught it. Little
more was thought about it and everybody laughed and then
danced as Miss Macbean played the piano. But next morning
Victoria was pronounced to have diphtheria, a dangerous and
highly infectious disease of which Alice, with all her nursing
experience, had a peculiar horror and dread. Alice personally
took charge of the nursing arrangements, with the help of the
staff and Lady Superintendent of her hospital. No sooner was
the eldest daughter out of danger than Alice was summoned
to examine six-year-old Alix. On her throat Alice could see the
dreaded patches of the white membrane. It was diphtheria in
its worst form, and Alix's condition looked as if it could easily
bring on one of the causes of death, obstruction through membrane formation in the respiratory tract.

As she redoubled her nursing efforts Alice was choked with
forebodings, especially for her little daughter May. The same
morning as Alix had caught the disease, May had clambered
up on her mother's bed to kiss her, before playing on the floor
in the highest of spirits. But by midday the sinister spots had
appeared on her throat as well. The thoughts of losing May –
'my little pet, my little darling' – drove Alice almost to despair. Ella escaped but Irene and Ernie both caught the infection, which finally overcame Louis as well. 'Well, Katie,' said
Alice to Miss Macbean, 'you and I are the only ones who are
not ill, and we must not be ill, there is so much to be done and
seen after.' The date was 15 November. 'It is not difficult to
realise the scene. The warm-hearted lovable man who was yet
mentally and morally his wife's inferior – brave as a lion on
the battlefield, yet beaten by "the pestilence which walketh
in darkness, and the destruction which wasteth at noon-day,"
so that he could only meet them, in the stricken house, with
half-delirious bravado.'[19]

Alice found time to send reports to her mother, sometimes

mentioning in her pathetic anguish that such letters were for
only the Queen and Princess Beatrice to see. On the terrible
day of 15 November she wrote: 'With a heart rung with pain
and fear I write a few lines. . . . And my sweet little May *so
bad* – so bad; will she get through it! My little one – my last!
Oh it is agony! . . . Husband and four children between life
and death. . . . [May God] protect them and teach us to say
"Thy Will be Done". This letter is only for you and Beatrice!
Please don't have it copied.'[20] That night she went to bed
exhausted, only to be disturbed soon afterwards: the doctor
came to report that a piece of the membrane had crossed May's
windpipe. Alice rushed to the nursery, but was too late. The
child had been choked – the second of her precious 'innocents'
to be snatched from under her eyes by the cold hand of death.
All she could do was to sit by her bed, distractedly kissing the
lifeless face and hands. The next day the Queen, at Balmoral,
was ignorant of the news until a telegram arrived from Darmstadt. She did not have to open it to realize its contents. It
was brought into her by her faithful servant John Brown, the
granite-like former gillie, now crying like a child. 'We guessed
at the truth!' the Queen wrote starkly in her *Journal*. 'Precious little May was gone!! I know how my darling child
adored that little angel.'[21] In her telegram Alice had said: 'The
pain is beyond words but God's will be done. Our precious
Ernie still a source of such terrible fear; the others though not
safe, better.'[22]

Two harrowing weeks followed for the bereaved mother,
whose greatest difficulty was in keeping the news about May
from the other children. They were constantly asking for her
and trying to send her their books and toys. Unsupported by
any of the family, in a palace that had become more like a
nursing home, Alice had to go through the ordeal of a virtually
secret funeral. Wearing the kind of long crêpe veil worn in
Germany on such occasions, she walked slowly between the
rows of court gentlemen and the servants at the bottom of the
staircase. She entered the room where the coffin was lying. It
was covered with white flowers; two large candles burnt on
either side and a great palm plant stood at the head. As she
prayed near the coffin her hand went out towards it; she
clutched a corner of the white satin pall and pressed it to her

lips. 'She paused in going back to her room and told her friend
to watch and let her know when the coffin was brought out.
Kneeling and looking through the bannisters, the Duchess
[*sic*]* saw it put into the carriage. Then from the Duke's
[*sic*]* sitting room she watched it go out of the gates. . . .'[23]
Could she ever have been more utterly alone than at this
moment? The thought that May was in a kinder world was her
only consolation; but she was still in a fever of worry over
Ernie. 'Our sweet May waits for us up there,' she wrote to her
mother, 'and is not going through our agony thank God. Her
bright happy sunshine existence has been a *very* bright spot
in our lives – but oh how short!'[24] That morning she had
visited the mausoleum, and prayed 'in tears of anguish to be
spared parting from Ernie too'.[25] Three days later she could
report that he was out of danger; he handed his mother a
book, asking her to give it to May. The effort of smiling back
as if nothing were wrong made Alice almost sick, but she still
felt that 'he must be spared yet awhile what to him will be
much sorrow'.[26] Apart from anything else it was Ernie's
tenth birthday three days later. But Alice had no festivities to
report; only: 'It seemed so long since the children have come
to my room – the lonely getting up – visiting the different sick
rooms – going past the locked doors of the bright nursery.'[27]
It was only at the beginning of December that Alice could
bring herself to tell him about his dead sister. The pain and
shock to the unusually sensitive little boy was even greater
than she had feared and he refused at first even to believe it.
As he sat up in bed with the tears running down his face[28] and
talked about May, her heart went out to him. Having so far
herself escaped infection, despite her constant involvement in
the nursing, she now broke the golden rule of avoiding, as far
as possible, actual physical contact with any of the patients.
The moment was immortalized in an address of condolence
made to the House of Lords a fortnight later by Benjamin
Disraeli, by then Lord Beaconsfield:

The Princess Alice – for I will venture to call her by that
name, though she wore a Crown – afforded one of the most

* The words, of course, should respectively read 'Grand Duchess' and
'Grand Duke's'.

striking instances that I can remember of richness of culture and rare intelligence combined with the most pure and refined domestic sentiments. . . . My Lords, there is something wonderfully piteous in the immediate cause of her death. The physicians who permitted her to watch over her family enjoined her under no circumstances whatever to be tempted into an embrace. Her admirable self-restraint guarded her through the crises of this terrible complaint in safety. She remembered and observed the injunctions of her physicians. But it became her lot to break to her son, quite a youth, the death of his youngest sister, to whom he was devotedly attached. The boy was so overcome with misery that the agitated mother to console him clasped him in her arms – and thus received a kiss of death. My Lords, I hardly know an incident more pathetic. It is one by which poets might be inspired and in which the artist in every class, whether in picture, in statue or in gem, might find a fitting subject of commemoration.[29]

But the 'kiss of death' did not have an immediate effect. She even started to make plans to take the family away. She got through her days in a sort of unreal calm, thankful that the rest of the family had been spared 'the dreadful reality I went through – and alone . . .'.[30] She went to see her elder sister at the railway station as she passed through Darmstadt on her way to England. The same day she wrote to her mother. It was a letter that, for the first time since the diphtheria had struck, contained a hint even of resumed cheerfulness.[31] But it was in fact the last letter she ever wrote to the Queen. She talked of the nurseries being repapered and their going away 'from Wednesday to Saturday week' to Heidelberg. It could hardly have been a more ironically worded forecast. Saturday would have been 21 December; the intervening Saturday was the ever-dreaded anniversary – even the same day of the week – on which the Prince Consort had died. By that date, in 1878, the kiss of death had taken its fatal effect on Alice, already weakened by the diphtheria she had caught a few days before. And on Saturday, 14 December, at 8.30 in the morning, she murmured like a sleepy child: 'From Friday to Saturday – four weeks – May. . . .' (It was exactly four weeks since her daughter had died.) And then she said, 'Dear Papa . . .'. These were the last words she ever spoke.

As one author has put it:

> It is needless to dwell on the grief caused by this event in the British Isles and throughout the Empire and in Germany, especially in Darmstadt and the district, where the deceased lady was universally beloved. It was severely felt by the Prince and Princess [of Wales] to whom the Princess Alice had been most dear, not only from natural ties, but from the beauty of her character, and above all, from memory of her devoted attendance on her brother when, seven years previously, he lay so near to death at Sandringham.[32]

Indeed the effect on the Prince and Princess of Wales was particularly shattering, but Alice's gifts as a peacemaker seemed to have power even after death. The former were at Windsor to attend the annual memorial service for the Prince Consort. The news from Darmstadt arrived and the Queen, coming in to see the Princess of Wales, clasped her in her arms. 'I wish I had died instead of her,' were the Princess's words. And 'during the sad days which followed, Queen Victoria learnt to love her daughter-in-law as never before and to turn to her more and more for support and comfort. . . . That evening the two sat alone together reading the letter which Princess Alice herself had written home of her children's illness. "Dear Alix has been a real devoted sympathising daughter to me" the Queen noted; from now onwards her daughter-in-law's place in her heart was unshakably secure.'[33] And the Prince of Wales wrote of Alice to Lord Granville (the letter was subsequently read out in the House of Lords): 'She was my favourite sister. So good, so kind, so clever! We had gone through so much together. . . .'[34]

The news had an overpoweringly emotional effect in Britain as a whole. 'The first break in my circle of children,' as the Queen described it to Disraeli,[35] produced many columns of eloquent comment – surrounded by heavy black borders – in the *Morning Post* and *The Times*. The latter reminded its readers: 'The humblest of people felt that they had the kinship of nature with a Princess who was the model of family virtue as a daughter, a sister, a wife and a mother. . . . Her abundant sympathies sought for objects of help in the great unknown waste of human distress. She had that rich store of pity which, even more than duty, is the route of philanthropic zeal.'[36] And the *Illustrated London News* felt that 'the lesson of the late Princess's life is as noble as it is obvious. Moral worth is far more of a distinction than high position.'[37]

For Queen Victoria every past quarrel or misunderstanding was erased from the memory as if it had never existed. This first death among her children shattered the monarch, who owed so much to the young girl who had become a woman overnight in 1861 and was now cut down in the afternoon of life. Her favourite son, Prince Arthur, had written to her from Berlin to say, 'How grateful one feels that dear Alice is going on so well. . . .'[38] The letter reached his mother on the very day of doom and was answered by the Queen, as if in melancholy 'monotone': 'I received your 2 dear letters on the 14th and today. . . . I am in the deepest grief for darling Alice was so devoted a daughter, so gifted and so necessary to husband and children. To think of them is too, too terrible. I am so overwhelmed with telegrams and letters that I am quite stunned by it. . . .'[39]

The grief that meanwhile fell on Hesse would have convinced Alice that she had, in her own mind – as indeed was the case – exaggerated the lack of sympathy felt for her by her adopted countrymen. That she had already, in her lifetime, captured the heart of the majority of them was abundantly evident on the morrow of her death. Darmstadters, silent with grief, lined the route of the procession as, after a service at the New Palace, her coffin, wrapped in a Union Jack, was carried to the chapel of the granducal palace. And on the following morning, in the presence of the Prince of Wales, as chief mourner, it was placed in the mausoleum at the Rosenhöhe. There is no more touching and evocative monument than that which stands over the spot where Princess Alice rests. The work of the sculpture Boehm, it is a recumbent statue of the dead Princess with her little daughter May lying in her arms. It is difficult, even now, to enter the Rosenhöhe Mausoleum and to look at this statue without a lump coming into the throat. But with sorrow once departed, the light, health, and love that Alice brought to so many must be her last earthly monument of all.

If her own life was short and often sad it was certainly not a failure. If she was the victim, to a great extent, of a small world and a cruel system, perhaps Providence saved her from becoming, in old age, a victim of herself. Premature though her death was, it came at a time when heart and head were at peace with each other. Many years before, Alice had turned the window from which her Frittie had fallen into a stained-glass memorial. Into its pattern were woven the phrases: 'Not lost, but gone before', and 'Of such are the Kingdom of Heaven'.

APPENDIX I

Letter from Sir James Clark to
Princess Alice, 6 July 1862

(DA Box 27 No. 5)

July 6th 1862

My Dear Princess,

I cannot feel satisfied to let Your Royal Highness leave this
country without giving you a few hints and cautions to guide you
on the subject of your health, as you must often be left to your
own guidance, especially while travelling. I will therefore put down
a few directions on the principal points upon attention to which
health mainly depends.

The first has reference to the necessity of healthy fresh air for the
maintenance of health. To secure this your rooms, both sitting and
bedrooms should be *at all times* well ventilated, a point requiring
the more attention in a country where the people seem to place
little value on pure air. This point Your Royal Highness will
require to impress upon your attendants.

The next point I wish to impress upon you is the steady perseverance in the use of the cold bath every morning, which you have
hitherto been accustomed to. Before going to bed also ablution
with tepid water should never be omitted, and the eyes especially
should be carefully bathed. The feet also often require bathing at
night. It will be your own fault if you have either corns or chilblains. A warm bath also, once a week at least, should never be
omitted when it can be had. This constant attention to the state of
the skin is quite necessary if you mean to keep it in a soft healthy
state, and it is also one of the most essential means of maintaining
the general health.

Exercise. Your Royal Highness will I trust keep up the habit of
daily exercise in the open air to which you have been accustomed
ever since you could walk. Walking is the best, and probably the
only active exercise you will have abroad; riding on horseback you

are not be likely to get, and driving in a carriage scarcely deserves the name of exercise for young persons.

Diet On this subject I have little to say as you do not err in that direction. Keep as much as you can to simply cooked and nutritious food, and do not fail to masticate carefully. Here I may give you a hint on the preservation of gums and teeth, which are now good and worth preserving. Do not fail to brush them very carefully after *every* meal – when you get up in the morning, and before you go to bed at night. By this frequent washing the teeth and gums will be preserved in a healthy state and decay prevented.

Medical Management
If your Royal Highness attends to the preceding directions little medicine will be necessary. You may occasionally require to take a mild aperient pill, especially when travelling, which generally has the effect of retarding the action of the bowels and treating the system generally. When the bowels have not acted for two, or at most for three days, a pill at bedtime should be taken, the object being, not to purge, but simply unload the bowels; and this may often be better and more speedily effected by a simple lavement of tepid water. This remedy administered before going to bed, after a hot days travelling, will often afford great relief, and may obviate the necessity of taking medicine. On this matter you will require my Dear Princess, to think a little, and you will soon come to manage generally in this respect while travelling, and obviate constipation and its disagreeable effects. While on a journey continue to have a little rest, or, at least, not to be called on to take active exercise during certain periods, as derangement of that function may be attended with unpleasant consequences. You must also bear in mind that the *period* may now cease from a natural cause. Should such an interruption occur, even for a single period, you should consider it a sign that you *may* be pregnant. If it is not so, no harm will arise from a little cease, and the period will most probably return next time. But until it does return you should act as if you are pregnant. In this case, as the best guide you can have I beg you to read with care, the second chapter of Combe's work, which you will receive with this. I will only add should you really find yourself pregnant to be careful not to take too much nor any active aperient, at these times when the natural periods should have returned. If at any time you should feel uneasiness in the lower part of the stomach, pain in the loins, or if an appearance of a return of the period should show itself, put yourself on the sofa

at once and send for the best advice you can get. Nothing of this kind however is likely to occur with ordinary prudence on your part and I could not have thought of going into such details had you remained in England. Should you have reason to believe yourself pregnant when in Switzerland, I would advise you either to return to Germany at once by easy journies, or, if you remain in Switzerland, to avoid most active exercise, especially ascending or descending mountains – But better return, as there is little pleasure in being in Switzerland when you are unable to do this – that is ascend mountains, etc.

Having concluded my hints in your health I might then properly put down my pen and say God speed you. But, as one of your ardent and most attached friends, I will venture to call your Royal Highness's attention to a few hints, which may be useful to you and which, at any rate, I know you will kindly take in good part as they originate in my anxious desire to promote your welfare and happiness. You are entering on a new stage of life, My Dear Princess, and are going among a strange people, who may not feel indisposed to watch your conduct, nor to mark what they may consider amiss in it. I know you will be careful to avoid remarks which might hurt their national feelings or prejudices. All nations have their prejudices, and we are not free from them, and, what is more, we are accused, and not I fear always without reason, of overbearing conduct and disregard of the feelings of other nations. Your good sense and right feeling will preserve you from falling into this error. You, I know, will be gracious to all and gain their good opinion. Be kind and considerate also to your attendants, and they will serve you from affection, the only motive of ensuring faithful and zealous service. Do not make them your confidants nor the recipients of your feelings and opinions, especially in regard to persons. Keep them in their proper position, but with all kindness and they will respect you the more and serve you the better. Of all things avoid being irritable with them, were it only that it tends to spoil your own temper, while it does them no good. – Endeavour to be methodical and punctual in all your arrangements. This will contribute greatly to your own comfort and to that of all those around you. It will prevent you from keeping your attendants and others wasting time in waiting unnecessarily than which nothing makes people more discontented, particularly persons who have other and sometimes important duties to perform and whose time is valuable. Methodical arrangement in all your affairs, as regards the distribution of your time, is of great consequence in your position, and will conduce greatly to your own comfort and that of those about you. I often had occasion to observe the want of method in your tormented father, as it greatly increased his mental labour. Do not fail to keep your papers, and particularly your letters, locked up. I would also venture to suggest a little caution in your correspondence. Letters written hastily and on imperfect information, or misunderstanding, often give, unintentionally, offence, and not unfrequently, do mischief. Write where you can at leisure. Letters written hurriedly, when the post is just about to start, are often incautiously confused. I have intended to make these few remarks to put you on your guard, but I feel assured they are unnecessary. I feel great confidence that your kind and amicable manner, your strict adherence to truthfulness and sincerity in all the relations of life will ensure you the love and esteem of all who know you, and that your example will produce a beneficial effect in the country.

But I fear I may have tired you by this long letter. I can only say it is dictated by an anxious desire to contribute to your Royal Highness' welfare and happiness. Had your dear father happily lived much of what I have written would have been unnecessary, but now I had the feeling that I was the only person in a position to say as much as I have.

I trust on this ground that your Royal Highness, will accept favourably what I have written, my sole object in troubling you with so much detail is the preservation of your health, and I do hope you will attend to what I have said on that point, as otherwise I fear you will fall into delicate health, which could interfere much with your happiness, and also with your usefulness where you would most wish to be useful.

> Believe me, my Dear Princess
> your attached and faithful
> servant
>   James Clark

Osborne July 8th 1862

APPENDIX II

Letters exchanged between
Princess Alice and
Miss Florence Nightingale, 1872–3

From Princess Alice
to Miss Nightingale

British Museum, Add 45750 Folios 75, 76

August 20 1872 SCHLOSS KRANICHSTEIN,
NEAR DARMSTADT

Dear Miss Nightingale,
Your answer was very welcome, and I thank you most sincerely
for it, and for the kind personal wishes for our darling youngest
child. I have the happiness of being able to nurse her as nearly all
my previous children, so that our quiet little country house is
pleasanter than ever. How I grieve to hear of your health getting
no better and being so precarious, yet I trust you may be long
spared for the good of others in which you yourself find your
happiness – But to come to business – during the last weeks (six)
I have come to the conclusion that to send the lady who is to
become superintendant alone, to st. thomas's will be after all the
best, and we could not think of effecting more, where we have been
so kindly and generously met. We should send the lady about new
year and communicate before hand with the gentleman you
mention.
   I shall shortly send you a small pamphlet which I have had
written to acquaint others with our New Institution and would be
very glad if it could be read in England also and find approval.
Would you please with our thanks let your Committee know that
the DARMSTADT Com: think to have found the suitable lady to send
for training to st. thomas's Hos: that she speaks good English, and
is going thro' a preparatory course of Nursing in the town hospital
here – to convince herself whether she thinks she is fit to go to

England and undertake so important a part as superintendant of a school for Nurses on her return. As soon as she is quite decided our Secretary will write to Mrs. B. CARTER enquiring at what time the lady can enter the Hospital after Xmas – with repeated thanks for the trouble and interest you take in this undertaking.

> Believe me ever,
> Yours most sincerely,
> Alice.

Add 45750   Folio 77

October 27 1872   DARMSTADT

Dear Miss Nightingale,

Two words of thanks for your letter, through which I am grieved to see that your health never improves. I would not for the world that this new association should add to your work. The way in which you can support and assist it – is by sending us all fresh and important printed statements on sanitary matters and nursing Institutes. I was very grateful for the papers you sent me through MISS CARPENTER. Your letter to the nurses is excellent and touches all the vital points which are so important in their arduous calling.

I will not trouble you by a long letter to-day.

> Ever yours most sincerely,
> Alice.

Add 45750   Folio 79

December 16 1872   NEUES PALAIS, DARMSTADT

Dear Miss Nightingale,

I trouble you once more with the affairs of our institution. Some weeks ago our Vice President FRAU STRECKER wrote to MRS. B. CARTER to enquire whether the Committee of ST. THOMAS's would consent to curtail the time of training for Miss HELMSDÖRFER from the usual year to 6 months.

Folios 80, 81

Not having received an answer I suppose this is not feasible, and venture therefore to ask again, and this time through your kind intervention whether the Committee will agree to a 9 months training or 10, if considered more desirable.

In such case Miss HELMSDÖRFER would be ready to enter the

training school in March, and to go through the *entire* system of training of every other nurse or probationer. As it is of importance for our local wants here that the Matron of the DARMSTADT nursing institution should likewise be experienced in district nursing, we mean to send her in JANUARY to LIVERPOOL to study the Working of Miss MERRYWEATHER's institution – a year is far too short for learning the important duties of a matron but the lady we shall send is very self sacrificing – highly cultivated and already possesses an amount of theoretical and practical knowledge which will enable her to seize more quickly all that she has to learn. Before closing these lines I can't help mentioning how much touched and elevated I was by reading the life of UNA. With your charming introduction, *how* I wish it were possible to give part of her noble soul and aspirations to more women – we should then not have so many difficulties to combat with – That it had been my lot to have remained single, it is the calling [*sic*] I should have most liked to have followed; but I still hope to learn much which can be of use to me – for my children and others – as soon as our little Hospital is finished. Begging for a *short* answer as *soon* as possible and hoping that you are pretty well.

Believe me ever,
Dear Miss Nightingale,
Yours most sincerely,
Alice.

Add 45750   Folios 83, 84   Christmas Day 1872

Dear Miss Nightingale,

Your kind letter reached me this morning, and my committee agree with me in accepting the proposal of MRS. B. CARTER and Miss HELMSDÖRFER will therefore enter the training school of ST. THOMAS's middle of January and is very glad to think that she will find a Lady there who can be a help to her. Should you feel well enough to receive her one day when she is at ST. THOMAS's I should be so grateful as a personal acquaintance with yourself would be to her of such great value! And it *would* be a pleasure to myself to think that she had had this advantage.

With repeated thanks for all the trouble you have so kindly taken.

Ever,
Yours most sincerely,
Alice.

Miss Nightingale
to Princess Alice

Private   (DA Box 27, No. 14p)
35 South Street
Park Lane
London W.   March 27/72

Madam,
   I have first to throw myself at the feet of your Royal Highness –
in spirit as I cannot alas! for me in body – and beg her to believe
that I did not lose one hour after receiving her kind and gracious
note in placing the matter before the Committee of the Training
School for Nurses at St. Thomas' Hospital and urging the consideration of how best we could carry out the desire which your
Royal Highness did us the honour to express of obtaining some
Nurses' training there for the Alice Frauenverein of Hesse, founded
by Your Royal Highness. We cannot yet call our school at new
St. Thomas' Hospital quite in working order. The new building,
having been opened by Her Majesty our beloved Queen last
Summer received its first Patients only in October could fill up the
beds by degrees (550) only . . . six months being but a short time
to organize all the Departments of an establishment of this size.
I merely mention this as some reason in your Royal Highness's
eyes for our delay together with my own severe state of illness and
yet I am unwilling to let my Committee's answer go, (which I
enclose), without a few words from myself to acknowledge, as I
ought, however imperfectly, your Royal Highness' gracious wish
for my 'advice and assistance'.
   Your Royal Highness is so well versed in all the arts of nursing
and so well understands the founding and fostering of an Institution that the truest respect on my part will be to speak to her as if
to one of the 'métier', certain that she will understand me better
than most who have passed their lives in it.
1.   The experience of 12 years in this Institution of St. Thomas'
and in many others founded by us from among our pupils trained
there, (together with much previous experience in England and
Europe), has confirmed one more and more every year in the conviction that only by training a nursing staff and their Superintendent together and sending them out together to undertake such
Institution as they are called upon, can this be properly founded
in good traditions of discipline and of training others. And we now

strongly deprecate and have generally declined supplying Institutions otherwise than by trained Staffs of Nurses. If this be impossible, then we train a Superintendent, as well as we are able, and send her out to train and govern her Staff as well as she can (Poor thing! She has generally a hard task of it – it is something like a Sisyphus and his stone – as Your Royal Highness is doubtless better aware even than I am.)

There is scarcely anything in which discipline is more wanted than in Hospital Nursing. Because whereas, on the one hand, we cannot, and do not wish to, make use of the Roman Catholic Arts for enforcing obedience, blind obedience – on the other, a want of discipline or training is of life and death importance to the Patients.

By discipline one means the art of inspiring intelligent obedience to the orders of the Medical authorities and to the governing spirit of the places, which includes I suppose, the art of carrying individual responsibility downwards thro' every Sister, Nurse, Servant, thro' every element and thro' every detail which may also be called the art of organisation for unless everybody is shown how to do his or her own work, so as to help and not to hinder everybody else's work, there can be no organization.

And one may remark, by the way, the greater freedom of Protestant or of mixed Institutions, as it requires or ought to require greater individual responsibility, so it requires greater or ought to require greater obedience. And I know of no way in which a Superior, unarmed with the terror of an 'infallible' Church can obtain legitimate obedience, except by inspiring confidence in her greater knowledge, skill, ability and powers of training; nor except by *having* these qualities can she inspire confidence in them.

It is much easier to obey a Religious Rule than it is to exercise with discretion either command or obedience, founded on our present views of freedom suited to this age.

From all this it results – and I should really feel a just scruple at writing dogmatic conclusions in this way to your Royal Highness, did I not know as all the world does that she is much better able to draw them than I am from all this experience – it results that it is but of small use to train a Nurse (or two or three Nurses) to go back to her parent Institutions, unless she is invested with the requisite authority and distinct charge as Superintendent to train others in the Hospital knowledge and ways of management she may have acquired. Either she breaks her heart at finding that she is unable to do so – or she falls back into the old ways *a fortiori*, because she sees that she is not expected to have charge to inculcate the new ones.

2. Experience has also taught that under a year's training nothing very material can be acquired by a nurse and for a superintendent to form her properly two years are better than one.

'Previous training' rather disqualifies than qualifies a *Nurse* to acquire the habits of a new School. With a *Superintendent* this is different. She cannot have had experience enough of different training Schools, in order to enable her to take the best of each. But this does not render less than a year's training at the new school desirable for her thoroughly to acquire its ways and system. I speak for myself when I say that it is scarcely possible to 'train too much'. And I would gladly, were I not entirely a prisoner to a couch, go myself for a year's training to any new and good Institution.

The more one learns, the more humble it makes one feel with regard to knowledge already possessed – and the more eager to acquire more. 'Previous experience' aids, more than anything else could do, a Superintendent to see and grasp these points in Hospital discipline or work which are most essential.

But I speak for one far dearer to me than myself who died at her post as the prisoner of Workhouse Nursing as the Superintendent of the largest Workhouse Infirmary in this Kingdom. She was trained at St. Thomas' after having had years of experience in England, Germany and elsewhere. She went through her *year's* training. She told me that she thought during the first 2 months, one only first 'learnt what a London Hospital is' – that she then felt she 'knew nothing'. And the year she died, she wished to come back to us for further training. 'How much', she said, 'I should be able to learn now! – Now that I have had my experience'.

But further I am certain that the Medical and Surgical Staff now *wish for* their Nurses to be trained to the highest possible degree.

In Germany, hitherto, I am constrained to confess the medical men have shewn a higher and nobler spirit in aiding all they can the instruction of these who are hereafter to act as their 'aides' in the great battle against disease and death than in England.

3. The theoretical training in the Institution at Darmstadt formed by your Royal Highness is such that, according to my best belief, there is little or nothing further to be learnt in this respect at St. Thomas' Training School.

The *practical* training, if I may say so, is probably all to be learnt. For in a large London Hospital where a system and machinery for imparting practical instruction to nurses has been organizing and working out for years, this only can be found as also if

I may say so, the ways of management of a large Institution, where there is a *secular hierarchy* of above 100 women at work from the Matron down thro' Ward Sister, Nurses, Assistant Nurses, to Ward Maids and scrubbers.

And it is this organized distribution of responsibilities and offices thro' a number of *secular* women with the duties and discipline attached which has appeared to be so much wanted and till lately so little regarded in large Institutions at home and abroad. Either there has been the Roman Catholic religious 'Order' or little of organization, discipline, system (in nursing and training) at all – above all, little of that organized gradation of a Corps in ranks, involving not *absence* of duty, but *defined* duties and responsibility, without which a Corps is not a Corps which is as necessary in a Nursing Corps to save life as it is in a Corps d'Armée to destroy life and which is if possible more essential among women than among men.

I will now merely commend to your Royal Highness' gracious consideration the Memorandum of my Committee* which I enclose praying that, if it does not meet with your approval, we may be permitted to modify it.

And I will release your Royal Highness from my tediousness knowing that, whatever may be true in what I have said, is not new to her, but rather only a truism.

I will only beg her to believe that, if I do not here allude to thankfulness for the Prince of Wales' recovery and to admiration for the Princess Louis' devoted Nursing, it is because all England was as one man and one woman on that score.

I will now but entreat your Royal Highness to lay all faults and omissions in this long note at the door of my severe illness and to put her own spirit into it.

And trusting that we shall be allowed the great favour of doing some little service to your Royal Highness in training one of these who must be considered her, not our, pupils, I hope to be believed.

Madam
the most faithful and devoted
(tho' most tedious)
of Your Royal Highness' servants
Florence Nightingale

* See letter following.

Her Royal Highness
the Princess Louis of Hesse Darmstadt
Princess Alice of Great Britain

Memo referred to in letter of 27 March   (DA Box 27, No. 14p)
91 Gloucester Terrace,
Hyde Park London W.
23 March 1872

Memo: respecting the submission of Probationers for the Darmstadt Hospital –

The Committee would be willing to render assistance in training for this hospital if satisfied that a really useful result would be attained.

They understand that it is asked that two Probationers should be submitted for four or six months, one having had considerable experience in nursing and understanding [sic] English family, the other new to the work and knowling little or no English.

The standing regulations for the submission of Probationers to the School at St. Norman's Hospital provide that the terms of training should be a complete year and moreover in handing out their trained nurses into service the Committee have found it necessary to avoid as much as possible sending Nurses singly or a few together to form part of the staff of an established Institution which has recruited its nurses from other sources.

The Committee judging from their own experience of Hospitals in this country and having received trustworthy information as to the system practised in German hospitals, see no reason to suppose that the circumstances of the Darmstadt Hospital would submit of a deviation from these principles without incurring the disadvantages which the observance of them was intended to obviate. They fear therefore that the introduction into that Hospital of one or two nurses trained here would be of little if any advantage to the Institution while they are satisfied that to the Probationers an [sic] useful instrument of training could not be afforded under any period much short of a year.

So far as regards the Medical and Scientific knowledge which the nurses are expected to acquire, it seems probable that the advantages offered at the Norman's are in no way greater perhaps than may be obtained under the Will Scheme which has been adopted at Darmstadt and Carlsruhe. The benefits to be gained by the course of training are to be accrued mainly by taking part in the practical work of a large well regulated establishment under the supervision of an experienced Briton, where a sound system of nursing has been in operation for many years.

It appears to the Committee that to make the desired experiment with the best prospect of success, an educated intelligent gentlewoman should be selected for training with a view to establish her as Superintendent of nurses with all necessary powers to organize a proper system of nursing. Such a Probationer the Committee would be prepared to submit for the usual course fortuitously.

If this be not practicable, the next best alternative would be to send only the proposed Probationer who understands English, also for the usual course or as little short of it as possible.

It should be observed that the arrangements for the staff of the New Hospital are not yet complete, the great increase in the number of Patients having caused considerable difficulty in making the corresponding enlargement of the Staff. Probationers are consequently placed under some disadvantages as to efficient training and supervision at present.

The unusual labour and anxiety which have been entailed upon the Matron will account for some delay in dealing with this application.

signed: Hy. Bonham-Carter
Secty.

(DA Box 27, No. 14p)
35 South Street
Park Lane
London W.   August 12/72

Madam,

    I have first to acknowledge Your Royal Highness' most kind and gracious letter relative to the admission of a Darmstadt lady and nurse for training at St. Thomas' Hospital and then to ask Your Royal Highness' pardon for my apparent delay in replying.

    I beseech your Royal Highness to believe that this has not been from negligence on my part and to believe this without my wearying Your Royal Highness with too long an explanation of how it arose. 1 – from Your Royal Highness having kindly announced her intention of herself writing again 'as soon as' she could 'say anything positive as to the Lady'.

2. because, owing to the enormous increase of numbers of all kinds in new St. Thomas' we have had to increase and re-organize our Staff, and shall scarcely be complete before October.

I am anxious to spare Your Royal Highness details which to her will be trite and superfluous and therefore proceed at once to answer her several questions: I have consulted with our 'Nightingale Committee' Secretary and Matron, who manage our Training affairs and they are of opinion that the two persons, nominated by Your Royal Highness, should not come before Christmas.

We understand from your Royal Highness that there is not yet a Hospital to train the nurses in of [*sic*] the 'Alice-Frauen-Verein'. And therefore, unless it is with the expectation of having one, our Committee beg to submit to your Royal Highness whether there is any object in sending especially the second woman, who is to be a mere ordinary nurse and whether Your Royal Highness anticipates that any benefit will be gained to the Darmstadt Institution by sending the second, unless for the purpose of assisting the Superior in establishing a Training School in a Hospital.

Our Committee hope that, as to the Lady being alone – there being several ladies among the Probationers – she would scarcely require companionship. Our Committee desire me to say 'that they are unable to admit the full number of Probationers' (for every one of whom they have to pay the full cost to the Hospital) 'without payment – and usually require payment from Lady Probationers who can afford it. The admission of the two free would therefore be a deviation from their ordinary rules'.

But if on further consideration the Darmstadt Committee still have the conviction that the admission and training of the two would be of great benefit in establishing a Training School and it is Your Royal Highness' own desire, I beg your Royal Highness to believe that I will undertake that they shall *both* be received *free*. (It will doubtless be a *sine qua non* that before admission they speak and understand English without difficulty.)

In answer to Your Royal Highness' questions:– any letters addressed to our Secretary

Hy Bonham-Carter Esq.
91 Gloucester Terrace
Hyde Park
London W

(who also understands German) upon this matter will receive immediate attention. But I would not have mentioned this, except in obedience to Your Royal Highness' desire – and because my own life is so precarious. While I live, Your Royal Highness' commands will always be welcomed by me with all my heart and with all my soul.

I must not take up Your Royal Highness' time but can scarcely conclude without humbly and fervently giving joy to the new little baby which calls you mother. A nation's prayers are with you – but of none more earnestly than of
Madam,
Your Royal Highness' most devoted servant
Florence Nightingale

Her Royal Highness
Princess Louis of Hesse Darmstadt
Princess Alice of Great Britain

(DA Box 27, No. 14p)
35 South Street
Park Lane
London W.   Dec. 22/72

Madam,
　　May I be permitted to express to Your Royal Highness how deeply grateful I feel for the kind letter which has been forwarded to me and how sincerely I regret Your Royal Highness's trouble in having to write to me again upon the same affair?
　　I was not aware that Frau Strecker had written to Mr. Bonham Carter, our Secretary, till I received Your Royal Highness' mission, and I am very sorry for the mistake and delay which has occurred – more particularly as it regards Your Royal Highness.
　　I immediately applied myself to obtain an answer, which I now enclose for Your Royal Highness' approval – a freedom I should not of course have allowed myself, had it not been for Your Royal Highness' gracious permission implied.
　　As our course of training is at present chiefly practical – perhaps too much so – we could not say that we think much less than a year would be much use – especially for a foreign lady. But our own Committee would wish to leave this to yours – that is, that if she should, after 6 months, believe that she has acquired enough, she should write home to the Darmstadt Committee and, upon its application, ours should release her from completing the prescribed term of a year's training.
　　We trust that this will meet Your Royal Highness' views.
　　I cannot but regret very much that Miss Helmsdörfer does not adhere to coming in *January*, as at first proposed (instead of in March). I fear that the first 4 months of the year will be our best

time at the Training School. A lady is going to leave us in April who will be a very great loss to it, although we trust that more workers will be raised up to us (like Una) to take posts of superintendence in our Schools.

Your Royal Highness speaks of this want – How deeply I echo the words, God only knows.

With my whole heart and soul I wish success to Your Royal Highness' noble works in the country so fortunate as to possess you. As an Austrian lady observed to me:– 'we have in Germany your two Princesses, daughters of a Reigning mother, leading in their own persons and with personal knowledge and ability every great and noble and useful work – while many of our little German "Fürstinnen" know and care nothing but about dress'.

I trust that Your Royal Highness will pardon and not think presumptuous this little but most true observation.

May Her royal children be like Herself is the prayer of many grateful hearts in the land of Her birth!

Your Royal Highness is good enough to ask after my health – business increases and strength declines – and it is a hard struggle especially as I am entirely a prisoner to my bed.

But I will not now take up more of that precious time but by begging
        Madam
that Your Royal Highness will believe me ever the most devoted of her servants
        Florence Nightingale

Her Royal Highness
the Princess Louis of Darmstadt
Princess Alice of Great Britain.

NOTES AND REFERENCES

Abbreviations

RA The Royal Archives, Windsor Castle
RA Add Victorian Additional Manuscripts, Royal Archives
DA State (formerly Grandducal) Archives, Darmstadt
LAL Letters from Princess Alice to Prince Louis
DPL Private Diary of Prince Louis
BA Broadlands Archives

All general and/or published sources referred to in the notes that follow – in which some book titles are abbreviated – are fully listed in the bibliography.

The expression *Alice Letters* refers, unless otherwise stated, to the 1884 edition of *Alice Grand Duchess of Hesse – Biographical Sketch and Letters* (London: John Murray 1884).

'Prince Ernest Louis', whose 'Private Memories' are quoted, signifies Princess Alice's eldest son, and 'Prince Louis of Hesse', whose 1953 and 1957 lectures are mentioned, her grandson. These lectures, on the 'Alice Hospital' and the 'Alice Sisterhood' respectively, were delivered in Darmstadt and privately printed. Prince Ernest Louis's unpublished 'Private Memories' are in the possession of Princess Margaret of Hesse, as are (also unpublished): the memoirs of Christa Schenck, entitled 'Loose Pages of Remembrance'; Sophie von Follenius's 'Life, Work and Testament of Princess Alice'; Dr Sigrid Schmidt-Meinecke's 'Short Biography of Princess Alice'; and Dr W. Wauer's 'Grand Duke Ernest Ludwig'.

I am extremely grateful to Princess Margaret for the loan of such papers and booklets, as also for being allowed to quote extracts from her copy of the unpublished 'Reminiscences' of Princess Louis of Battenberg, the first Marchioness of Milford Haven.

PART I

Chapter One

1 Princess Marie Louise, *My Memories of Six Reigns,* p. 15
2 RA, Queen Victoria's Journal, 25 April 1843
3 RA Y55/9, confidential family papers, 25 April 1843
4 RA, Queen Victoria's Journal, 25 April 1843
5 E. Longford, *Victoria R.I.,* p. 66
6 D. Cecil, *Lord M,* p. 181
7 RA Y91/10, 16 May 1843
8 Cecil, *op. cit.,* p. 314
9 RA M51/118, 25 April 1843
10 RA Y91/10, 16 May 1843
11 G. M. Willis, *Ernest Augustus,* p. 414.
12 Kronberg Letters, 4 September 1843
13 RA, Queen Victoria's Journal, 26 April 1843
14 *Ibid.*
15 *Ibid.*
16 Longford, *op. cit.,* p. 150
17 RA, Queen Victoria's Journal, 24 May 1843
18 *Ibid.*
19 RA Z294/45, 2 June 1843
20 RA Y91/12, 6 June 1843
21 RA, Queen Victoria's Journal, 2 June 1843
22 RA Y147/106, 18 July 1845
23 RA M12/50, 8 December 1846
24 RA M12/55, 3 January 1847
25 *Alice Letters,* p. 8
26 *Ibid.,* p. 9
27 RA M17/7, May 1852
28 RA Y391/26, 21 April 1849
29 *Alice Letters,* p. 13
30 *Ibid.,* p. 10
31 M. Ponsonby, *Mary Ponsonby,* p. 17
32 RA Y101/11, 4 April 1856
33 E. Fitzmaurice, *The Life of Granville,* p. 172
34 RA Y101/12, 8 April 1856
35 RA Y101/18, 20 May 1856
36 RA Y80/56, 23 May 1850
37 RA Y140/179, 3 May 1856

Chapter Two

1 RA T1/31, undated
2 RA T1/32, undated
3 RA T1/36, undated
4 RA T1/72, undated
5 RA T1/75, undated
6 RA T1/92, undated
7 RA T1/96, undated
8 RA T1/96, undated
9 RA T1/84, undated
10 RA T2/49, undated
11 RA T2/104, 13 December 1859
12 RA T3/14, 18 February 1860
13 RA T2/104, 13 December 1859
14 RA T2/100, 13 November 1859
15 R. Fulford (ed.), *Dearest Child*, p. 148
16 Strachey, etc. (eds.), *Greville Memoirs*, Vol. vii, pp. 156–8
17 S. Erskine (ed.), *Twenty Years at Court*, p. 364

PART II

Chapter Three

1 *Alice Letters*, p. 7
2 *Alice Letters* (1885), p. 7
3 *Queen Victoria Letters*, iii, p. 235
4 RA T1/30, 15 September 1856
5 RA Y103/14, 27 April 1858
6 *Alice Letters*, p. 13
7 RA Y104/6, 15 February 1859
8 RA Y104/12, 12 April 1859
9 RA Y104/13, 19 April 1859
10 R. Fulford (ed.), *Dearest Child*, p. 98
11 S. Erskine (ed.), *Twenty Years at Court*, p. 351
12 *Ibid.*, p. 352
13 A. L. Kennedy (ed.), *My Dear Duchess*, p. 106
14 F. Curtis (ed.), *Memoirs of Prince Hohenlohe*, p. 88
15 Earl of Malmesbury, *Memoirs*, p. 157

16 RA Y80/89, 7 November 1856
17 RA Y101/19, 27 May 1856
18 RA Z8/71, 2 November 1859
19 Kennedy, *op. cit.*, p. 67
20 *Ibid.*, p. 79
21 RA Z9/11, 30 December 1859
22 Anon., *Uncensored Recollections*, pp. 148ff.
23 RA Y105/12, 25 April 1860
24 RA Y82/52, 27 April 1860
25 Kennedy, *op. cit.*, pp. 102–3
26 E. C. Kenyon, *Scenes in the Life of Princess Alice*, p. 46
27 Kennedy, *op. cit.*, p. 106
28 RA Z3/25, 8 June 1860
29 DA DPL Box 21 Fa, 29 May 1860
30 DA DPL Box 21 Fa, 7 June 1860
31 DA DPL Box 21 Fa, 9 June 1860
32 DA Box 26 6a, 13 June 1860
33 DA Box 26 6a, 17 August 1860
34 DA Box 26 6a, 16 September 1860
35 RA Y100/22, 31 July 1860
36 RA Add U/32, November 1860
37 Erskine, *op. cit.*, p. 379
38 DA DPL Box 21 Fa, 24 November 1860
39 *Ibid.*, 29 November 1860
40 *Ibid.*, 30 November 1860
41 RA Add U/32, 1 December 1860
42 RA Z261/160–9, 1 December 1860
43 RA Z10/20, 30 November 1860
44 RA Add U/32, November 1860
45 RA Y105/39, 29 November 1860
46 F. Bunsen, *A Memoir of Baron Bunsen*, II, p. 328
47 RA Add U/32, 1 December 1860
48 RA Add U/32, 1 December 1860
49 DA DPL Box 21 Fa, 30 November 1860
50 RA Z261/160–9, 1 December 1860
51 RA Z261/160–9, 1 December 1860
52 DA DPL Box 21 Fa, 30 November 1860
53 DA DPL Box 21 Fa, 1 December 1860
54 *Ibid.*
55 Prince Ernest Louis, 'Private Memories'
56 Kennedy, *op. cit.*, p. 170
57 RA A10/21, 3 December 1860
58 Kennedy, *op. cit.*, p. 136

59 DA DPL Box 21 Fa, 30 December 1860
60 DA Box 26, No. 4 (I), 29 December 1860
61 DA Box 26, No. 3 (I), 30 December 1860
62 DA Box 26, No. 3 (II), 31 December 1860
63 DA Box 26, No. 3 (VI), 10 January 1861
64 RA Y105/41, 4 December 1860
65 Kennedy, *op. cit.*, p. 136

Chapter Four

1   R. Fulford, *The Prince Consort*, p. 252
2   *Ibid.*, p. 253
3   *Alice Letters*, p. 6
4   K. Jagow (ed.), *Letters of the Prince Consort*, p. 233
5   RA Z502/48, 1 July 1858
6   *Alice Letters*, pp. 13–14
7   RA T2/104, 13 December 1859
8   Prince Ernest Louis, 'Private Memories'
9   RA C19/94, 14 May 1861
10 RA C19/95, 21 May 1861
11 E. C. Kenyon, *Scenes in the Life of Princess Alice*, p. 64
12 *Ibid.*, p. 66
13 Windsor, etc. (eds), *Letters of Lady Augusta Stanley*, p. 219
14 *Ibid.*, p. 233
15 *Ibid.*, p. 234
16 *Ibid.*, p. 239
17 Kenyon, *op. cit.*, p. 74
18 DA Box 26, No. 4 (II), 3 December 1868
19 G. Barnett-Smith, *Queen Victoria*, p. 351
20 G. Villiers, *A Vanished Victorian*, p. 309
21 C. Jerrold, *The Widowhood of Queen Victoria*, p. 20
22 Stanley, *op. cit.*, p. 245
23 *Alice Letters*, p. 20
24 DA Box 23, No. 1, 1 January 1862

Chapter Five

1   H. Maxwell, *Clarendon*, p. 253
2   H. Bolitho, *A Century of British Monarchy*, p. 75

3   G. Villiers, *A Vanished Victorian*, p. 309
4   'The Alice Hospital', Prince Louis of Hesse's 1953 lecture
5   E. C. Kenyon, *Scenes in the Life of Princess Alice*, p. 81
6   E. Fitzmaurice, *The Life of Granville*, p. 405
7   RA Y201/15, 19 December 1861
8   *The Times*, 17 December 1861
9   *Alice Letters*, p. 398
10 G. Barnett-Smith, *Queen Victoria*, p. 356
11 Kenyon, *op. cit.*, p. 85
12 Windsor, etc., *op. cit.*, p. 259
13 E. Sheppard, *George Duke of Cambridge*, p. 227
14 Villiers, *op. cit.*, p. 313
15 *Ibid.*, p. 312
16 E. Longford, *Victoria R.I.*, p. 313
17 *Alice Letters*, p. 20
18 S. Erskine (ed.), *Twenty Years at Court*, p. 394
19 *Ibid.*, p. 395
20 DA Box 26, No. 4 (III), 1 February 1862
21 A. L. Kennedy (ed.), *My Dear Duchess*, p. 187
22 Longford, *op. cit.*, p. 309
23 Kennedy, *op. cit.*, p. 197
24 H. Dyson and C. Tennyson (eds), *Dear and Honoured Lady*, p. 51
25 *Ibid.*, pp. 60, 65
26 H. Bolitho (ed.), *Further Letters of Queen Victoria*, 26 May 1862
27 RA Add O/17–19, 7 June 1861
28 DA Box 26, No. 4 (III), 20 June 1862
29 Kennedy, *op. cit.*, p. 193
30 *Ibid.*, p. 187
31 C. Schenck, 'Memoirs'
32 Sheppard, *op. cit.*, p. 321
33 Erskine, *op. cit.*, p. 398
34 Schenck, *op. cit.*
35 *Ibid.*
36 RA, Queen Victoria's Journal, Z368/163, 1 July 1862
37 *Ibid.*
38 Schenck, *op. cit.*
39 RA, Queen Victoria's Journal, Z368/163, 1 July 1862
40 *Ibid.*
41 DA DPL, 1 July 1863
42 D. Duff, *Hessian Tapestry*, p. 85
43 *Ibid.*, p. 86
44 DA DPL, 1 July 1863

45 R. Fulford, *Dearest Mama*, pp. 85–6
46 DA Box 23, No. 1; Box 26, No. 11
47 DA Box 23, No. 1, 11 December 1860
48 DA Box 23, No. 1, 12 February 1862
49 DA Box 26, No. 11, 21 February 1862
50 DA Box 23, No. 1, 27 April 1862
51 R. Fulford, *Dearest Mama*, p. 86
52 RA, Queen Victoria's Journal, Z368/171, 8 July 1862
53 DA Box 27, No. 5, 6 July 1862
54 R. Fulford, *Dearest Child*, p. 267
55 R. Fulford, *Dearest Mama*, p. 88

PART III

Chapter Six

1   M. Wauer, *Grand Duke*
2   *Ibid.*
3   DA DPL Box 21 Fa, 12 July 1862
4   *Alice Letters*, 13 July 1862, p. 28
5   RA Add C2/7, 17 July 1862
6   *Alice Letters*, 16 July 1862, p. 29
7   RA Z/261, pp. 253ff.
8   *Alice Letters*, 19 July 1862, p. 30
9   RA Add C10/69, 15 July 1862
10 *Alice Letters*, 25 July 1862, p. 33
11 Windsor, etc. *op. cit.*, p. 269
12 Schenck, *op. cit.*
13 DA LAL, 19 January 1863
14 DA LAL, 20 January 1863
15 DA LAL, 21 January 1863
16 DA LAL, 9 February 1863
17 RA T3/41, 23 May 1860
18 DA Box 26, No. 61, 3 June 1863
19 DA DPL Box 21 Fa, 5 April 1863
20 Schenck, *op. cit.*
21 RA Y109/26, 14 April 1863
22 E. Sheppard, *George Duke of Cambridge*, pp. 244–5
23 RA Y110/12, 14 September 1863
24 RA Y113/3, 15 November 1864

25 RA Y113/10, 1 December 1864
26 RA Y113/24, 12 January 1865
27 Schenck, *op. cit.*
28 *Alice Letters*, 21 November 1863, p. 61
29 *Alice Letters*, 5 March 1864, p. 69
30 RA Y114/34, 4 October 1865
31 A. L. Kennedy (ed.), *My Dear Duchess*, p. 232
32 DA Box 26 6b, 11 April 1865
33 RA Y113/3, 15 November 1864
34 RA Y114/34, 4 October 1865
35 RA Y114/37, 25 October 1865
36 RA Add A25/328, 29 January 1871
37 RA Add A17/537, 19 June 1872
38 RA Add A17/538, 26 June 1872
39 RA T4/74, 11 November 1865
40 *Alice Letters*, 21 April 1865, p. 95
41 DA LAL, 17 April 1865
42 DA LAL, 18 April 1865
43 DA LAL, 22 April 1865
44 DA Box 26 12a, 19 April 1865
45 *Alice Letters*, 11 December 1865, p. 112

Chapter Seven

1 *Alice Letters*, 10 February 1866, p. 122
2 *Alice Letters*, 17 March 1866, p. 125
3 S. von Follenius, 'Life, Work and Testament of Princess Alice'
4 *Alice Letters*, 3 May 1866, p. 128
5 *Ibid.*
6 DA LAL, 2 July 1866
7 DA LAL, 5 July 1866
8 *Ibid.*
9 DA Box 26 12a, 14 July 1866
10 DA LAL, 16 July 1866
11 DA LAL, 17 July 1866
12 *Ibid.*
13 DA LAL, 19 July 1866
14 DA LAL, 21 July 1866
15 DA LAL, 21 July 1866 (a second letter written the same day)
16 DA LAL, 22 July 1866
17 DA LAL, 28 July 1866

18 DA LAL, 4 August 1866
19 DA Box 26 12a (letters from Louis to Alice, 14 July to 3 August 1866)
20 DA Box 26 12a, 3 August 1866
21 *Alice Letters*, 17 August 1866, p. 144
22 British Museum, Add MSS 45.750, 64–6, 29 September 1866

Chapter Eight

1 RA Add U/2, 1 February 1867
2 DA LAL, 19 July 1866
3 *Alice Letters*, 21 December 1866, p. 158
4 Prince Louis of Hesse, 'Lecture on the Alice Hospital' (1953)
5 S. Schmidt-Meinecke, 'Short Biography of Princess Alice'
6 S. von Follenius, 'Life, Work and Testament'
7 Prince Louis of Hesse, *op. cit.*
8 C. Woodham-Smith, *Florence Nightingale*, p. 508
9 Prince Louis of Hesse, *op. cit.*
10 D. Duff, *Hessian Tapestry*, p. 113
11 Follenius, *op. cit.*
12 Fr. von Holtzendorf, *Memoirs*, Deutsche Frauenanwalt (magazine), 21 December 1878
13 DA Box 27 14p

Chapter Nine

1 *Alice Letters*, 13 May 1867, p. 171
2 DA Box 23, No. 1, 4 Febraury 1867
3 C. Schenck, 'Memoirs'
4 H. Maxwell, *Clarendon*, p. 336
5 DA Box 26 6b, 28 May and 5 June 1867
6 DA Box 23, No. 1, 16 June 1867
7 *Alice Letters*, 4 August 1867, p. 172
8 DA LAL, 5 September 1867
9 DA Box 27 14f, 4 September 1867
10 *Ibid.*, 14 September 1867
11 DA Box 26 6b, 6 October 1867
12 *Alice Letters*, 14 October 1867, p. 185
13 DA Box 26 14f, 16 October 1867

14 DA LAL, 16 April 1868
15 DA LAL, 18 April 1868
16 DA LAL, 20 April 1868
17 DA Box 26 12a, 20 April 1868
18 DA LAL, 21 April 1868
19 DA Box 26 12a, 22 April 1868
20 D. Duff, *Hessian Tapestry*, p. 143
21 DA LAL, 5 December 1869
22 DA LAL, 31 October 1869
23 DA Box 26 12a, 13 October 1869
24 DA LAL, 17 November 1869

Chapter Ten

1   RA I63/177, 26 July 1870
2   DA Box 26 12b, 2 August 1870
3   *Ibid.*
4   *Alice Letters*, 28 July 1870, p. 243
5   DA LAL, 28 July 1870
6   DA LAL, 4 August 1870
7   DA LAL, 13 August 1870
8   DA LAL, 16 August 1870
9   DA LAL, 18 August 1870
10 DA LAL, 22 August 1870
11 DA Box 26 12b, 22 September 1870
12 DA Box 26 12b, 23 September 1870
13 DA Box 26 12b, 25 September 1870
14 DA LAL, 26 September 1870
15 DA Box 12b, 29 September 1870
16 DA LAL, 28 September 1870
17 DA LAL, 8 September 1870
18 DA LAL, 24 September 1870
19 DA LAL, 30 September 1870
20 C. Schenck, 'Memoirs'
21 DA Box 26 12b, 1 December 1870
22 DA Box 26 12c, 6 January 1871
23 DA LAL, 18 January 1871
24 DA LAL, 12 March 1871
25 RA I68/13, 7 January 1871
26 *Ibid.*, 25 January 1871
27 DA DPL Box 21 Fa, 9 April 1871

28 DA LAL, 25 April 1871
29 *Alice Letters*, 29 August 1866, p. 147
30 DA Box 23, 25 September 1871
31 E. F. Benson, *Daughters of Queen Victoria*, p. 164
32 DA LAL, 22 November 1871
33 DA LAL, 23 November 1871
34 DA LAL, 24 November 1871
35 DA LAL, 25 November 1871
36 DA LAL, 27 November 1871
37 G. Battiscombe, *Queen Alexandra*, p. 114
38 *Ibid.*, p. 115
39 DA LAL, 2 December 1871
40 G. Battiscombe, *op. cit.*, p. 116
41 DA LAL, 4 January 1872
42 G. Battiscombe, *op. cit.*, p. 117
43 *Alice Letters*, 9 November 1871, p. 274

Chapter Eleven

1 D. Duff, *Hessian Tapestry*, p. 167
2 F. Warwick, *Afterthoughts*, p. 272
3 *Alice Letters*, 13 May 1867, p. 172
4 *Ibid.*, 31 May 1865, p. 99
5 *Ibid.*, 24 July 1865, p. 104
6 *Ibid.*, 30 December 1865, p. 114
7 *Ibid.*, 3 May 1866, p. 128
8 *Ibid.*, 20 March 1866, p. 125
9 *Ibid.*, 5 August 1870, p. 244
10 *Ibid.*, 15 September 1870, p. 249
11 *Ibid.*, 12 November 1870 and 14 February 1871, p. 251 and p. 264
12 *Ibid.*, 19 August 1870, p. 246
13 DA LAL, 13 February 1871
14 D. Duff. *op. cit.*, p. 164
15 E. Zeller, *Strauss and Renan*, pp. 30–1
16 E. Zeller, *D. F. Strauss*, p. 108
17 *Ibid.*, p. 84
18 T. Ziegler, *Strauss*, p. 653
19 E. Zeller, *op. cit.*, pp. 127–8
20 Ziegler, *op. cit.*, p. 655
21 *Alice Letters*, p. 231

22 Ziegler, *op. cit.*, p. 656
23 Opinion (given privately to author) of Professor H. J. Eysenck
24 DA Box 27, No. 16

PART IV

Chapter Twelve

1   Marchioness of Milford Haven, 'Reminiscences'
2   R. Fulford (ed.), *Dearest Mama*, 8 April 1865
3   E. Sheppard, *Duke of Cambridge*, p. 239
4   E. C. Kenyon, *Scenes in the Life of Princess Alice*, p. 99
5   *Alice Letters*, 16 January 1864, p. 66
6   *Ibid.*, 7 November 1864, p. 77
7   Prince Louis of Hesse, 'Lecture on the Alice Sisterhood' (1957)
8   Dr M. Wauer, *Grand Duke Ernest Ludwig*
9   Prince Louis of Hesse, *op. cit.*
10 *Alice Letters*, 15 June 1865, p. 101
11 *Ibid.*, 3 May 1866, p. 127
12 Kenyon, *op. cit.*, pp. 137, 141
13 Prince Ernest Louis, 'Private Memories'
14 *Ibid.*
15 *Ibid.*
16 *Ibid.*
17 DA Box 27, No. 10

Chapter Thirteen

1   A. J. Quick, *The Hemorraghic Diseases*, p. 192
2   DA LAL, 9 October 1870
3   *Alice Letters*, 17 June 1872, p. 279
4   *Ibid.*, 14 August 1872, p. 281
5   Marchioness of Milford Haven, 'Reminiscences'
6   Prince Ernest Louis, 'Private Memories'
7   *Ibid.*
8   RA Z379/163, 29 May 1873

9   Marchioness of Milford Haven, *op. cit.*
10 DA Box 27 14c, 11 May 1873
11 DA Box 27 14c, 30 December 1873
12 Prince Ernest Louis, *op. cit.*
13 DA Box 27 14a
14 *Alice Letters*, 26 April 1874, p. 321
15 E. C. Kenyon, *Scenes in the Life of Princess Alice*, p. 162
16 Rev. C. Bullock, *Doubly Royal*, pp. 34–5
17 E. Longford, *Victoria R.I.*, p. 234
18 *Granville Papers*, 4 April 1873 (Public Record Office)
19 Longford, *op. cit.*, p. 235
20 RA S27/129–30, 26 July 1873
21 *Alice Letters*, 26 July 1873, p. 308
22 *Ibid.*, 17 December 1874, p. 331
23 R. K. Massie, *Nicholas and Alexandra*
24 *Ibid.*
25 G. H. Green, 'A Royal Obstetric Tragedy and the Epitaph', *New Zealand Medical Journal*
26 Quick, *op. cit.*, p. 193
27 Green, *op. cit.*, p. 303
28 *Ibid.*, p. 304

Chapter Fourteen

1   Prince Ernest Louis, 'Private Memories'
2   *Alice Letters*, 24 September 1874, p. 327
3   *Ibid.*, 26 August 1874, p. 325
4   DA LAL, 7 September 1874
5   BA, 6 November 1876
6   DA Box 27 14r
7   DA LAL, 11 June 1876
8   DA LAL, 14 June 1876
9   DA LAL, 11 September 1876
10 DA LAL, 22 September 1876
11 DA LAL, 3 October 1876
12 DA LAL, 4 October 1876
13 *Alice Letters*, 7 June 1876, p. 354
14 DA LAL, 20 June 1877
15 DA LAL, 28 July 1877
16 DA LAL, 29 July 1877
17 DA LAL, 1 August 1877

18 DA LAL, 2 August 1877
19 DA Box 26 12e, 3 August 1877
20 DA LAL, 5 August 1877
21 DA LAL, 9 August 1877

Chapter Fifteen

1   *Alice Letters*, 13 December 1877, p. 359
2   *Ibid.*, 21 December 1877, p. 359
3   *Ibid.*, 9 September 1877, p. 358
4   *Ibid.*, 30 October 1877, p. 359
5   DA LAL, 31 October 1877
6   *Ibid.*
7   RA Z79/95, December 1877
8   DA LAL, undated except for 'Friday'; probably late November 1877
9   D. Bennett, *Vicky*, p. 211
10 RA H20/95, 20 February 1878
11 DA Box 23, No. 1, 8 February 1878
12 G. F. Chambers, *East Bourne Memories*, p. 54
13 DA LAL, 3 August 1878
14 DA LAL, 28 October 1878
15 DA LAL, 3 November 1878
16 DA LAL, 4 November 1878
17 *Alice Letters*, 6 November 1878, p. 367
18 S. Tytler, *The Queen*, pp. 110–12
19 *Ibid.*, p. 111
20 BA, 15 November 1878
21 RA, Queen Victoria's Journal, 16 November 1878
22 BA, 16 November 1878
23 Tytler, *op. cit.*, p. 112
24 BA, 19 November 1878
25 *Ibid.*
26 BA, 22 November 1878
27 BA, 25 November 1878
28 BA, 2 December 1878
29 *Hansard*, 17 December 1878
30 *Alice Letters*, 6 December 1878, p. 374
31 BA, 7 December 1878
32 E. Sanderson and L. Melville, *Edward VII*, p. 164
33 G. Battiscombe, *Queen Alexandra*, pp. 148–9

34   T. Martin, *Queen Victoria As I Knew Her*, p. 113
35   W. F. Monypenny and G. E. Buckle, *Disraeli*, p. 1,341
36   *The Times*, 16 December 1878
37   *Illustrated London News*, 21 December 1878
38   RA Add A15/2942, 12 December 1878
39   RA Add A15/2946, 17 December 1878

BIBLIOGRAPHY

Alice, Grand Duchess of Hesse, Biographical Sketch and Letters (London: John Murray 1884)

Alice, Grand Duchess of Hesse, Letters to Her Majesty the Queen, new and popular edn. with a Memoir by HRH Princess Christian (London: John Murray 1885)

ANON., *Peerless Princess A* (London: Nisbet 1878)

ANON., *Uncensored Recollections* (J. P. Lippincott 1924)

ARTHUR, SIR GEORGE, *Concerning Queen Victoria and her Son* (London: Robert Hale 1943)

ARTHUR, SIR GEORGE, *Queen Alexandra* (London: Chapman & Hall)

BARNETT-SMITH, G., *Queen Victoria* (London: Routledge & Kegan Paul 1887)

BATTISCOMBE, GEORGINA, *Queen Alexandra* (London: Constable 1969)

BENNETT, DAPHNE, *Vicky* (London: Collins 1971)

BENSON, E. F., *Daughters of Queen Victoria* (London: Cassell 1939)

BOLITHO, H., *A Century of British Monarchy* (London: Longmans Green 1951)

BOLITHO, H. (ed.), *Further Letters of Queen Victoria* (London: Thornton Butterworth 1938)

BUCKLE, GEORGE EARLE (ed.), *Letters of Queen Victoria* (second series) (London: John Murray 1926)

BULLOCK, REV. CHARLES, *Doubly Royal: Memorials of the Princess Alice* (London: Hand & Heart 1879)

BUNSEN, FRANCES (Baroness), *A Memoir of Baron Bunsen* (London: Longman 1868)

BUXHOEVEDEN, SOPHIE (Baroness), *The Life and Tragedy of Alexandra Feodorovna* (London: Longman 1926)

CARPENTER, J. ESTLIN, *The Life and Work of Mary Carpenter* (London: Macmillan 1879)

CECIL, DAVID, *Lord M* (London: Constable 1954)

CHAMBERS, G. F., *East Bourne Memories of the Victorian Period, 1845–1901* (Sumfield 1910)

COOKE, C. KINLOCH, *Memorial of Princess Mary Adelaide, Duchess of Teck* (London: John Murray 1900)

CURTIS, FRIEDRICH (ed.), *Memoirs of Prince Clodwig of Hohenlohe Schillingsfuerst* (London: Heinemann 1906)

DE MONTALEMBERT, Count, *The Life of Saint Elizabeth of Hungary* (Dublin: Duffy)

DUFF, DAVID, *Hessian Tapestry* (London: Frederick Muller 1967)

DYSON, HOPE, and TENNYSON, CHARLES (eds.), *Dear and Honoured Lady*, correspondence between Queen Victoria and Charles Tennyson (London: Macmillan 1969)

ERNLE, LORD, *Whippingham to Westminster*, Reminiscences (London: John Murray)

ERSKINE, MRS STEUART (ed.), *Twenty Years at Court* (London: Nisbet)

FITZMAURICE, LORD EDMUND, *The Life of Granville George Leveson Gower, Second Earl of Granville, 1815–1891* (London: Longman 1905)

FULFORD, ROGER (ed.), *Dearest Child. Letters between Queen Victoria and the Crown Princess of Prussia, 1858–1861* (London: Evans 1964)

FULFORD, ROGER, (ed.), *Dearest Mama. Letters between Queen Victoria and the Crown Princess of Prussia, 1861–1864* (London: Evans 1968)

FULFORD, ROGER, *The Prince Consort* (London: Macmillan 1949)

GOWEN, REV. H. H., *Church Work in British Columbia* (London: Longman 1899)

GREEN, G. H., 'A Royal Obstetric Tragedy and the Epitaph', *New Zealand Medical Journal*, 69 (1969)

HARRAEUS, KARL, *David Strauss* (Leipzig: Hermann Seemann Nachforger 1901)

JAGOW, DR KURT (ed.), *Letters of the Prince Consort* (London: John Murray 1938)

JERROLD, CLARE, *The Widowhood of Queen Victoria* (London: Eveleigh Nash 1916)

KENNEDY, A. L. (ed.), *My Dear Duchess. Social and Political Letters to the Duchess of Manchester, 1858–1869* (London: John Murray 1956)

KENYON, EDITH C., *Scenes in the Life of Princess Alice* (London: W. Nicholson 1887)

LEE, SIR SIDNEY, *King Edward VII*, I (1841–1901) (London: Macmillan 1925)

LEE, SIR SIDNEY, *Queen Victoria* (London: Smith Elder 1903)

LONGFORD, ELIZABETH, *Victoria R.I.* (London: Weidenfeld & Nicolson 1964)

MALMESBURY, EARL OF, *Memoirs of an ex-Minister* (London: Longman 1884)

MANSON, J. A., *Sir Edwin Landseer* (London: Walter Scott 1902)

MARIE LOUISE, HRH PRINCESS, *My Memoirs of Sir Reigns* (London: Evans 1956)

MARTIN, SIR THEODORE, *Queen Victoria as I knew Her* (for private circulation) (Edinburgh: Blackwood 1901)

MASSIE, R. K., *Nicholas and Alexandra* (London: Gollancz 1968)

MAXWELL, SIR HERBERT, *Life and Letters of George William Frederick, Fourth Earl of Clarendon* (London: Edward Arnold 1913)

MONYPENNY, W. F., and BUCKLE. G. E., *The Life of Benjamin Disraeli, Earl of Beaconsfield* (London: John Murray 1929)

MORLEY, JOHN, *Life of William Ewart Gladstone* (London: Macmillan 1903)

PANKHURST, E. SYLVIA, *The Suffragette Movement* (London: Lovat Dickson & Thompson 1931)

PONSONBY, ARTHUR, *Henry Ponsonby, Queen Victoria's Private Secretary. His Life from his Letters* (London: Macmillan 1942)

PONSONBY, SIR FREDERICK, *Letters of the Empress Frederick* (London: Macmillan 1928)

PONSONBY, MAGDALEN, *Mary Ponsonby: A Memoir, Some Letters and a Journal* (London: John Murray)

QUICK, A. J., *The Hemorraghic Diseases* (Springfield & Baltimore: Chas C. Thomas 1942)

ROYSTON, PIKE, E., *Human Documents of the Victorian Golden Age (1850–1875)* (London: Allen & Unwin 1967)

SANDERSON, E., and MELVILLE, L., *King Edward VII* (London: Gresham 1910)

SHEPPARD, EDGAR, *George Duke of Cambridge, A Memoir of his Private Life* (London: Longman 1906)

STRACHEY, LYTTON, and FULFORD, ROGER (eds.), *The Greville Memoirs*, 8 vols (London: Macmillan 1938)

TYTLER, SARAH, *The Life of the Queen* (J. S. Virtue and Company)

VICTORIA, QUEEN, *More Leaves from the Journal of a Life in the Highlands. 1862–1882* (London: Smith Elder 1884)

VILLIERS, GEORGE, *A Vanished Victorian. The Life of George Villiers, Fourth Earl of Clarendon* (London: Eyre & Spottiswoode 1938)

WALSH, WALTER, *The Religious Life and Influence of Queen Victoria* (London: Swan Sonnenschein 1902)

WARWICK, FRANCES, COUNTESS OF, *Afterthoughts* (London: Cassell 1931)

WILLIS, G. M., *Ernest Augustus of Hanover* (London: Arthur Barker 1954)

WINDSOR, DEAN OF, and BOLITHO, HECTOR (eds.), *Later Letters of Lady Augusta Stanley* (1864–1876) (London: Jonathan Cape)

WOODHAM-SMITH, CECIL, *Florence Nightingale, 1820–1910* (London: Constable 1950)

WOODHAM-SMITH, CECIL, *Queen Victoria, Her Life and Times*, Vol. I, *1819–61* (London: Hamish Hamilton, 1972)

ZELLER, EDUARD, *David Friedrich Strauss in His Life and Writings* (London: Smith Elder 1874)

ZELLER, EDUARD, *Strauss and Renan* (London: Trubner 1866)

ZIEGLER, THEOBALD, *David Friedrich Strauss* (Strasbourg: Trubner 1908)

INDEX